I0605349

SCREAM WITH ME

ALSO BY ELEANOR JOHNSON

Nonfiction

Practicing Literary Theory in the Late Middle Ages

Dramatizing Contemplation

Waste and the Wasters

Poetry

The Dwell

Her Many Feathered Bones

SCREAM WITH ME

HORROR FILMS AND THE RISE OF AMERICAN FEMINISM (1968–1980)

ELEANOR JOHNSON

ATRIA BOOKS

New York Amsterdam/Antwerp London
Toronto Sydney/Melbourne New Delhi

ATRIA
BOOKS

An Imprint of Simon & Schuster, LLC
1230 Avenue of the Americas
New York, NY 10020

First Atria Books hardcover edition September 2025

ATRIA BOOKS and colophon are trademarks of Simon & Schuster, LLC

Simon & Schuster strongly believes in freedom of expression and stands against censorship in all its forms. For more information, visit BooksBelong.com.

For information about special discounts for bulk purchases, please contact Simon & Schuster Special Sales at 1-866-506-1949 or business@simonandschuster.com.

The Simon & Schuster Speakers Bureau can bring authors to your live event. For more information or to book an event, contact the Simon & Schuster Speakers Bureau at 1-866-248-3049 or visit our website at www.simonspeakers.com.

Interior design by Davina Mock-Maniscalco

Manufactured in the United States of America

5 7 9 10 8 6 4

Library of Congress Control Number: 2025008858

ISBN 978-1-6680-8763-3
ISBN 978-1-6680-8765-7 (ebook)

This book is dedicated to my mentor, Lyn Hejinian 1941–2024

You wrote your name in every one of his books.

CONTENTS

SCREAM WITH ME

INTRODUCTION

In spring 2022, I was preparing a lecture on *Rosemary's Baby* for my History of Horror class. As I watched the film for the umpteenth time, I experienced vertigo. Watching Rosemary get raped and impregnated by Satan; watching her be controlled and abused by her husband and neighbors; watching her husband grab her and shake her for not adhering to the restrictive regimen that he and the neighbors had endorsed throughout her agonizing pregnancy: All I could see in the film was a parable about the dangers of denying women their reproductive agency. So, I wrote my lecture about *Rosemary's Baby*, reproductive control, and the history of abortion rights in New York State—where the film is set, and where I teach. I taught the film as *reproductive horror*, in which the monstrous, horrific acts in question all have to do with a woman's sexual and reproductive autonomy—or, rather, with the violation of her sexual and reproductive autonomy. It was the best lecture I gave that semester; by the end, many of my students were in tears, and so was I. The next day, the US Supreme Court leaked its intention to reverse *Roe v. Wade*. I cried again, and much harder this time. And then I did what I always do when I get alarmed about a social or political situation: I turned to art. This time, I turned specifically to horror.

Now, this turn to art may seem avoidant or apolitical; for me, it's anything but. I have long believed—and long argued, both in my teaching and my writing—that art is where the most complex social problems and traumas get worked through and processed, sometimes long before a culture is fully prepared to grapple with those problems and traumas in mainstream public discourse. Art is where we store, analyze, and hone our secret social fears and hopes, our desires and demons, long before we're ready to talk about them clearly or articulately on the news. Studying and teaching art, for that reason, is always political, and always has the capacity to do real activist work.

Moreover, the power of art to represent and immerse us in complex social problems exceeds—and sometimes confounds—what an author's or director's own vision may have been, because art takes on its fullest life once it interfaces with an audience. Sometimes, it takes years—even decades—for a culture to consciously recognize that a particular work of art was handling some thorny, complex, or not-fully-articulable topic. Often, innovative works of art speak to contemporaneous sociopolitical dynamics that are *just* starting to get serious attention in the public eye. The power of art is to create an experiential arena within which readers or viewers can witness—and to some extent experience—those dynamics. Art, that is, both *reflects and accelerates* social change, and it does so by inviting readers or viewers to participate in the imaginative world the artwork creates.

Horror, though long saddled with a bad reputation as schlock or lowbrow, is no different. In fact, as a genre, horror is one of the most acutely participatory art forms out there: By design, horror triggers a physiological response in a reader or viewer. Even though we know we are merely witnessing events on the screen or the page, we *feel* endangered, we *feel* like we're right there with the horror protagonists. When I watch *Rosemary's Baby*, I *feel* Rosemary's entrapment, her dehumanization, her vulnerability, and her fear.

So I asked myself: Was *Rosemary's Baby* the only horror film so clearly tied to the battle for women's reproductive rights in the 1960s or 1970s? As I began racking my brain, I quickly realized the answer was no. Without half trying, I came up with a set of six films—all released between 1968 and 1980—that were inextricably linked with the fight for women's rights in the United States. All the films had in common a gut-twisting awareness of women's vulnerability to physical, reproductive, and psychological torture *in their own homes*—an awareness that something was rotten in the state of American domestic life. Those films are *Rosemary's Baby* (1968), *The Exorcist* (1973), *The Stepford Wives* (1975), *The Omen* (1976), *Alien* (1979), and *The Shining* (1980).

These six films are some of the greatest horror movies in American film history—classics of the genre that have inspired countless subsequent films. All of them have been sequeled, prequeled, remade, or reinvented more than once. Many of the originals were nominated for and awarded prestigious film awards. The blazing hot soul of horror in these films was the restriction and controlling of women's bodies, minds, and rights. And in *all* these films, this restriction took place in the domestic sphere. In fact, in these films, the supernatural—a mainstay of the horror genre—simply offered a lens through which to view the altogether too quotidian and too private realities of domestic violence and reproductive abuse. The true horror of the films was not ultimately otherworldly but *domestic*.

These films depict horrific acts—sadistic, predatory, dehumanizing acts—of violence against women. Violence against women, of course, is typical of the horror genre writ large: As Hitchcock himself famously said about how to make horror films, the crucial thing was to "torture the women!" Given that horror gleefully fetishizes the torture of women, it's not obvious to think of horror as a feminist genre. To be sure, there is some excellent feminist philosophy out there that teaches us to think about the "final girl" who survives to the end of a slasher movie in a triumphal light, and there is other work that teaches us to think about female monstrosity as something powerful and countercultural. But if you ask the average person—especially those who do *not* gravitate toward horror films naturally—whether horror is more feminist or misogynist, odds are high that they will say misogynist, and maybe even degrading. And with good reason: You do see a lot of torture of female bodies in horror.

But horror also has a deep and enduring relationship with American feminism. In fact, American feminism and American horror have been—for more than half a century—allies on issues of domestic abuse, reproductive control, and women's restricted rights relative to men.

I say "allies," though, with two qualifications: First, although the *films* in this book do make viewers witness, fear, and lament the entrapment of women in the domestic sphere, the *directors* of several of these films are notoriously misogynistic and predatory. This is an irony I'll talk about in depth later, but for now, I simply want to remind us that a work of art should not be reduced to the intention of the person who made it. All works of art wind up meaning more and different things than their creators intended, because art, once it escapes the artist's studio or writer's pen, goes on to interface with a broader culture. In that environment, the work of art takes on meanings that far exceed the conscious planning of any single creator.

Second, in most cases, the female characters in the 1970s films are not resistant; they are victimized, usually unwilling or unable to fight back very much against the domestic horrors that consume or control them. Their *power* is generally not what we're being invited by the films to witness. Instead, we're supposed to witness their fear, their entrapment, their *vulnerability*. And we're supposed to witness those things *as emergent properties of the domestic sphere*. For centuries, the home has been set up as the safe place for women—safe from violence, safe from sexual assault, safe from danger. These films are all taking issue with that ideology. These films are all, in fact, centrally concerned with the home and the family as places of horror. For that reason, we should think of them as *domestic horror*.

We can all probably conjure up a list of horror subgenres, some better known than others: haunted house horror, sci-fi horror, serial killer horror, monster horror, slasher horror, and zombie horror, just to name a few. But *domestic horror* has consistent and particular characteristics that set it apart from many other modes of horror.

1. It takes place largely within a *confined dwelling place*, in which a *female protagonist* has restricted freedom.
2. There is at least one *male antagonist* who is also within the dwelling place, and he cannot easily be removed.
3. The horror that the film inflicts on its female protagonist centers on *children, reproduction,* or *sex*, and it includes an element of physical battery.
4. All the films are either explicitly or implicitly thinking through contemporaneous legal conflicts in the United States about *women's rights*.

Indeed, the six films featured in this book reflect and seek to advance three intersecting legal and sociocultural changes that happened in the US in the 1970s. First, they are concerned with reproductive rights. In fact, these six movies—released from 1968 to 1980—neatly flank the passing of *Roe v. Wade*, in January 1973. Second, they are concerned with the Equal Rights Amendment (ERA) and with the efforts throughout the

1970s to pass it. Third, they are concerned with early legislation that criminalized domestic violence and with the change in American consciousness that made that possible. In fact, these domestic horror films highlight the deep, thrumming interconnection between these three bodies of law: equal rights, reproductive rights, and the right to physical safety. In the worlds these films create, if you deny a woman any one of these, you deny them all, and, in so doing, you create horror.

I'm throwing around the term *horror* here as if its meaning is obvious and well established. But in truth horror is a big, baggy genre with countless examples, and no watertight definition. Some critics say horror is about abjection; some say it's about the experience of the uncanny. According to many critics and viewers, horror is closely linked with pornography, since both are designed to trigger a physiological response in viewers. I think that's a fair baseline, that horror is defined in part by making us feel things in our bodies. But American *domestic* horror is a wonky subgenre. In my view, it is ultimately much more akin to tragedy than it is to something like pornography.

Aristotle defined tragedy by saying that it makes viewers feel fear and pity, so that they can experience a catharsis at the end. The Greek words for fear and pity are *phobos*, cognate with *phobia*, and *eleos*, which means "compassion," "mercy," and "clemency." So, it's not just straight "pity," with all the condescending freighting of that term in Modern English. No one wants to be pitied; everyone wants to experience compassion, mercy, and clemency. *Eleos* is a social and interpersonal good, because it teaches people to feel empathic about and merciful toward their fellow citizens. Tragedy makes you a better person and a better citizen. Tragedy is prosocial.

Domestic horror works similarly—as we'll see. We feel *phobos* and *eleos*: fear in the obvious sense, and *eleos* in the sense of feeling deep compassion for the endangered protagonists. We feel not just pity for them, but actual *compassion and empathy*. Shared feeling. Like tragedy, domestic horror makes us experience another person's vulnerability as our own, so that we wish for their suffering to end. Like tragedy, domestic horror trains us to care about people who are maybe not *exactly* like us but share in the commonwealth we recognize as our humanity.

But there is a crucial difference between tragedy and horror. Tragedies tend to end neatly. Sure, everyone dies, and there's often quite a lot of blood on the floor at the end (think of *The Oresteia*, *Hamlet*, *Macbeth*, *Romeo and Juliet*, or *The Atheist's Tragedy*), but there's usually an accompanying sense that the violence is done now. The social order will be restored, maybe even improved upon, because of the tragic events foregone. Tragedy is defined, remember, by its creation of *catharsis*—purification, cleansing, or purging—in the audience. We have our catharsis, and we move on. We can release a hard-earned sigh of relief at the end of the play.

In horror, by sharp contrast, we do not get our catharsis. Instead, we get what I call the *horror hangover*. Things end messily and chaotically, with a sense that the horror hasn't ended—and that maybe it never will. When we leave the theater after seeing a horror film, we feel nervous as we walk up the steps to our house. We wonder if someone is lurking in our apartment. There is no sense that order is restored, no sense that we are safe now; the unease lingers. Horror stays with you, keeps you hypervigilant against threats, keeps you in a state of activation and vulnerability, for some period after the film is over. And in some cases, the activation and vigilance and vulnerability stay with you a long time. That's the *point*, in fact, of horror. And that's why horror and tragedy, though analogous in so many ways, are radically different in ultimate effect.

What's so important about the domestic horror films in this book is that they make viewers—whether or not the viewers are female—carry the fear and vulnerability *embodied by the women in the films* home with them. They center on a woman's perspective, making audiences feel wracking physiological and psychological compassion for the women characters who are abused and terrorized. The films, although they showcase women's suffering, do not simply fetishize that suffering, but rather *humanize* it, make it palpable, exportable to the viewers' own minds and bodies. They invite viewers into the lived, embodied experiences of abused women; women barred from power, barred from speaking for themselves, barred from defending themselves; women who weren't taken seriously by the people from whom they sought aid—doctors, police, lawyers, psychiatrists, husbands, coworkers. These movies took what was going on in American cultural, political, and legal history in the late 1960s and 1970s, and they made those things *feelable*. They made women's suffering *come alive* to viewers who might not otherwise ever have stopped to think about what or how women suffered in the United States, behind closed doors, in the twentieth century. They made that suffering seem like an emergency. And then they made that suffering follow viewers all the way home and nest there.

The original six domestic horrors in this book gave voice to kinds of domestic violence that pervaded American culture but were essentially unnamed and unspeakable in the 1970s, because the available language for describing domestic and reproductive violence then was far, far less developed than it is now. These films amplified the emergent political discourse around women's rights to domestic safety, as well as to reproductive and bodily autonomy. They highlighted and narrativized the power disparities between women and men, women and doctors, women and the church, and women and the patriarchy. In doing so, they turned isolated whispers and tense conversations into loud, public screams. This is the great power of art: to give voice to those social and cultural problems for which a critical vocabulary does not yet exist.

But even within the wide-ranging category of "art," there was something uniquely powerful about cinema in the 1970s. When you're reading a book or viewing a sculpture at a museum, you're doing it, in effect, alone. Nowadays, when we watch movies, we often stream them in our homes, also alone. But in the 1970s, when the films that are central to this book were released, when people watched films, they watched them *together*, in a pop-up community of filmgoers at a movie theater. When you watch a film in the theater, and you see someone next to you crying, it affects you. And when you watch a *horror* film in the theater, when you hear everyone around you screaming or groaning, or see them jumping around in their seats, that affects you, too. Cinema has an amplifying effect on affect, on emotion, on an audience's empathy with the main characters on the screen. So when I say that these six films turned whispers into screams, I mean it quite literally. These films turned whispers about reproductive violence and domestic abuse into screams that reverberated around movie theaters, among millions of shocked viewers, all around the United States, creating a durable, widely disseminated, highly public meditation on the dangers facing women in their own homes throughout the 1970s. And in doing so, horror became the cinematic genre that did the most to organize and give voice to the burgeoning discourse against domestic violence, against reproductive control, and against the dehumanization of women in the 1970s.

To write a book about horror and feminism in the 1970s might seem a little quaint, a little out of vogue. The truth is, I wish it *were* quaint. I wish it *were* a random little antiquarian project undertaken by a fusty scholar. But the vertiginous reality is that now, in the 2020s, we are once again living through the 1970s. Since the *Dobbs* decision was handed down in 2022, women's bodily autonomy is in a grave state of peril. Because of that decision, now, again, American women live in a political reality in which their reproductive agency is under systematic threat. Whether you believe unflinchingly in a woman's right to choose, whether you believe that a fetus is ensouled as soon as its heart beats, or whether you are somewhere on the complex spectrum that separates those two positions, it should be terrifying that governments, rather than a woman and her doctor, are making lifesaving or life-threatening medical decisions on a woman's behalf for the foreseeable future. Before abortion was decriminalized, as we will see in this book, many, many American women simply died during their pregnancies. We've forgotten that history; we've forgotten what it was like to read newspaper articles about young women being found dead through botched, illegal abortions. But we're living through our own version of that era now, with death rates of pregnant women *and babies* climbing again, since 2022.

The return to the '70s isn't only about reproductive rights, either. The numerous laws that passed in the 1970s and 1980s to protect women from violence in the home are gradually being undermined by complex legal and social forces; on top of that, the modes by which domestic violence takes place are ever evolving and are getting harder and harder to detect and prosecute. Very, very few states in the US have laws capacious enough to protect women—particularly married women—from things like cyberstalking, hacking, cyberbullying, surveillance, technological abuse, sexual violence, or other controlling and dehumanizing behaviors that a domestic partner may inflict upon them. On top of that, women *still* haven't won equal rights under the law: Despite the fact that the ERA came before the Senate again as recently as 2023, it still failed to be made into law. Joe Biden's Hail Mary proclamation that the ERA should be considered ratified does not, in fact, have the force of law. And the ERA seems unlikely to get ratified by the current legislature. So now, again, American women live in a reality in which their political, physical, medical, and legal equality are under threat. In truth, they have always been. But now, we're looking at a regression to an environment the likes of which we haven't seen since the early 1970s.

That is precisely why, in the past few years, we've seen a resurgence in domestic horror genre. The penultimate chapter of this book will analyze the bridge films that bring ideas of domestic horror into the twenty-first century—*Paranormal Activity*, *Creep*, and *Creep 2*—showing how, by holding misogynist filmmakers accountable for their exploitation of women in situations of domestic peril, they helped make room for a new generation of powerful feminist domestic horror directors. The final chapter will examine the three thrilling domestic horrors of 2024: *Immaculate*, *The First Omen*, and *Apartment 7A*. Each of these films either explicitly or implicitly remakes at least one of the original six domestic horrors from the 1970s, and all of them—inspired by the 2022 *Dobbs* decision—centrally address reproductive rights. These three films recognize the weird cultural vertigo we're all living through right now: Our calendars tell us we're living in the 2020s, but our political discourse feels of a different era.

My greatest hope in writing this book is that I can impart some of the horror I felt watching and teaching *Rosemary's Baby* in the spring of 2022, when I realized my students won't grow up confident that women have autonomy over their own bodies, when I realized that they will likely grow up reading newspaper articles about young women dying from illegal pregnancy terminations. We are descending into a new, twenty-first century domestic horror. As an educator, a scholar, a mother, a woman, and a feminist, I will be damned if I let that happen without making some noise about it. And that, of course, is exactly what these films have trained Americans to do. They have trained us to scream at the horrors inflicted on women's bodies. So come: Scream with me.

CHAPTER 1

This Is No Dream; This Is Really Happening: *Rosemary's Baby*

Rosemary's Baby (1968) is an uncontested classic. Directed by Roman Polanski, adapted from Ira Levin's immensely popular 1967 novel of the same name, and starring a diaphanous Mia Farrow (Rosemary Woodhouse), a seething John Cassavetes (Guy Woodhouse), a manic Ruth Gordon (Minnie Castevet), and a terrifying Sidney Blackmer (Roman Castevet), this film is routinely cited by fans and critics alike as one of the greatest horror films of all time. The story is simple enough: A young couple moves into a New York apartment building; the wife gets pregnant by Satanic rape; she struggles through her pregnancy; she gives birth to the Antichrist. It's so simple—albeit disturbing—that it almost sounds silly. But in its fully realized form, it's a brilliant film on all counts, from cinematography to script, acting to sound design, direction to editing, as horror buffs and critics have recognized for fifty years. Roger Ebert wrote in 1968 that it was a "brooding, macabre film, filled with the sense of unthinkable danger . . . It is a creepy film and a crawly film, and a film filled with things that go bump in the night. It is very good."

Ebert's review is fairly typical: What most critics admired about the film was its creepiness—the witches, the Satanism. But *Rosemary's Baby* isn't just a film about witchy Satanists; it's a film about violence toward women. The film both reflected and consolidated public attitudes toward forced pregnancy, toward the relationship between women and the medical establishment, and, most of all, toward a woman's right to be in charge of her own body, her own mind, and her own pregnancy. In fact, *Rosemary's Baby* gave voice to a reality already well known to but unnamed by many American women: a reality in which they were forced to become pregnant and then to stay pregnant by their abusive husbands. Nowadays, we call this type of abuse *reproductive coercion*, or *reproductive violence*, but that language didn't exist in 1968.

Reproductive violence happens when a man forces his female partner to engage in sexual activities she does not wish to engage in with the goal of impregnating her, or when a man sabotages a woman's birth control. It also happens when a woman is denied appropriate access to gynecological or reproductive medicine in an attempt to control whether or not she has a baby. *Rosemary's Baby* was the first American film to thematize reproductive violence and reproductive control *as horror*. It's a film in which a young woman is drugged by her husband, raped by Satan, and forced to endure a pregnancy of intense physical pain until she gives birth to an inhuman child. No matter the supernatural elements at play, the message is the same—Rosemary is in danger for one reason and one reason only: She is a woman of childbearing age.

To see *Rosemary's Baby*'s reproductive horror in sharpest relief, we need to look at the battle for reproductive rights in New York State in the years leading up to the film's release. *Rosemary's Baby* is set in New York City, and that's no accident: New York was where a great deal of the loudest and most successful protesting about reproductive restriction was happening in the United States. Abortion was illegal in New York State in almost all cases in the 1950s and 1960s, permissible only if the mother's life was in provable and immediate medical danger. Getting an abortion legally, in practice, was next to impossible. Of course, the illegality of abortion didn't mean abortions didn't *happen*; it simply meant that abortions didn't happen *safely*. There were examples of this in the news everywhere—and in particular, they were plastered all over *The New York Times*. In April 1951, police raided a Stuyvesant Town apartment, in which an "abortion ring" had been operating, consisting of three doctors and three aides; the doctors were taken into custody and interrogated and eventually brought up on charges. In 1953, a doctor was arrested on a murder charge because a woman had died during an abortion procedure he illegally performed on her at his office. In April 1954, a Bronx woman was found dead in her apartment, with abortion as the presumed cause of death. In 1956, two abortion providers accidentally killed their patient, and then so feared prosecution for providing an abortion in the first place that they dismembered her and hid her body parts. Case after case emerged of women being found dead, where abortion was known or strongly suspected as the cause of death.

Dozens of these articles were published in *The New York Times* and other papers throughout the 1950s, creating an atmosphere of fear and terror. New Yorkers were regularly reading horrific accounts about young women's bloodied bodies, left to die, by doctors who were imagined as rogue, renegade madmen, helped by nurses of the night. Mainstream media showcased lack of access to legal abortion in safe hospital settings as what it was: truly, a horror show.

In June 1960, the American Medical Association (AMA) decried abortion law as too strict and began to advocate for doctors' rights and obligations to provide abortion care to pregnant women. The American Medical Association called for abortions to be legalized whenever medically or humanely necessary. The AMA pointed out that the main 1960s argument against abortion—that it was dangerous for the pregnant woman—was grossly exaggerated, and that women were far more likely to die through a botched abortion than a medically sanctioned abortion, and far more likely to suffer psychiatric illness after a live birth than after an abortion. Notwithstanding this plea from the AMA, abortion remained illegal in every state throughout the 1960s. But the pressure was on to change things.

The controversy around thalidomide intensified that pressure. In the early 1960s, many pregnant women were prescribed thalidomide, a drug later proven to cause severe birth defects in children. Doctors, women, and advocates began to suggest that women who took thalidomide should be allowed to access abortion in order to prevent the birth of severely deformed children. One particularly well-publicized case was that of married actress Mrs. Robert Finkbine, who found out she was pregnant after having taken thalidomide and sought legal permission to get an abortion in the state of Arizona. It was denied, and she and her husband publicly announced that they would seek a legal abortion for her elsewhere. Two weeks later, in Sweden, a panel agreed that Mrs. Finkbine's mental health justified an abortion; when the fetus was aborted, the Swedish surgeon confirmed that it was indeed severely deformed. This narrative was papered all over mainstream news media, largely because of Mrs. Finkbine's celebrity status as Miss Sherri, from the children's television show *Romper Room*. Everybody loved Miss Sherri, which made it harder to hate her decision.

In response to the thalidomide controversy, the New York Academy of Medicine urged the legalization of all "therapeutic abortions," which would be performed any time the mother's physical or mental well-being was endangered by the continuance of the pregnancy or any time a fetal deformity was suspected. The next year, the *Times* ran an editorial advocating for the legalization of all therapeutic abortions, noting that 87 percent of people polled about the New York Academy of Medicine's recommendations favored their passage. In later 1965, a full-scale war erupted in the editorials page of the *Times*, with some taking strong stances about the urgent need to decriminalize abortion and others stating that aborting fetuses on the chance they might develop abnormalities in the wake of things like thalidomide usage or German measles (also known to cause birth defects) was murder. By the end of June 1965, the *Times* ran an article about doctors becoming more and more willing to stretch the law, ostensibly reflecting a softening in public and medical attitudes toward the procedure; by the end of that year, the *Times* ran strongly worded editorials condemning the "cruel" laws of forty-five states in which abortion was illegal unless performed to save a woman's life. This article pointed out that approximately ten thousand American women died per year due to illegally performed abortions. Let that statistic sink in: ten thousand women *per year*.

In 1966, there was a widespread effort to liberalize abortion law in New York. Doctors and psychiatrists spoke up to back abortion law reform. Polls showed that most Americans—even Catholics—supported the liberalization of abortion laws. That summer, the New York Obstetrical Society backed the liberalization of abortion law. In the fall, the American Lutheran Church came out in support of therapeutic abortions; two weeks later, the American Medical Women's Association spoke up in favor of liberalizing abortion law. Toward year's end, the New York County Medical Society urged New York law to change so that a woman could legally obtain a therapeutic abortion, as well as in cases of rape or incest; the New York State Council of Churches spoke out in support of that position a week later. *Enough is enough*, even ecclesiastical organizations started to say; *we have to do something to protect women from untimely and preventable death*.

Despite efforts to liberalize New York's abortion laws, in March 1967, the abortion bill was killed on the legislative floor in New York State by a vote of 15–3. Fifteen to *three*: It wasn't even close. All those dead women; all those deformed fetuses; all those stories of maniacal, murderous doctors operating terrifying abortion rings . . . Somehow, it hadn't done the trick yet. People weren't quite horrified *enough*. They needed a little push.

One New Yorker was poised and ready to push: novelist Ira Levin. In 1967, at the height of the abortion controversy, he published his wildly popular novel *Rosemary's Baby*. He has said of the genesis of his novel that he "was struck one day by the thought . . . that a fetus could be an effective horror if the reader knew it was growing into something malignly different from the baby expected. Nine whole months of anticipation, with the horror *inside* the heroine!" For Levin, from the beginning, it was the unwanted *baby*, not the Satanism itself, nor the witchy neighbors, that was the real horror. To the best of my knowledge, Levin never came out and called *Rosemary's Baby* a topical novel about the overstrict abortion laws in New York or in the United States broadly. But maybe he felt he didn't need to announce it so baldly: His much earlier novel, *A Kiss Before Dying* (1953), also centers on a young woman who dies because of an unwanted and unplanned pregnancy. So, writing novels that were about abortion availability was kind of Levin's modus operandi.

Just after Levin released *Rosemary's Baby*, things in New York shifted a little more: Governor Nelson Rockefeller urged his legislature in 1968 to liberalize abortion law in New York.

Referring to the then-current state of affairs as a "human tragedy" because of the needless loss of women's lives due to unsafe abortion, he begged his colleagues to modernize the state's eighty-five-year-old abortion statute. Within the month, Governor Rockefeller appointed a ten-person committee to study the potential effects of liberalizing New York's laws; that committee was rumored to be pushing toward far broader and more capacious reforms than those that had been rejected the year before. Despite this, the abortion reform again failed in the New York State Senate in April.

But over the course of 1968 and 1969, something shifted in New York, so that, by 1970, New York became the second state not to *liberalize* abortion law, but in fact to *legalize* abortion. The something that shifted was multivariate: grassroots organizing, ongoing controversy surrounding thalidomide, the ever-accelerating women's rights movement. But a piece of that shift, signal-boosting the changes in consciousness and attitude that were already circulating around the United States and were particularly intense in New York, was the release of *Rosemary's Baby* in mainstream theaters across the US in summer of 1968.

Rosemary's Baby's Dark Catholicism: The Unholy Family of Guy and Rosemary Woodhouse

Rosemary's Baby opens with a panoramic shot of the Manhattan skyline, culminating at an archaic-looking building—the now-famous Dakota building, called the Bramford in the film. At its base, from a camera positioned far above them, we see two people turning to walk into the building. Set almost entirely within the confines of the Bramford, domestic horror is coming for us, initially signaled via a creepy lullaby that rolls on during the opening shots. The lullaby is simply a breathy soprano, chanting "La, la, la, la, la, la" for several minutes, with very spare, slightly discordant organ music underneath. It is not especially soothing, and it points toward the general emotional tone of the film: things *seem*, on the surface, to be calm and gentle, but there's a turbulence and dissimulation just underneath. Something that feels just a little off.

The two people entering the Bramford are a young couple named Rosemary and Guy Woodhouse (Mia Farrow and John Cassavetes), who are looking at apartments around New York. We learn that Guy is a struggling actor—a B-list actor, at best. He makes most of his money doing commercials, but he has big dreams of being a leading man. When their Realtor asks Guy, "Have I seen you in anything?" Guy responds—lying—that he's been in *Hamlet* and *The Sandpiper*. Rosemary steps in to set the record straight, saying, "He's joking. He was in *Luther* and *Nobody Loves an Albatross* and a lot of television plays and commercials." It's a brief exchange, but an important one—Rosemary undermines Guy in front of another man, bruising his ego, the ramifications of which have devastating consequences.

Rosemary's costuming in this scene is noticeably childlike, innocent, and even virginal. She sports a blunt, blond bob and bangs. She's clad all in white, with a white dress, a white purse, and white shoes. She carries white gloves in her hand. Everything about her projects stereotypical female purity. She's beautiful, but also delicate and pale; she smiles constantly and talks in a lilting, gentle, childlike voice. A young, innocent woman, soon to be the mother, we imagine, of a young, innocent family.

Through these costuming choices and the decision to have Mia Farrow play up her childlikeness, the film accentuates a dynamic also present in Levin's novel: Rosemary parallels history's most famous and childlike mother, the Virgin Mary, mother of Jesus. Rose*mary*'s name of course registers that parallel; her costuming throughout further emphasizes the connection. Indeed, not just in the opening scenes but throughout the film, Rosemary almost always appears in white or white and blue, the archetypal colors of the Virgin Mary in Christian history. Farrow pulls off this Modern Mary aesthetic effortlessly, looking like a delicate lily bobbing around her apartment after she and Guy move in. Moreover, it is not an accident that Guy's last name is Woodhouse; Joseph was, famously, a carpenter. The novel and film offer a modern reboot of a very old, very familiar, and acutely Christian story: a carpenter and his virtuous young wife, looking for a place to stay so they can start their family.

In all of these Christianizing choices, of course, Levin's novel and Polanski's adaptation of it run headlong at the institution most directly responsible in the 1960s for the ongoing horror inflicted on American women by the criminalization of abortion: the Catholic Church. Indeed, long after Protestant churches and synagogues had lined up to advocate for the liberalization of abortion laws in New York, the Catholic Church steadfastly opposed it. Levin himself has said that he was perfectly conscious that he was "standing the story of Mary and Jesus on its head" in how he told Rosemary's story, and he certainly had reason to in 1967.

In the 1968 film, Rosemary's Marian purity contrasts sharply with the ponderous darkness of the apartment she and Guy move into. On their first night in their new home, Rosemary and Guy order Chinese takeout and eat it on the floor of the living room. The shot is dark; the floors are dark; the scene is set in room tone, highlighting the young couple's sudden separation from the world outside, the starkness and unfamiliarity of this new place, its eerie quiet. Throughout their interaction that night—even after Rosemary has proposed that they "make love"—Guy seems stilted, disengaged. And Rosemary, in all her purity and sweetness, seems somehow isolated and vulnerable, even though her husband is right there with her. Or maybe *because* he's right there with her.

Even so, in the days that follow, Rosemary is eager to make a bright, clean, safe home for the family she so desperately wants—she covers drawers with white and yellow contact paper, she whitewashes the walls. The whole place gets a facelift, but as we watch Rosemary do all this domestic labor, we still can't help but notice how painfully *alone* she is. She feels it, too, so she accepts an invitation to have dinner at their much older neighbors' apartment next door. Roman and Minnie Castevet—the neighbors—are exceptionally weird people. They chat up Rosemary and Guy all evening, plying them with compliments and conspicuously overfilled cocktails.

Roman, in particular, butters Guy up, saying he saw him perform in *Nobody Loves an Albatross*, and that he had been "struck by a gesture" that Guy had made during the performance. Roman goes on to assert, "You have a most interesting inner quality, Guy. It appears in your television work, too, and it should carry you very far indeed; provided, of course, that you get those initial 'breaks.'" Guy's sense of inferiority about his profession—recently agitated by Rosemary's comment to the Realtor—makes him vulnerable to the form of seduction that Roman Castevet exercises over him. His wounded male ego is the fertile ground into which the metaphorical seed of Satanism is planted, though it will be Rosemary's body that bears its fruit.

After dinner, Minnie starts pumping Rosemary for information while they do the dishes. She wants to know Rosemary's family's fertility history and whether she expects to have children soon. Rosemary appears understandably taken aback by these intrusive questions, but Minnie is such a loudmouthed person to begin with, we can almost see Rosemary convincing herself that it's not *so* unusual for Minnie to pry like this. Through the conversation between Rosemary and Minnie, we learn that Rosemary comes from a large and markedly fertile family of devout Catholics, though Rosemary herself is a lapsed Catholic. She wants to get pregnant soon; Guy is more hesitant about it.

Meanwhile, Guy is in the living room talking with Roman. We don't see or hear what goes on between them—they are out of our sight line, and out of Rosemary's as well, though she does angle her head around to try to see what's going on in there. What Rosemary and the audience *do* see is a thin ribbon of smoke that bends around the door frame from the living room into the hallway, signaling that the two men are deep in a hushed conversation, smoking. The smokiness, on second or third viewings of the film, seems a clear anticipation of the diablerie soon to come.

After talking with Roman, Guy suddenly gets a huge boost in his career, after which he suddenly grows excited about having a baby with Rosemary. He says to her, "I've been a creep . . . I've been tearing my hair out about my career. Let's have a baby. Let's have three babies, one at a time, all right?" Rosemary is understandably stunned at this sudden shift and doesn't respond. Irritated by her lack of response, Guy instantly becomes belligerent: "A baby, you know? Ma-ma, Da-da, poo-poo, you know . . . ?" Rosemary, in the trembling voice of someone without power being given something she desperately wants by the person who has power over her and who might take the gift back at any second, says quickly, "You mean it? . . . You really mean it, really?" Unable to contain his unkindness, Guy responds, "No, I'm kidding," and then, "Sure, I mean it," causing Rosemary to cry in what looks like a combination of relief, gratitude, and submission to Guy's idiosyncrasies.

After Rosemary has been carefully tracking her menstrual cycle, she and Guy both know when she should be fertile, and they have a romantic dinner at home in preparation for the baby making to follow. That night, Rosemary wears not blue or white but red—top to bottom. It's a jarringly conspicuous and very pointed costume change, one that again anticipates the devilry around the corner. Guy lights the fire in the fireplace, briefly illuminating his face with the match flame and causing a transient devilish glow to play on his facial features. The flue turns out to be closed, so the room begins to fill with smoke—again, anticipating the Satanic events to come. The couple drink their cocktails by the fire; they eat their candlelit dinner, but throughout, there is an awkwardness between them, a formality, a rigidity. Rosemary seems nervous; Guy seems like his mind is elsewhere. Eventually, Minnie brings over some chocolate mousse for them. Turning suddenly despotic, rather than detached, Guy insists vigorously that Rosemary eat it despite her detecting what she calls a "chalky undertaste." "That's silly," he says. "There is no undertaste . . . Come on! The old bat slaved all day! Now *eat it*!" Watching the film, even on a first viewing, the viewer knows Rosemary is being drugged; we just don't know why. And we certainly don't know why Guy is so aggressively on board with the drugging. He starts criticizing her for being picky; with a sigh of surrender, Rosemary picks up the mousse again and digs in. Surreptitiously, when Guy is turning over the record on the record player, she dumps the mousse into her napkin, like a sneaky child, and pretends she ate it all, asking, "Do I get a gold star, Daddy?" This line always makes me puke a little, but it does important work for the film: It reminds us that we are in the deep belly of patriarchy, and that Guy is the patriarch—the *paterfamilias*, the father who is head of the household—and that Rosemary is in his thrall. Very soon after this, we see her stumbling around the apartment, clearly drugged. Guy carries her to bed, unsurprised and unconcerned about his wife's stupor.

Rosemary then has what seems at first to be a hallucinatory dream. The camera continually rotates, surveying a small yacht crowded with people. A rippling water effect is superimposed on the shot, too, giving off a feeling of submersion and drowning. The scene is silent, and our visual field keeps rotating—the film is trying to impart to us the feeling of the spins that Rosemary is having while drugged. It is making us physiologically align with her, amplifying our bodily empathy with her. Rosemary sees herself on the boat, belowdecks; but at the same time, she can tell that Guy is untying her clothes. She is told in the dream that "Catholics only" can come along on the journey. The camera keeps moving around in circles through the next several shots; we feel a little sick, a little off balance. Her wedding ring is unceremoniously pulled off her finger. Soon she finds herself in a dark, subterranean room. There is a mattress in the room, which she is laid down on, surrounded by her naked neighbors, most notably Roman and Minnie. Guy is there, too. The camera continues to spin. The neighbors begin chanting in an angry-sounding whisper; it's almost as though they are threatening her. Her legs are lashed down—and that is when it becomes clear: Rosemary is at the center of some kind of rape ritual, supervised by Roman, Minnie, and numerous other inhabitants of the Bramford. All eyes are on Rosemary. She, meanwhile, looks stoned, catatonic.

Now, we see Guy walking toward her, half in darkness. As he approaches, he begins to look crusty, like he has a skin disease. His hands rake over her body. Suddenly, it's not *his* hands, but the hands of some kind of demon, complete with claws, hair, and dark brownish carbuncles. These hands claw mercilessly along Rosemary's flesh, and we watch it all in an extreme close-up. This demonic creature mounts her slowly and begins to rape her.

Rosemary looks feverish throughout much of this scene but has a moment of clarity when she sees his red and yellow face, his goatlike eyes, and she says, "This is no dream! This is really happening!" She is being raped by Satan. Her husband sanctions it; her neighbors facilitate it. She sees it clearly, with the camera zoomed close on her eyes, then Satan's, then back to hers. Her eyes are wide with horror; she is alert and clearheaded. Someone covers her head with a dark cloth, however, and knocks her unconscious.

So, just to make things very plain: This film recounts a story of a virtuous, modern-day Mary who becomes pregnant through *rape*. This choice is significant, and not just because of its aggressive anti-Catholic messaging. By New York State's own abortion laws in 1968, Rosemary would *not* have been able to get an abortion on grounds of rape alone. Rape was not justification enough for abortion in 1968 in New York, nor was physical danger, nor psychological harm. Nor, indeed, was the prospect of having a baby born with deformities—which would seem likely when the child's father is a claw-handed, leather-skinned, goat-eyed demon. The Satanic fetus, whose true range of deformities could only be known after the birth of the child, allegorizes the thousands of thalidomide pregnancies across the United States that women were forced to carry to term, anxiously waiting to see how compromised their babies would be by the drug the women had taken. Like them, Rosemary is going to be forced to carry to term a pregnancy of unknown viability.

This was no dream. This was really happening.

So *Rosemary's Baby* takes on the two major justifications

for the abortion liberalization that New Yorkers advocated for in the 1960s: the rape justification and the fetal anomaly justification. Rosemary's experience, while unique in its supernaturalness, would have been arrestingly familiar to an audience in the 1960s, an audience that knew that New York State was having such trouble liberalizing abortion law. Even for audiences outside of New York State, the legal landscape of the abortion-law liberalization movement was well known: Many states were discussing abortion reform since abortion-related deaths were happening all over the country, every day. *Rosemary's Baby* depicts the situation facing women across the country—their lack of control over their bodies, their lack of ability to choose whether to carry a baby that was forced on them to term. What happens to Rosemary in the film is no dream: It was *really happening* to countless American women, who had no legal grounds to fight back in 1968.

The morning after the Satanic rape, Guy roughly wakes up Rosemary, telling her she passed out from too much liquor the night before. Groggy and disoriented, Rosemary inspects her body and finds deep claw marks all over her side, back, and belly. Guy quickly claims responsibility, saying his nails were jagged when they had sex. Rosemary is affronted at the idea that he forced himself on her while she was unconscious: "You . . . while I was *out*?" Unabashed by what his wife obviously feels to be a violation, Guy informs her that it was "fun" for him, "in a necrophile kind of way." She tells him that she dreamed someone inhuman was raping her; Guy's response, which he hollers from across the room, is "Thanks a lot!" She turns her back to him, clearly traumatized by his conduct. He comes over, clumsily traces his finger down her back, and she jerks away.

For the next several shots, Rosemary is alone, driving home the larger point: She is isolated, trapped in her building, in her marriage, and in some kind of supernatural conspiracy whose contours she can't quite perceive.

Predictably, Rosemary and Guy's relationship deteriorates—he can't bring himself to look at her, and he's entirely preoccupied with his newly flourishing acting career. When Rosemary finds out she is indeed pregnant, she is alone; when she tells Guy, he has a bizarre reaction. He tries to avoid touching her body, even as he passes narrowly by her while she stands in a doorway. He acts happy, but his tone sounds forced and distracted. Rosemary makes a pathetic bid that this should be a "fresh start" for them, which Guy absently agrees to, preferring to run and tell Minnie and Roman, rather than stay and rejoice with Rosemary about their coming baby. Of course, he knows it's not *his* baby but Satan's. As a result of Guy's avoidance, Rosemary is reduced to looking at herself in the mirror and saying, her face perched on her two hands like a little girl, "You're pregnant!" She is so alone, so terribly alone. And in her solitude, she echoes the experience of far, far too many other American women in 1968 and now.

But she's not alone for long, because soon Minnie and Roman get involved, telling her whom to use as an obstetrician, what she can drink and eat, and what jewelry to wear. Rosemary finds herself constrained to cede basic control over her body to her neighbors—Guy supports it, so she must obey. She begins to develop terrible, crippling pains in her abdomen, and she loses weight at an alarming rate for months. Numerous shots show her clad in gauzy blue-and-white housecoats, reeling with pain, the soundtrack keening mournfully behind her. Something is terribly wrong with this pregnancy; we know it, Rosemary suspects it, and Rosemary's friends—on the rare occasions when she is allowed to see them—can see it immediately. But her fancy obstetrician Dr. Sapirstein (Ralph Bellamy), who's in cahoots with Minnie and Roman, instructs her not to talk to her friends. So, even though she's surrounded by intrusive neighbors, on a deeper level, Rosemary is completely isolated.

Eventually, she tires of this forced seclusion and decides to throw a party. Upon seeing her emaciation and pallor, her shocked girlfriends gently urge her to consider abortion, telling her that pregnancy isn't supposed to hurt this much nor to make a woman so sick. They worry that her life may be in danger—and maternal mortality is the one justification for legal abortion in 1968 in New York State. Resistant, Rosemary says to her friends, "I'm not going to have an abortion." Rosemary loves her growing baby. This is true because, of course, she doesn't know (or consciously accept) that the baby isn't Guy's but Satan's. How could she? It's a ridiculous idea, impossible, supernatural.

But the film, by raising abortion explicitly as an option for Rosemary, and having her reject it, does something extraordinarily sophisticated, shedding light on the insanity of antiabortion laws in the 1960s. Rosemary may not want an abortion, but she *should* get an abortion, even and perhaps especially by any Christian or Catholic standard. Because *we* know, as she will eventually know, too, that she was raped by Satan, and that her baby is the Antichrist. To root for Rosemary to take her pregnancy to term is to root for evil to enter the world. This story forces Christian readers or viewers to examine the limit of their antiabortion beliefs. No Christian could *possibly* endorse Rosemary's carrying that pregnancy to term; she is carrying Satan's baby, after all. She is *wrong from a theological standpoint* to protect the life of this unborn child. In positing this scenario, *Rosemary's Baby* has created a thought experiment in which the pope himself would have to advocate for Rosemary to terminate.

Of course, Rosemary doesn't realize this, because of the web of cruelty and gaslighting to which Guy subjects her. Over the course of the film, it becomes clear that Guy, though he is not the baby's father, certainly *is* the source of Rosemary's problems. In a brilliantly realized scene, late in the film, Rosemary is reading books about witches that her recently deceased friend Hutch had left for her. She's reading because she's trying to figure out what kind of weirdness is going on in her apartment building and whether she should be afraid for her unborn child. In a spasm of patriarchal control, Guy snatches the book Rosemary has been reading, *All of Them Witches*, and places it high up on a bookshelf, out of Rosemary's reach. The camera follows Guy's hand up the bookshelf. We can see that the book—as Guy shelves it horizontally—touches only two other books on the shelf. The books are Alfred Kinsey's *Sexual Behavior in the Human Male* and *Sexual Behavior in the Human Female*. The film's suggestion, with the juxtaposition of the three books, is that all this malign, demonic, witchy abuse to which Rosemary is subjected has at its root something dark and malevolent in male sexual behavior and its interaction with female sexual behavior. Roman, Minnie, and Satan might *seem* to be the monsters of this film, but the real point of origin for all its domestic horror is Guy, his brittle ego, and the dark, dehumanizing opportunism lodged deep in his sexual mind—an opportunism bent on taking sexual advantage of his own wife.

Guy's brittle ego is not the only thing that endangers Rosemary; the other is her own maternal instincts. After she delivers her baby, at home and in extreme duress, Guy tells her the baby died. Even in her wild grief, soon enough Rosemary knows it's a lie: Rosemary can hear her baby crying through the walls. Through a drug-induced haze, she realizes that the Castevets have her baby, alive. Looking lost, febrile, and panicky, she manages to sneak into the Castevets' apartment to find him.

As she enters the apartment, Rosemary is once again wearing a long, blue housedress. She sees a coven of modern-day witches assembled around her baby's black cradle. As she peers into the cradle, we don't see the baby but instead only Rosemary's face. Her eyes widen, much as they did at the moment when she realized her Satanic rape was "no dream" but "really happening." Silent at first, she covers her mouth with her hand. "What have you done to it? What have you done to its eyes?" she asks the coven. Roman explains, parroting in twisted form the logic of the Virgin Birth, "Satan is his father, not Guy. He came up from hell and begat a son of mortal woman. Satan is his father; his name is Adrian!" Going on in this Satanic mockery of the story of Mary, Minnie then jumps in to say, "He chose *you* out of all the world. Out of all the women in the world, he chose you! He arranged things, because he wanted *you* to be the mother of his only living son."

Something in Rosemary shatters. She looks catatonic as she is convinced by Roman to go and rock her baby in his cradle. She is stripped of agency and personhood, powerless, a pawn in the incarnation of the Antichrist. The film makes her a cog in a massive Satanic conspiracy that relied upon domestic betrayal and sexual assault to produce its desired outcome. The film dehumanizes her to the bitter end and forces us to reckon with that dehumanization as absolute and irreversible. Rosemary will not come back from this. She will not heal from what has been done to her. And, significantly, neither will everyone else: part of what is so powerful about this story is that we—the citizens of the world—are every bit as endangered by this monstrous birth as Rosemary is. Her lack of reproductive agency and autonomy will destroy us all.

Reactions to *Rosemary's Baby* and New York's Abortion Laws, 1968–1970

Rosemary's Baby was one of the biggest cinematic hits of 1968. It was nominated for and won numerous national and international film awards—for direction, for best actress, best supporting actress, best film, and others. The average ticket price in 1968 was $1.31 (*USA Today*), and *Rosemary's Baby* made $33 million at the box office worldwide, which means approximately 25 million tickets to the film were sold. Even assuming that some of those tickets were bought by viewers who saw the film more than once, that's still a lot of individual people, mostly Americans, viewing the film.

Rosemary's Baby was on screens in the United States for more than a year. During that time, Americans shrieked together at the physiological and psychological stresses of her pregnancy, they cringed at Rosemary's loneliness and isolation, they shuddered at her rape, and they worried about the pregnancy that seemed apt to kill her. They screamed at the domestic horror she found herself trapped in—the realness and plausibility of it all, at least as much as they did at the supernatural wonder of it. Renata Adler said in her *Times* review, "Mia Farrow is quite marvelous, pale, suffering, almost constantly onscreen in a difficult role that requires her to be learning for almost two hours what the audience has guessed from the start. One begins to think it is the kind of thing that might really have happened to her, that a rough beast did slouch toward East 72nd Street to be born." The horror of *Rosemary's Baby* is the horror of reproductive agency being denied to women, and the movie, rather than making it seem unbelievable and unreal, made it seem like something "that might have really happened to her."

The enormity of the film's popularity both reflected and concentrated abortion reform sentiment in New York. Watching this film means watching someone who is raped, and then forced to carry a rape-induced pregnancy to term. Watching this film is thus watching a woman forced to comply with actual state and national regulations about abortion in 1968–69. Watching this film, moreover, isn't just *watching* the film; it's *empathizing* with

Rosemary, worrying that she will die, worrying that her baby will be born demonic. Everything in the film is geared to activate our sympathy with Rosemary—she is in no way depicted as a selfish, promiscuous, contemptible woman. Quite the contrary, she is consistently depicted as a modern Virgin Mary, who is raped by Satan and bullied by malevolent neighbors, a cruel husband, and a corrupt doctor into carrying the Antichrist to term. Through their encounter with this film, viewers were forced right into a reproductive disaster along with Rosemary. They were forced to live, imaginatively and empathically, through a worst-case scenario of a woman being denied adequate medical care and access to abortion during a pregnancy that began with rape. This film urges viewers to shift their thinking around reproductive rights. Rosemary, we think, has a right to better care than she receives. She has a right to see a real doctor, and not a quack or a "sadistic nut," as her friends call him. She has a right to her own health. She has a right to the truth. Rosemary is the poster child for why abortion should be legal.

One reviewer from *Time* magazine specifically clocked the film's relationship to reproductive agency, calling the film "a wicked argument against planned parenthood." Now, on first blush, to my twenty-first century ear, that sounds incorrect, backward: Planned Parenthood is today known as an abortion-providing institution. But it wasn't that in 1968, because abortion was illegal, except in hospital contexts, when the mother's life was demonstrably in danger. Founded in 1916, Planned Parenthood started as a birth control clinic. In the 1930s, Planned Parenthood lobbied for the destigmatization of birth control and actively advocated for and funded the development of the birth control pill in the '40s and '50s. In 1965, two years before Levin wrote his novel, partially through the advocacy of Planned Parenthood, the birth control pill was legalized in ten states. The idea of the pill, of course, was that you should be able to "plan" your parenthood, not just to have it fall into your lap against your wishes. But Planned Parenthood was *not* an abortion provider in 1967–68, or, at least, that wasn't its public face, as it is now. The claim that the film is a "a wicked argument against planned parenthood" means that Rosemary's is the ultimate "planned" pregnancy—planned and prepped for by a whole coven of witches and one very bad husband. In a tongue-in-cheek way, this reviewer clearly sees the film as a defense of the mother's being allowed to choose her own reproductive fate. Pregnancy isn't something that should be "planned" for by entities outside of the mother herself.

In the few months after the release of the film, there was a tidal wave of public will to rethink New York State's antiabortion laws. By November 1968, five months after the movie's June release, while it was still in theaters around the country, *The New York Times* ran an article about how "abortion experts" convened at a conference to argue that women should have control over whether to carry a pregnancy to term, noting that doctors routinely provide abortion to "known patients who can afford it," regardless of what the laws are in their state, and pointing out that the newly loosened abortion laws in six states were not loose enough. In November, the *Times* ran an editorial calling for the radical reform of abortion law; it then ran a response letter that even urged for the total *repeal* of abortion law, arguing that a decision about terminating a pregnancy should be left entirely to a woman and her doctor. In December of that year, an article critical of California's reformed abortion laws argued not that the reform was too much but that it was too *little*, citing numerous cases in which women who, by law, should have been able to access abortions (for medical reasons or rape), were denied them. Public sentiment was shifting, and fast. People had come to understand the horrific costs of anti-abortion legislation for women. They had come to believe that the decision about whether to terminate a pregnancy should be just that: a decision. It shouldn't need to be an emergency situation because it should be a private matter decided between a woman and her physician.

The frustration with abortion law, particularly in New York State, picked up momentum in 1969, while *Rosemary's Baby* was still in theaters. In early 1969, the Presbytery of New York City began to advocate not reforming, but *repealing* New York's abortion laws. Women stormed the New York State Legislature in late winter 1969, demanding abortion law repeal. The Episcopal Diocese of Rochester advocated the repeal of New York's abortion laws, arguing that abortion was a matter to be decided on the basis of individual conscience, not by law. A scorching editorial ran in March in the *Times*, critiquing New York's "savage and antiquated abortion laws" and noting that Jewish and Protestant authorities, medical and legal authorities alike were now championing not just reform but repeal, and that the "intransigent" opposition of the Roman Catholic Church was the main obstacle to letting abortion be decided according to "individual conscience." In October, 125 people in New York sued the state to declare New York State abortion law unconstitutional; the suit said that the laws violated women's right to privacy—a relatively new move in the fight against abortion law. By November, a judge had decided the suit had enough merit to be heard by a Federal Supreme Court panel. Where people had been talking about the dangerousness of illegal abortion and about the needless death of women, now they were talking about women's rights to privacy, to equal opportunity, to freedom of choice.

Emphasizing the enormity of the shift in attitude that took place in 1968–69, an article in the *Times* ran, which opened as follows: "As recently as two years ago, the idea that American women have a constitutional right to have abortions was heard only from the radical fringes of the feminist movement. Today, a growing number of lawyers and judges are predicting that this right will eventually be recognized by the Supreme Court." An article in *The New York Times* from early 1970 rang the same bell: "A right to abortion. Such a notion, at first hearing, sounds fantastic, illusory," but it then goes on to recount how the state of California and the District of Columbia had both, in the previous year, challenged abortion laws, on grounds that they violated women's rights to privacy and autonomy. These cases, according to the article, were good precedent for a federal decision that might overturn the New York State abortion laws as unconstitutional. Where people had been talking about making safer abortions slightly more available in some cases, now people were talking about how abortion restriction was, on its face, unconstitutional, because it violated the rights of women, their rights to privacy, to bodily autonomy, to decision-making about their own lives.

In 1970, the floodgates opened. Washington and Vermont moved to ease abortion restrictions. California's judiciary decided that antiabortion laws were unconstitutional. Arizona's State House approved a bill lifting all curbs on abortions performed by licensed doctors. Hawai'i passed a law decriminalizing abortion entirely and making it a medical matter between a woman and her doctor, manifesting what a *New York Times* journalist called "the revolutionary change in public attitudes toward abortion." Finally, in 1970, that revolutionary change came home to roost in New York. In mid-March, having failed to pass even a modest reform bill for the previous three years, the New York State Senate roundly endorsed *a total repeal of abortion laws*, by a margin of 31–26. The new law would make abortion a matter to be decided wholly and exclusively by a woman and her doctor. A few weeks later, the Assembly approved the radical repeal by a margin of 76–73; New York State would now make abortion a legal right of women and a decision to be made between her and her doctor, privately, and without interference from the law or the police. By 1970, abortion criminalization was seen as cruel toward women and archaic. It was seen, in effect, as a form of state-sanctioned abuse of women, a restriction of their rights and humanity, and a danger to their well-being.

Many things contributed to this cultural shift: grassroots

organizers, protests, medical associations, religious institutions, local politicians, news media pressures. I would never want to minimize the importance of those movements, institutions, and activists. But *Rosemary's Baby* also played a major role, because over the course of a year, tens of *millions* of Americans—male and female alike—watched Rosemary get raped and forced to maintain a pregnancy at extremely high physical and psychological cost to herself as well as to the world around her. They watched her innocence get exploited by a flock of abusers. They felt her pain, her fear, and—perhaps most of all—her solitude. It's much harder to make reproductive decisions for someone else once you've been through a reproductive crisis yourself. And, through the empathogenic magic of *Rosemary's Baby*, millions and millions of Americans *had* been through a reproductive crisis. And they had seen its result: to destroy Rosemary psychologically and to bring Satan's spawn into the world. Something had to change, and, mercifully, it did.

Conceiving of Coercive Control

Moreover, whereas the film's critique of abortion policy was on pace with what was going on in the press and in women's rights activism, its take on *how* reproductive violence could be committed by a male malefactor was years—decades, really—ahead of its time. Because, whatever supernatural horrors may arise in this film, there is an acutely interpersonal domestic horror at its heart: Guy is a betrayer, a liar, and the facilitator of acute sexual violence toward his own wife. He may not be the one raping and impregnating her, but he certainly does bawd her out—and to the devil, no less. Domestic horror is something to scream about, something deeper than the Satanism, deeper than evil neighbors. As a domestic abuse survivor I know said to me, when I asked her what she'd felt when she saw this movie in the 1960s, "That movie was terrifying. She is *so trapped* with that husband. So helpless. He breaks her down bit by bit, until there's nothing left." When viewers scream with Rosemary, they're also screaming *about* Guy.

But why is Guy so disquieting as a character? He doesn't actually rape Rosemary himself. He doesn't hit her or throw her around while she's pregnant—though he does shake her fiercely at one point. Guy is what scholars and domestic violence activists and advocates now call a *coercive controller*. Coercive control, a term coined by domestic violence researcher Evan Stark, describes a kind of domestic violence that, while it may not ever escalate to battery or rape, nevertheless keeps a woman in a state of perpetual fear, dehumanization, and entrapment. Stark argues that coercive control is a crucial part of understanding the interpersonal dynamics at work in any domestic abuse situation, because what's ultimately at stake for the abuser is his ability to control his victim. He may use verbal abuse, psychological torture, or emotional terrorism on his domestic partner; he may restrict her access to her friends or family, or to her finances. He may restrict her access to knowledge or education. He may interfere with her reproductive life, either by tampering with her birth control or by restricting her agency once she becomes pregnant. He may control what the woman eats or drinks, or what she wears. He may control what doctors she sees and under what circumstances she is permitted to seek medical help in the first place. He may control her access to transportation, as by hiding her car or her car keys. He may lock her in her home; he may drug her to keep her under his control. The ultimate goal of this kind of coercion is to induce the victim to question her own reality, her own humanity, and her own basic rights, so that she grows ever more entrapped in the abuser's web of distortion, mistreatment, and control.

This language of coercive control wasn't any more available in 1968 than was language about reproductive abuse, but even so, that's a big part of what we witness when we watch the film. Guy *does* control what Rosemary eats and drinks, whom she sees, what doctor she visits. When Rosemary cuts her hair short, and Guy openly criticizes her appearance, telling her it's an "awful" haircut, he is already trying to make her feel small, weak. When Rosemary wants to see her friends, Guy insists they socialize only with the Castevets; Guy wants to restrict her access to her usual and preferred social supports. When Rosemary wants to choose her own doctor, Guy insists she see the doctor the Castevets recommend. When she points out the "chalky undertaste" of the mousse, Guy denies that it's there and forces her to eat it anyway. When Rosemary wakes up from her drug-induced haze, Guy pretends he was the one who forced himself on her—not Satan. Guy's chronic gaslighting and undermining of Rosemary's reality facilitates and enables her becoming pregnant with the Antichrist and carrying it to term. After the Satan-child is born, Guy does actually lock Rosemary in their home and drug her. Rosemary is trapped, controlled, dehumanized, not so much by Satan but very much by Guy, colluding with their evil, scheming neighbors.

Even though there was no technical language for coercive control in the late '60s, that doesn't mean people didn't see it. In fact, in 1968, reviewer Kathleen Carroll registered that the central horror of *Rosemary's Baby* wasn't Satanism but interpersonal betrayal, which resulted in Mia Farrow's entrapment and dehumanization. "Miss Farrow's special magic is her fragility. She reminds one of a fawn in captivity. What she does so remarkably well is draw sympathy to Rosemary who is herself a captive fawn, a totally helpless heroine surrounded by evil on all sides with no way out." To Carroll, *Rosemary's Baby* isn't just a supernatural horror story about witches and Satanists. In fact, it isn't *primarily* a supernatural horror story: Instead, it's an empathogenic story about female helplessness, when an innocent woman is surrounded and conspired against by an enclave of domestic malefactors. Carroll does not talk about the "evil" as sexual assault, reproductive violence, or even as wife battery, but she does see Rosemary as "a captive fawn," surrounded by evil on all sides. What Carroll responds to, and what the novel and film both seek to highlight, is *coercive control*.

So, in the end, what's absolutely astonishing about this film isn't just that it forces viewers to contend with reproductive violence and rape, and to think differently about abortion and reproductive rights, but that it *associates reproductive violence with other, as-yet-unnameable forms of domestic violence*. Without Guy's coercion, Satan never would have had access to Rosemary's womb. *Rosemary's Baby* made readers aware that reproductive violence was not only a horror that women were subjected to entirely against their will, but also that controlling behaviors were largely to blame when that violence happened. Though directed, paradoxically, by a notorious violator of women's rights—a complexity I'll return to in chapter seven—the film *Rosemary's Baby* itself stands as perhaps the single most powerful and important filmic contribution to American feminism of the late 1960s.

CHAPTER 2

There's a Demon in My House: Domestic Violence in *The Exorcist*

The Exorcist was released just after Christmas in 1973, like a horrifying gift wrapped in thick layers of blood, urine, and, famously, vomit. It was released five years after *Rosemary's Baby*, and eleven months after *Roe v. Wade* was decided in the Supreme Court. Like its Satanic predecessor *Rosemary's Baby*, *The Exorcist* played an important role in American feminism, working through and signal boosting a major area of activism in the 1970s. Specifically, it showed American audiences what a broad culture of women's liberation might look like in practice, and how that liberation might both trigger and be imperiled by domestic violence. As we will see, the film conveys some deep anti-feminist sentiment, suggesting that liberated women might be something American culture should fear, not welcome. But, as the film goes on, its shrill critique of liberated women will be undermined and complicated by a far more blistering critique of the kinds of violence and control that women's libbers were desperate to eradicate from American culture. Like *Rosemary's Baby*, this ostensibly supernatural horror film forced American audiences to participate imaginatively in the catastrophic domestic abuse of women. As such it, too, stands at the vanguard of American feminist cinema in the early 1970s.

The Horror of the Liberated Woman

Early in *The Exorcist*, we meet a beautiful woman with short, modish hair, who is writing notes while in bed. Chris, played memorably by Ellen Burstyn, is a young, independent, urban, professional woman—very focused and in control. She also appears to be quite comfortable in her home—her room is slightly messy but very cozy and lived-in. Suddenly, she hears a rattling sound and looks up from her work. She gets out of bed, looking not afraid but curious, and checks out the house, clad in her bathrobe. She does the very thing that men were traditionally meant to do in such situations—check out the strange noise from elsewhere in the house. It's implied to the viewer in this early sequence that Chris is single.

After she determines that the sound originates in the attic, she goes to check on her daughter. So, now the viewer knows that this single, working woman is also a mother. The working mother was a dicey social category in the 1970s: National survey after national survey found that even voters who supported equal rights for women believed strongly that when women were career-oriented, it disadvantaged their children. But that's not what we see in this film—at least not at first. When Chris gets upstairs, she finds her daughter, Regan (Linda Blair), lying on top of her blankets with the window open, in the winter. Chris carefully replaces the covers on her sleeping child and then she whispers to her, "Sure do love you," in a way that conveys comfort, ease, and love.

The next morning, we see Chris on location, shooting a new film as the lead actress. The scene is chaotic, with hundreds of extras milling about, and Chris is eager to get the attention of the director, Burke. She emerges from her trailer with her makeup still in process, and she starts critiquing the script. Chris is exasperated and frustrated, and she clearly expects to be taken seriously by Burke, who gazes upon her with frank admiration. Burke calms her down, their conversation ending with the two of them sharing a joke and embracing. This scene humanizes Chris; she appears warm, friendly, easygoing, funny, and a touch self-deprecating. She may be a single working mother, and she may swear a lot, but she certainly seems like someone with whom you'd want to be friends.

More than that, wealthy, powerful, dominant, and large of feeling, Chris is a force to be reckoned with. We see her yelling at people numerous times in the film, often with a heavy smattering of profanity. She's not going to be pushed around by anyone, it's clear—she is going to make her voice heard, like it or not. She is a women's libber for sure, with all the telltale markings. Chris manifests exactly the kinds of social gains that the women's liberation movement promised to women: She has independence, professional security, personal wealth, happiness, and control over her domestic sphere. And she has a child. Miracle of miracles: She has it all.

But she also manifests exactly the kinds of social *losses* that opponents of women's liberation worried about: She's sassy, she's domineering, she's coarse, she's "unfeminine." And, although a loving mother, Chris is about as far from the iconic or *traditional* American mother as possible. She's not fettered to the domestic sphere but is very much out in the world, surrounded by adoring fans and respectful colleagues. Again, national surveys would predict that her child would suffer from those things. And indeed, she's about to.

The film complicates this presentation of Chris when it shows what kind of character she plays in the film she's shooting. In the film, Chris plays a teacher, involved in some kind of student protest, seemingly at a university, in Washington. Somewhat surprisingly, given Chris's own liberated ways, her character's role in the film is more conservative—she's trying to get the student protesters to stand down. "We're all concerned for human rights, for God's sake! But the kids who want to get an education have a right, too!" she says, and then "If you want to effect any real change, you have to do it *within the system*!" In her on-screen role, Chris is more of a reformist than a radical, advocating against challenging the status quo *too* much. In her real life, by contrast, Chris is a professional woman who swears constantly, bosses people around, shoves away the hands of makeup artists who try to make her look perfect, feels no need to apologize for her feelings, and commands respect from all the men around her.

The tension between Chris's on-screen self and her real-life self is pointed: The film is asking us to think seriously about what we feel about liberated women and what kinds of limits should be imposed on them. Maybe we can tolerate an outspoken teacher who's not trying to overthrow the system; maybe we feel a little differently about a foulmouthed single mother who doesn't hesitate to stand up for herself and holler at those around her. Whether viewers in the 1970s would have liked her or not would have depended almost entirely on what their political stance was on women's liberation going into the theater. Put bluntly, Chris serves as a mechanism for stress testing Americans' feminism and their level of allegiance with or hostility toward the women's liberation movement.

Chris gains more dimensionality a couple of scenes later when she arrives home from work and starts interacting with Regan. We learn that Regan is twelve, charming, sweet, and maybe just a little bit spoiled. She asks in pleading tones if she can have a horse as a gift; rather than saying no, Chris says that a horse isn't possible while they're on location in DC, but "we'll see when we get home," presumably to Los Angeles. The scene is warmly lit, and Regan and Chris are close to each other, very much at their ease. Impishly, with a big smile on her face, Regan steals a cookie and runs off; Chris runs after her. Eventually, Chris and Regan wind up rolling around on the floor, laughing hysterically as Chris tries to pull the cookie out of Regan's hand so she won't ruin her appetite. Whatever we might feel about the dangers of liberated, working women to their young daughters, the bond between them is solid and beautiful.

This warmhearted feeling offers the perfect setup for what comes in their next interaction. They're down in the basement, in an area marked out as Regan's craft room. Chris learns that Regan has been playing around with a Ouija board that she found in the basement and suggests they play together. Before Chris can put her hands on the sliding device on the board, however, it lurches away from her and toward Regan. Chris looks up, visibly surprised, confused, and a little scared. She concludes that Regan somehow pulled it away from her. Regan says she's been talking to someone through the Ouija board named Captain Howdy. Chris is curious and mildly concerned about Regan's play with the board and explores it a bit with her, but, finding nothing obviously amiss, puts it out of her mind. This turns out to be a catastrophic error.

About thirty-five minutes into the film, while Chris is hosting a fancy party, Regan comes downstairs in her nightgown and urinates on the floor. The urination scene is designed to be shocking: Regan is backlit, and we see a stream of urine rocketing down between her legs, caught in an extreme close-up, so that Regan's feet fill the screen, the urine splashing loudly on the carpet between them. It is important here to remember the cultural context of 1973 America: Seeing a pubescent girl urinating on the floor wasn't something that happened in mainstream American films—and it still isn't. Pauline Kael's scathing review of the film in *The New Yorker*, which ended by musing about the awfulness of the urination scene, noted her shock that the film wasn't given an X rating. In the film, Chris channels that shock with a horror-stricken expression, leaves her own party, and rushes Regan upstairs to give her a bath and get her back to bed.

In the bedroom, things get dramatically worse, edging decisively into the realm of the supernatural. Regan's bed shakes violently under her. Uncontrollably. Inexplicably. The idea of a shaking bed not so subtly invokes the idea of sexual intercourse, but this bed isn't shaking the right way. Rather than rocking back and forth in rhythm with the movement of lovers, the bed is violently banging and wobbling around, conspicuously out of rhythm with anything Regan is doing. So the kind of sexuality that's invoked by the shaking bed is violent, nonvolitional, abnormal, and dangerous. Watching Chris—who jumps onto the bed with Regan—try to still the shaking of the bed with her body, trying to physically shield Regan from danger but being unable to, gestures toward a kind of too-early, too-violent sexual awakening in Regan—which Chris is unable to temper and which will only prove more distressing as the film progresses.

So, we have a liberated single mother with a child whose pubescent body doesn't behave right. We have an independent woman who loves her daughter but is losing her grip on her domestic situation, particularly as something about her daughter's body changes right before her eyes. There's an allegory here—only thinly veiled—about the insufficiency of Chris, as a single mother, to grapple with and curb her daughter's emergent sexuality, a dark parable about the dangers to children of growing up in a household with a single, liberated mother. The film is lining up to be a critique of women's liberation, no matter how beautiful and dynamic Chris may be. Look out, the movie seems to say: Liberated women have libertine daughters.

Regan's physical and mental health deteriorate rapidly. Chris does what any responsible parent would do: She assumes the problem originates in Regan's physiology and takes her to the hospital. Regan is not, however, an easy patient. The hospital scene opens with a close-up of Regan screaming and struggling against the doctors, who are trying to give her a sedative injection. As the needle pierces her arm, Regan spits in the doctor's face and screams "You fucking bastard!"—the first time in mainstream American cinema that a child says the word "fuck" onscreen. Chris looks abashed and horrified, unable to believe her little girl has become such a dysregulated, degenerate, and foul-mouthed creature. Somehow, despite her obvious adoration for her child, she is not doing a good enough job caring for Regan. Even when the doctors attempt to reassure her that the problem lies in the temporal lobe of Regan's brain, we can see that Chris doesn't totally buy it. And it's not only fear but agonized self-reproach playing across her face. *The Exorcist* is starting to feel rabidly anti-feminist, highlighting the dangers of single motherhood, the risks of living in a household run by a liberated woman who can't keep things in order.

That anti-feminist flavor quickly grows more acrid. After a series of tests Regan endures in the hospital, Chris gets a couple of doctors to make a house call. When they arrive, Regan is writhing around in her bed, convulsing like a rag doll on a string. Eventually, she shouts, "Fuck me, fuck me!" and picks up the front of her nightdress to reveal her genitals to the doctors (though not to the camera). The implication of the earlier bed-shaking scene is now fully realized: Regan is hypersexual, sexually aggressive, and extremely out of control. She is becoming a nightmare rendering of what many Americans feared women and girls would become in the wake of sexual liberation: lascivious, obscene, and uncontrollable.

Desperate for answers and having exhausted physiological explanations for Regan's transformation, Chris hires a hypnotist to work with Regan to explore whether there may be a psychological cause for her dysregulated behavior. When everyone thinks Regan is under hypnosis, she surprises them by grabbing the hypnotist by the balls and squeezing while she pushes him to the floor. We see him fall backward onto the floor in agony—the camera follows him all the way down, from Regan's point of view. In that moment, Regan becomes an abuser, and the camera forces viewers to enter into her rapacious and aggressive vantage point and to consider sexual vulnerability in *men*. Look out, America, indeed: These libertine bitches are going to grab you by the balls and push you down.

But Regan's tendency toward sexual violence is most acute and most troubling toward herself. In the most famous and most horrifying scene of the film, Regan begins stabbing herself in the genitals with a crucifix, saying, "Let Jesus fuck you! Let Jesus fuck you!" Chris, her face the picture of horror, runs over to try to prevent her daughter from mutilating herself any further. Regan then grabs Chris's head and shoves her face down to her now bleeding genitals, screaming, "Lick me!" Regan then throws Chris across the room, and we watch her hit the ground—hard—and scream for dear life. As viewers, we are horrified: Regan, a twelve-year-old girl—clearly possessed by an agent of evil and an enemy of Christ—is engaging in genital self-mutilation, attempting lesbian incest, and physically assaulting her own mother. Roger Ebert said of the film, echoing the sentiments of Pauline Kael, "That it received an R rating and not the X is stupefying." This film is designed to be *shocking*. You're not supposed to feel just a little afraid; you're supposed to feel scandalized, horrified, harmed, traumatized, and broken open.

The Horror of Domestic Imprisonment

The panicked anti-feminism surrounding Chris and Regan is not, however, the film's only commentary on the status of American women. The other is a strong critique of the patriarchal structures of power—and, specifically, of the structures of power in a domestic sphere—that keep Chris (and Regan) imprisoned in their shared tale of horror and violent suffering. Because although the film is, on one level, an anti-feminist screed, eager to lambaste both working mothers and pubescent girls, it is also, on a deeper level, a crushing exposé of domestic violence and what sustains it in America culture. Regan, after all, is not the only person in the film who is being physically and sexually tortured. Chris, too, at the hands of the demon who seems to have taken possession of Regan, is abused. Regularly and brutally. Furniture is thrown at her, she's hit, she's pushed. Chris is being battered, tortured, domestically abused. Her daughter is a pawn in that abuse pattern. Whether William Friedkin intended it or not (and I seriously doubt he did), the demonic abuse narrative in the film amplifies the emerging feminist awareness in the 1970s about the all-too-real and all-too-quotidian horror of domestic violence.

As we watch Chris's transformation over the course of the film, we see a liberated woman get broken—both physically and psychologically—by a demon who has entered her home. We watch her suffer at the mercy of this male demonic figure because she cannot leave her child, and that child, in turn, cannot leave their home. The film lays bare Chris's complete and total helplessness and her inability to find help from the outside. Like *Rosemary's Baby*, *The Exorcist* showcases motherhood as a central site of vulnerability for domestic abuse—a social reality that, by the time the film premiered, had just begun to be acknowledged in scholarly conversations and at professional conferences. To show how the film mounts its avant-garde critique of domestic violence, however, I need to take us on a brief tour of Anglo-American legal history.

For close to a thousand years, the beating of wives and children was a recognized and accepted fact of domestic life, first in English law and then in the American legal system that emerged directly from it. Domestic battery was understood as a good and necessary thing, if not done to excess. Two pieces of logic underpinned the accepted practice of wife beating and child beating. The first was the idea that wives and children were in need of "correction"; women and children were understood to be mentally and morally weaker than adult men, so it was incumbent upon adult men to discipline, correct, and control women and children. The second was that wives and children were the property of their husbands—and I mean that quite literally.

By the doctrine of *couverture* (covering), when a woman married a man, she became of one flesh with him, and he had total legal control over her, her body, her children, her property, and her rights. Legal commentator William Blackstone argued in the eighteenth century that "By marriage, the husband and wife are one person in law: that is, the very being or legal existence of the woman is suspended during the marriage, or at least is incorporated and consolidated into that of her husband: under whose wing, protection, and *cover*, she performs every thing." Women belonged to their husbands, because their legally independent status died when they married, and their bodies became, literally, his to do with as he saw fit.

So, given this ideological bedrock of Anglo-American family law, if a man beat his wife, how would you prosecute him? For punishing his own body? A body he owned, by marriage, in the eyes of the law? The short answer is that you wouldn't—even well into the twentieth century. The head of the household in almost all of Anglo-American legal history was the absolute and uncontested *paterfamilias*, the "father" who ruled the family as a quasi-divinity and who had the power to correct, discipline, and harm his underlings as he wished. As a result of these beliefs and doctrines, the battering of wives and children was rampant in America throughout most of history.

Although rampant, it was also cruelly silent. Even in the relatively liberal 1960s, domestic violence was seldom featured in public writings or in legal and medical writings. Indeed, a 1977 article from *The New Women's Times*, which interviewed a domestic abuse survivor, noted that the survivor had only ever read or seen one article on wife beating during the time she was married. An influential 1980 review essay noted that there was not one single article on family violence in the *Journal of Marriage and the Family* in the first thirty years of its existence—which is to say, up to 1969. There was precious little legislation that sought to curb the domestic abuse of wives, and there were far more articles in psychiatric journals about how wives provoked their husbands' beatings than about how to support the wives who were being abused. In fact, a very common and very erroneous belief among even psychiatric practitioners into the 1970s was that women in violent relationships were masochists who wanted to be there, and that, therefore, there was precious little a practitioner could do for them. Even for more sympathetic medical practitioners and psychologists, there were no clear guidelines about how to help women who were clearly being abused. Doctors routinely told women who reported being victims of domestic abuse that they, the women, were probably causing the problems, that they should try to reconcile with their husbands, or that they were simply "nervous" and needed medication.

Knowing the biases against abused women that existed broadly in American culture, abused women simply hid. They hid their bruised faces under large, dark sunglasses. They wore scarves to cover head lacerations and bald patches where their hair had been torn out by the roots. They wore bulky sweaters and coats to conceal injuries to their arms, chests, and necks.

And more often than not, they simply stayed indoors, concealed from public view—which, of course, is where they were getting hurt in the first place. But they often stayed indoors anyway, often because it was an embarrassment to *them* if they were seen in such a state.

It was an embarrassment to them in part because so many Americans overtly supported the practice of spousal violence as a mechanism for corralling unruly wives. Indeed, 25 percent of American adults in a University of Wisconsin survey in the 1960s confirmed that they supported husband-wife physical battles—with a higher rate of approval among better-educated respondents. A Harris poll from 1968 showed that 25 percent of people with a college education approved of a husband slapping a wife. Now, 25 percent may seem like a small fraction, but think about it: If 25 percent of highly educated people actively *approve* of slapping a wife, how many are willing to turn a blind eye, especially if it happens behind closed doors? Perhaps 75 percent? Maybe 90 percent? The high approval ratings of physical violence were part of what made it hard to prosecute—many people simply didn't have a problem with it as a social practice, because they felt it was necessary and normal to correct the behavior of women. And, of course, it happened behind closed doors, where no one could see it and no law could hope to regulate it.

Compounding and complicating the dual culture of shame and condonation around domestic violence, there was the logistical difficulty of doing anything through law enforcement or litigation to curb wife battery. In 1972 and 1973—right when *The*

Exorcist was filming—there were fourteen *thousand* complaints of wife battery in the Family Court system in New York City alone; the reported figure is estimated to be approximately 10 percent of the true total—140,000. Almost none of these 140,000 suspected instances of spousal battery were successfully prosecuted, and not only because so few of them were reported. The legal system routinely dismissed cases or ruled that the husband was well within his rights to do whatever act of violence he did to his wife. It is worth noting that, until 1966 in the relatively liberal state of New York, it was not possible for a woman to obtain a divorce because of beatings and, even *after* 1966, she had to establish a "sufficient" pattern of physical battery. Let me pause to emphasize that: in a *liberal* state, if a husband battered his wife *once*, it was not even grounds for *divorce* in 1966. In New York State in the 1960s, to get a divorce, let alone for criminal prosecution of her own abuser, which was entirely out of reach for most women, a woman had to establish *habitual* beatings.

So, given the amount of shame surrounding wife battery, given the hesitation of police to get involved, given the inadequacy of legal mechanisms for combating it, and, of course, given the social agnosticism about whether it should be classed as criminal behavior in the first place, how could American public and legal culture go about changing things? What *did* change? First, there were scholarly conferences and studies in the works, many of which led to mass market book publications. Second, there was a rapidly exploding grassroots movement in the early and mid-1970s to support beaten women and help them escape violence, while also raising the consciousness of the average American about what intimate partner violence really was.

One of the books that spurred the rapid and public awakening about wife battery was *Violence in the Family*, published in 1974. This essay collection opens by targeting three "myths" it wanted to debunk: first, the "class myth," which was that the physical battery of people within a family was a "working class phenomenon." Second, "the sex myth," that sexual drives were what produced violence toward women in the family. And third, the "catharsis myth," namely, that the battery of wives and children was the outgrowth of normal male aggression. From there, the book argues that violence, while not normal or healthy, has its origins in pro-violence American culture and in families in which there are generational patterns of violence—that is, men who witnessed battery in their childhood homes are more likely to beat their wives and children. Although these are truisms of twenty-first-century discourse around domestic abuse, they were revolutionary in 1974 because they suggested that intrafamilial violence was pathological, heritable, and linked with cultural patterns and mindsets that needed to evolve. They suggested domestic violence was not something a woman was ever "asking for," nor was it something for her to be ashamed of. It was an undesirable by-product of cultural and intrafamilial dysfunction, and it was rooted in the violent psychology of the abusive male.

Meanwhile, grassroots organizations had begun opening women's shelters—the first to appear in the United States—and circulating information in small-scale publications to help women understand their rights, and to help women make escape plans from abusers. In 1974, one of the first battered women's shelters opened in St. Paul, Minnesota. In 1975, Abused Women's Aid in Crisis was founded, an organization based in New York to help women exit violent marriages. By 1978, the "We Will Not Be Beaten" movement had inspired the founding of more than 150 battered women's shelters across the United States.

So, 1974 was a watershed year for women's rights to safety and for anti-violence cultural awareness. And in movie theaters across the country, with viewers watching Chris and Regan get brutalized, that awareness had begun to consolidate and to pick up momentum. You couldn't see into your neighbors' homes, but you *could*, thanks to the silver screen, see into Chris MacNeil's home, and what you saw there would stop you dead in your tracks.

The Exorcist's aggressive staging of the dangers of women's liberation sets up an equally strenuous critique of domestic violence as a habitual practice in the US. As Chris gets brought to heel by the demonic forces in her home, as she gets unmade as a women's libber, Chris's and Regan's imprisonment in their home reflects the real-life situation of countless American women in the 1970s. Although it was legally possible in many states in the 1970s—albeit very difficult—for a woman to leave her abusive spouse, it was often extremely difficult logistically. Women in the 1970s often did not have incomes of their own, had many children to care for in their flight from violence, and did not have a place to seek shelter. Indeed, in 1973, there were only a couple of domestic violence shelters *in the entire United States*. There was no way to escape a domestic abuse situation for the vast majority of women who were in one. Chris and Regan's entrapment, however harrowing and supernatural, actually reflected a situation of domestic battery with shocking accuracy. For so many mothers and their children, there was no way out.

One might protest that the violence in *The Exorcist* is not *really* domestic violence against Chris, in the traditional sense of wife beating, because it's her daughter who's doing it to her, not some evil husband. But in the fiction of the film, it *is* a "powerful man" who is abusing her—the police officer whom Chris speaks with in the latter half of the film says so, verbatim. More specifically, it is a male demon who has entered her house and made her daughter his own personal plaything. A male demon who has decided, in effect, to construe Chris's house as his own domain. A male demon who has turned Chris's daughter into an instrument of torture for both Regan herself and for Chris. A male demon whom the surprisingly helpful, kindhearted, and well-meaning police officers in the film cannot detect, let alone capture or remove from Chris's home.

This diabolical plot element is crucially important to the film's critique of domestic violence. In fact, it's right in the intersection between the possession narrative and the ideologies of domestic violence in the United States that the film's energy turns from being anti-feminist to being pro-feminist and extraordinarily sophisticated in its feminist critiques. First, the demon clearly understands himself to be "correcting" Chris. He's curbing her, subordinating her, and breaking her down because she fails to acknowledge his complete and total right to her daughter and to her daughter's body. Second, and most important, the possession narrative taps into and literalizes the core and horrific truth of Anglo-American legal history: Women were property. Women were owned; they were, literally, *possessed by men*—as were children. The possession narrative of this film isn't just supernatural; it's also a representation of lived reality for married American women and their children. The supernatural possession plot of *The Exorcist* is not extraneous to its feminist critique; it *is* its feminist critique.

The film represents how women are *further* trapped by their fundamental vulnerability to the danger their children are facing. Regan is physically possessed by this new, male, powerful, interloping presence in the domestic space. And, because of her possession, there is nothing Chris can do, either to save her child or to save herself. Because the reality is that Chris, too, is possessed by proxy: There is no way for Chris to escape because there is no way she will ever abandon her child. No matter how much the demon beats her, no matter how much the demon terrorizes her, Chris cannot leave her child. She is vulnerable to demonic abuse because she is a mother who loves her child. This film recognizes something that the battered women's movement was desperate to get Americans to see: When a woman stays in a physically abusive situation, it is often because she believes staying there to be *essential to the safety and survival of her children.*

That reality wasn't just psychological for women; it was also logistical and legal. In the 1960s and 1970s (and before), if a woman fled her abuser but didn't bring her children with her—even in the heat of abuse—she ran the very real risk of losing custody of them to her abuser. Moreover, if a woman did flee with her children, it was not clear there was anywhere to go—precious few domestic violence shelters and even the most sympathetic and supportive friends and family typically couldn't house a woman and her children for an extended period of time. In *The Exorcist*, Regan's possession results in her being so physically dysregulated that she has to be tied down to the bed, imprisoned in the house. So her mother can't leave because she can't leave Regan behind, alone, to be tortured or killed by the demon.

Through the possession dynamic and its staging of domestic violence, the film forces viewers to connect with a version of domestic violence in which the woman is *in no way at fault* for the physical battery she and her child endure. However liberated Chris may be and however foulmouthed, however "unpleasant" she may have appeared to some anti-feminist viewers, we cannot in good conscience say that she or her daughter deserve to be brutalized like they are. Moreover, the male character who commits the violence has *zero* moral complexity: He is an allegory of pure evil who possesses and violates a little girl and beats the living hell out of her mother. He is, literally, a demon, as well as a child rapist, a batterer of women, a murderer, and a sociopath. As the degree of his demonicness is confirmed, our ability to condemn Chris as the reason for Regan's problems drains away. There is no room for sympathy toward the demon or understanding for why he might be committing this domestic violence. It's brutal, horrible battery, pure and simple. No way to justify it. No way to pretend it's complicated. No way to say Chris was asking for it. No way to say Chris needed correction as violent as the demon is doling out—even if a viewer had initially found Chris to be brash, abrasive, unpleasant, unfeminine, or in any other way offensive to patriarchal norms of femininity or womanhood.

In its allegorical presentation of domestic violence, *The Exorcist* was fifty years ahead of its time. It forced Americans to view the torture and abuse of women by a malign, inexcusable male force, and to recognize how utterly and completely trapped both Regan and Chris were. Doctors and psychiatrists fail to help her. The police fail to help her. This pervasive failure, of doctors, of police, and of law, is made all the more horrible because it reflects *reality* in the early 1970s: There were no social institutions that a woman could easily turn to for support in a situation of domestic violence. Chris's case of abuse wasn't *exceptional* for being unprosecutable and irremediable—it was *typical*. In forcing the American people to witness the torture of a woman and her child in their own home, to witness the total impotence of the police to help, *The Exorcist* created itself as a masterpiece of consciousness-raising. Through the film—with all its supernaturalness—we actually bear witness to a totally quotidian, familiar, tragically pervasive reality. The only place a woman could turn, often, for help in situations of domestic violence was a priest.

Paralleling reality again, Chris eventually finds help in the very place from which the logic of couverture, the logic that, in the domestic space, man and woman are of one flesh, originated: the Church. And even though the film's turn to the Church seems only to reinscribe Chris and Regan within the patriarchal power systems that got her into trouble in the first place, it is her choice to turn to the Church that allows Chris to appear in full relief as exactly what she is: a battered supplicant who seeks the support of the institution that is, in principle, supposed to advocate for the weak, the desperate, and the disempowered. By this point in the film, Chris certainly is all those things. And so, in weary resignation, having become convinced that no doctor or psychiatrist can help her or her child, Chris arranges to meet Father Damien Karras (Jason Miller), a disenchanted Catholic priest whose life has formed the secondary plot of the film up to this point.

In the scene where she meets Father Damien, we see Chris *radically* physically transformed from her first appearances in the film. Initially, she was brash, loud, sexy, and liberated, wearing formfitting clothing and classy makeup. Now, she wears a headscarf, tucked tight to her face, and a heavy coat, collar turned up. And in a stark symbolic gesture, she dons big, dark sunglasses to cover her eyes and cheekbones. She looks, for all the world, like a victim of domestic abuse who is trying to hide the signs of her battery from the world. Which, of course, she is. And like countless tens of thousands of other women in the 1970s, she is ashamed of her brokenness, her vulnerability, her own pain, and she seeks to hide it from public scrutiny. Indeed, when she talks with Damien, at one point, she pulls off her glasses, and we can see that her face is in fact all bruised and beat up. This scene is a revelation of domestic violence. There is *no way* that women who were living through domestic abuse and watching the film would have failed to notice this iconography.

Although skeptical that he can help, Father Damien agrees to meet Regan at their home. Upon seeing him, the demon reveals that he cannot tolerate the priest's presence. After all, the demon's structural and symbolic role is that of the *paterfamilias*, "correcting" those whom he has taken possession of, whether bodily (Regan) or psychologically (Chris). When Father Damien comes in, a true "father" enters into the domestic sphere and challenges the demon's right to exert his patriarchal power over Chris and Regan.

Of course, that's a problematic place for the roiling feminism of the film to turn: Chris cannot help herself, and she can't help Regan. But Father Damien, who steps into the role of the *paterfamilias* for the rest of the film—*he* can help. By challenging the primacy of the demon for the role as the father in the home, Father Damien is the only one who can help Regan and Chris out of their plight. Chris, the liberated, profane, professional mother, has to be reinscribed within the norms of Christian domestic space in order for her and her child to be saved, soul as well as body. And that dual soul-body salvation of Chris and Regan is made possible—as it is in traditional Christian doctrine—only by an act of supreme self-sacrifice on the part of a Christian male. In the end, Father Damien takes the demon into himself, seeing that there is no other way to end the gradual destruction and dehumanization of Regan. The demon appears to penetrate into Father Damien's eyes, which grow wide and wild, and then take on a demonic cast. But Father Damien retains enough of his humanity at this critical moment to choose to leap out the window to his death, and that of the demon.

So, can we call this film a feminist masterpiece, determined to showcase in allegorical form the true horrors of domestic abuse? Yes. Can we also call this film an anti-feminist screed, determined to showcase the dangers to the family posed by the liberation of women and the necessity of that liberation being limited and regulated by Catholic Christianity? Yes.

This tension is not unusual in domestic horror. Domestic horror is often ambivalent toward women and their suffering. When we gaze on Rosemary's suffering, we cannot help but notice her beauty, her sweetness; there is a fetishism in that film, as well as a resistance to the dehumanization to which Rosemary is subjected. Here, *The Exorcist* revels in disciplining Chris for her unfeminine ways. But it also forces us to align affectively with her in the end. In *The Exorcist*, we may or may not like Chris at the start, but we definitely want her and Regan to escape their hell. And they do—with the audience being shown, all the while, the true entrapment and horror of being "possessed" by a demonic male. But they only escape through their willing submission to Catholic ritual and to the reinstatement of Catholic paternalism within their household.

After Father Karras's self-sacrifice, Regan heals, and she and Chris pack up to leave Washington, DC, we assume forever. In the final scene, Chris is a restrained, depressive version of her former self; she wears conservative clothes, little makeup, and the tight-lipped expression of someone who expects pain and fear to come raining down on her again at any time. In my own work with abuse survivors who have extricated themselves from the demons in their own homes, I'm all too familiar with that particular facial expression. It is very, very hard to accept that the demon is really gone. Because all too often, he isn't.

So, however much the film may have raised awareness about the domestic violence inflicted on women and children who are "possessed" by demonic men, trapped in their own homes to be "corrected" by that man's law of violence, it simultaneously critiqued and cast doubt on any vision of a future in which a women could be truly independent or free from such domestic horror. Chris may get out from under the demon's violence, but she only does so with the help of the Church, and her face clearly tells us, in the final scene, that she will never feel truly safe again.

Reactions to *The Exorcist*

The Exorcist was one of the most profitable horror films ever made. It cost twelve million dollars to make, and it made well over one hundred million dollars in its first year of release. The film was on theater screens for more than two years. Moreover, it was the first horror film ever nominated for Best Picture by the Academy Awards; it earned nine other nominations beside. People were utterly captivated by this film: critics and casual filmgoers alike. Roger Ebert gushed about the film: "*The Exorcist* is one of the best movies of its type ever made; it not only transcends the genre of terror, horror, and the supernatural, but it transcends such serious, ambitious efforts in the same direction as Roman Polanski's *Rosemary's Baby*."

Some responses to the film—equally powerful—were not nearly so intellectual. An article in the *Times* in January 1974 noted that "It's been reported that once inside the theater, a number of moviegoers vomited at the very graphic goings-on on the screen. Others fainted, or left the theater, nauseous and trembling, before the film was half over. Several people had heart attacks, a guard told me. One woman even had a miscarriage, he said." People who saw this film responded with a profound physiological aversion. They were sickened by it; they were harmed by it. They were broken open. Theater officials reported that it was rare for a screening of the film *not* to end with at least one person fainting or vomiting. Countless audience members sought the support and reassurance of priests and clergy in the wake of seeing the film. This film made people feel things—too many things, and too intensely for many audience members to tolerate.

And yet they kept going back, for two years. What people who went to see the film again and again responded to most was the horrific supernatural dynamic of the horror that befalls Regan, and the salvific power of Father Damien, as representative of Catholic order. The public, in-print response to the domestic violence in this film was muted, to say the least. But of course, not everything that *happens* in a culture makes it into print or explicit public consciousness—at least not right away.

What slowly filtered into American consciousness, with two years on the big screen, was the abuse that Chris and Regan suffered. Americans got to witness and imaginatively participate in the domestic torture of two women—a daughter and a mother—

in a way they could witness, think about, and take home with them. People watched Chris transform from a powerful, stylish, assertive woman into a bruised, battered, beaten, terrified, and trapped domestic pawn. Thousands and thousands of women, who were silently enduring regular beatings in their own homes, watched this externalization and literalization of their own experience, of being possessed, tortured, and abused, on the silver screen. They watched it in the theater, in public, in community with others. They looked around during the scenes where Chris gets beat up. They looked around during the scene where Chris appears in a scarf, a coat, and sunglasses. They thought about the possibility that this wasn't just happening to Chris, but that there were countless other "demons" out there, inflicting crushing physical and sexual harm on the wives and daughters in their lives. They were registering, even subconsciously, that for many women, as for Chris in the film, "home" was not a safe space but a dangerous prison where no human authority could intervene on the woman's behalf—not the police, not the doctors, no one. Only God and his ambassadors.

The Exorcist played a shaping role in American consciousness about domestic violence and sexual abuse, coming out, as it did, *just* before the massive uptick in protests against domestic violence and sexual abuse of women. The film came out in the final days of 1973. Earlier in 1973, the Rainbow Retreat, the first shelter for women in the US, had opened in Arizona; in 1974, a second battered women's shelter opened in California. In that same year, the aforementioned groundbreaking essay collection *Violence in the Family* was published. In 1975, prominent feminist Del Martin started publishing her findings in major venues, like *The New York Times*, and in 1976 she published *Battered Wives*, arguably the single most influential popular press work on domestic violence up to that point. In 1975 the National Organization for Women formed a task force on domestic violence. In 1976, it was found that nearly two million American women were in situations of severe domestic battery. In 1975 and 1976, numerous articles ran in *The New York Times* about battered wives and the challenges they faced. These articles clamored for change at local, state, and federal levels; they demanded more resources, more shelters, changes of social consciousness. By contrast, between 1970 and 1972, *The New York Times* had run zero articles about the problem.

Although many of the books published in the mid- and late '70s that helped guide reformist public policy were in the works before *The Exorcist* came out, and although there was some cultural and legal movement toward reform prior to 1973, it is equally clear that this film was reading the writing on the wall and screaming it at the top of its lungs: The sociocultural and legal sanctioning of domestic abuse needed to come to an end. It's one thing to read a powerful feminist study on the incidence of domestic battery in the United States; but watching Chris get terrorized, abused, beaten, and slowly broken, watching Regan transformed by a demonic male in their household from a healthy young girl to a bloody, brutalized creature, and watching their transformations on a huge screen, in a theater with scores of other people who were yelling their lungs out at the pain and suffering these women endured? That was something else entirely.

Moreover, the sheer popularity and visibility of the film exceeded the popularity or visibility of any scholarly work or activist publication by orders of magnitude. We're talking about a film that earned $193 million in its initial theatrical release—millions and millions of Americans saw this film. Both through its innate artistry and through its wide cultural reach, *The Exorcist* changed public awareness about domestic battery in a way that, I believe, the public couldn't bounce back from.

I have interviewed a number of women who either watched *The Exorcist* in the theaters in 1973–75 or who have seen it since. Many of them commented that, for them, the most horrifying part of the film was watching Chris's conversion from a powerful woman into a helpless victim. Many commented that the brutal violence directed toward her body and Regan's body were the parts of the film that really frightened them. Some commented that the doctors were totally unsympathetic to Chris and didn't help her enough with her situation. All commented on the entrapment and physical torture of mother and child. What male reviewers generally responded to—the Catholic crisis of faith, the male actors in the film—wasn't central to the terror felt by women who watched this film in 1973 or now. Women's horror hangovers were and are tightly pinned to the domestic violence they witnessed onscreen. As one woman I interviewed stated, "I recognize that demon. I lived with him, too."

Perhaps more important, however, than its ability to speak to victims and survivors of domestic violence is that this film enabled men and women who had *not* lived with this demon to grasp some portion of what it might be like to be imprisoned by a sadistic torturer in your own home, with your own child. This is what is so politically powerful about art, and about horror art in particular: It can make viewers feel their way into the action. It gathers up and performs human vulnerability in a way that is psychologically and physiologically participatory for audiences. It gives us that horror hangover so that we go home, having seen Regan and Chris ultimately escape the hell on earth of their domestic torture, but we go home feeling just a little less comfortable climbing into our beds at night, a little more aware that this whole notion of the domestic space as a safe place might just be a fiction. Maybe this place that we've been taught to think of as a refuge is actually a place of peril.

CHAPTER 3

Trad Wives Forever: *The Stepford Wives* and the Equal Rights Amendment

Welcome to Stepford (1972)

In 1972, Ira Levin, author of *Rosemary's Baby*, published his second domestic horror novel: *The Stepford Wives*. Levin flags it as a feminist work early on, opening with a lengthy quotation from iconic feminist Simone de Beauvoir's *The Second Sex*. The quotation describes how women are imprisoned by men and seek to escape, but men won't let them go. Starting from this premise, *Stepford*—much like *The Exorcist*, which was in production when Levin's novel was released—is a horror story that takes the rise of the liberated woman as a provocation. Or, rather, it takes the reactionary *responses* to the liberated woman as a provocation. This book was met with a huge audience, leading Bryan Forbes to direct it as a film that hit theaters in the winter of 1975.

Like *Rosemary's Baby*, *The Stepford Wives* is a New York

City novel, albeit more obliquely. In the first pages, we learn that a young family is moving from Manhattan to a town called Stepford in the Connecticut suburbs. The town is quiet, with generously proportioned houses, sprawling emerald-green lawns, and lots of space between neighbors. Ideal and picture-perfect Americana. The mother of the family, Joanna Eberhart, is at peace with the move. Her relationship with her husband, Walter, is initially loving and mutual; their sex life is happy, they share political and specifically feminist values, and they've decided together that a move to the country will make life easier for them and for their children. Once they're in Stepford, he'll be the primary breadwinner; she will largely shelve her aspirations to be a professional photographer. But she won't entirely jettison her liberated values. She tells a woman in her new town, "I'm a semi-professional photographer . . . And I'm interested in politics and in the Women's Liberation movement. Very much so in that. And so is my husband." Not subtle, the feminism of this woman. But all of the novel's seeming feminism is a setup for the abject domestic horror yet to come at the hands of the Stepford men who have had it with all this talk of women's lib.

Soon enough, Walter announces that he's "joining the Men's Association" in Stepford, though he assures Joanna that he's done so only to change the archaic organization "from inside." As Joanna meets her neighbors, she realizes that the women in the neighborhood are all housewives. She also comes to understand that they are all docile, almost aggressively pretty, and quite vacuous as conversation partners. She determines that she won't become "a compulsive hausfrau" nor an "asking-to-be-exploited patsy," so she teams up with the other outwardly liberated woman in town, Bobbie Markowe. They spend their days together talking and bonding over the extreme political backwardness of Stepford. Doing some research at the local library together, they discover that there *used* to be a women's organization, too, in Stepford, but that it disbanded for mysterious reasons. Bobbie and Joanna begin to get nervous that something's wrong with Stepford. As Bobbie puts it, "A few years ago, they were *applauding Betty Friedan*, and look at them now . . . There's something here, Joanna! I'm not kidding! This is Zombieville!" Something bad happened in Stepford, something that chastened or corralled all the liberated women, just as the demon had chastened and corralled Chris in *The Exorcist*. But this time, the demon isn't a supernatural demon. Here, the demon is simply the men of Stepford.

The conversion of the town's female residents happens, we later learn, because the Men's Association records the Stepford women's physical appearances and voices and uses those two things to build robotic replacements for the women of the town. The entire novel is a meditation on what it would be like if women were turned into the robotic domestic servants that reactionary groups in the 1970s wanted them to be—entirely at the sexual and domestic beck and call of their husbands. It's a thought experiment, really, about the trad wife movement, but fifty years early. Like the internet-famous trad wives of the twenty-first century, the Stepford wives voice nothing but happiness in their domestic life, centering all their sense of self around their children and husband. There is no arena beyond the home that they care about; they have no being beyond that of homemaker.

In his film adaptation of Levin's novel, director Bryan Forbes revises the plot in subtle but important ways. He takes great pains to show us that our protagonist, Joanna Eberhart (played by Katharine Ross), is ambivalent about the move from Manhattan to the suburbs from the get-go—it's almost like she *knows* how much she's going to be giving up by leaving the city. She's unsmiling in the opening shots; we see her staring at herself in a mirror in her newly emptied apartment—a visual anticipation of what's to come at the end of the film when we find her empty, robotic doppelgänger staring blankly into a mirror. We see that her husband, Walter (Peter Masterson), is highly dissimilar to Levin's realization of him in the novel. In the film, Walter tends to be flip and dismissive of others, and he likes to pick fights with Joanna. He's not the loving husband and reflexive feminist ally of the beginning of Levin's novel. Instead, he's kind of a boor. He's also the one who pushes for the move from the city to the suburbs, while Joanna voices her wish to move back to Manhattan. And her instinct is entirely correct: For her, the city means freedom; it's the move to the suburbs that puts her in danger.

When the family arrives in Stepford, everything is organized around Joanna's point of view. From the car window, we see what she sees. She appears tense and ill at ease when they arrive. We see Joanna's reaction to her bizarre and old-fashioned, perfectly coiffed and domestic-goddess-like neighbor, Carol Van Sant; Joanna is confused by her, put off balance, perhaps even slightly repulsed. When she's interviewed by a local reporter about her feelings about her new home, Joanna says she misses the noise of the city, and, indeed, there really is a lot of quiet in the film, a lot of scenes where Joanna isn't talking but simply witnessing the strange social practices in her new town. In one scene, she sees her neighbor Carol being groped by her husband in their yard; Joanna is shocked and somewhat aroused, it seems, by what she sees. She goes home and tells Walter about it; he responds by telling her about the Men's Association that exists in Stepford and reveals that he's already joined it. Joanna spins around to stare at him in shocked disappointment, saying, "I give up on you . . . You pretend we decide things together, but it's always *you*, what *you* want." In the book, by contrast, they discuss it together, both acknowledging that it's weird and sexist that women aren't allowed to join; Forbes's film makes Walter more obviously scheming and traitorous from the start. In so doing, Forbes makes the precariousness of Joanna's situation clearer from the beginning. He sees the panicked feminism of the novel and doubles down on it.

Soon thereafter, Walter goes to his first meeting of the men's club. Whatever he learns there shakes him up. He comes home to swear to Joanna, "I really love you. Do you know that? I really do." It sounds very much as if he's trying to convince *himself* that this is true. By the end of the film, we've worked out that, at that initial meeting, Walter was offered the opportunity to have Joanna replaced with a sexy, passive, domesticated robot Joanna—an exact replica of her but empty of thoughts, feelings, or desires. In retrospect, Walter's protestation that he really does love Joanna strikes the viewer as evidence that he has already decided to replace her with a robot but feels some degree of guilt or remorse about it.

In the next scene, Joanna meets and befriends Bobbie (Paula Prentiss). As in the novel, she is liberated, sassy, and fun; she comments constantly that she doesn't hold with the hyper-domesticated, passive, servile women of the town any more than Joanna does. "Given the freedom of choice," she says, in reference to the local wives' obsessions with commercial products for the domestic sphere, "I don't wanna squeeze the goddamn Charmin." Both Joanna and Bobbie resist the commodification of homemaking. That resistance gets extra sharpness in her phrasing, "given the freedom of choice": Bobbie parrots the logic of the pro-choice movement. Bobbie and Joanna celebrate their new friendship, and its resistance to the gravitational pull of domestic servility, by eating Ring Dings and drinking scotch during the daytime at Joanna's kitchen table.

Over the course of the film, Bobbie and Joanna become increasingly restless in their town. Bobbie is eager to avoid being turned into a Charmin-squeezing automaton of domestic consumerism. Joanna wants to be taken seriously as an artist; Bobbie wants, it seems, to have fun. What the film and novel showcase is how two liberated women—women who want to have at least some kind of life separate from their husbands and children, separate from the domestic sphere—try to come to terms with the misogynist and consumerist culture in which they live.

For the rest of the film, we build up to a crescendo of imperiling women's rights that, pointedly, ends in violence. But as is the case with domestic violence in real life, things start slowly and gradually. Walter invites the Men's Association over for dinner, despite Joanna's extreme disappointment that he joined their number in the first place. At the party, Joanna appears to be the object of everyone's gaze: clad in a clingy flesh-toned dress, she almost appears naked as she attempts to converse with the men as an equal. They, of course, are less interested in her words than her appearance. One of them, in fact, creates a sketch of Joanna, and it's disquieting how accurately the sketcher captures her likeness, because it makes her seem somehow vulnerable to actual, bodily capture. Another one of the Men's Association guests gets her to agree to having her voice recorded for some experiment he's doing. The viewer doesn't yet know why, but Joanna's bodily freedom is being compromised, recorded, and controlled.

In the coming weeks, Joanna and Bobbie continue to commiserate over their town and decide to form a Women's Association, not so much to compete with the Men's Association as to provide some kind of response to it. Despite their efforts, they soon find out that, although many of the women in their town used to be high-powered, career-oriented women, they've all been somehow *domesticated*—judges, scientists, politicians have all just become housewives. They also find out that there used to be a Women's Club in the town, but that it has mysteriously disappeared. Bobbie and Joanna visit many of the other women in the town, and when they meet them, Joanna and Bobbie consistently find that the women are somehow blank in their expressions, ambitionless in the public sphere, and wholly focused on the trivialities of domestic life—folding towels, finding the best cleaning supplies.

In one scene, Bobbie, Joanna, and Carol Van Sant are sitting in a sanitized, white room, while Carol speaks in smiling platitudes about how silly and useless the Women's Club had been and says the women disbanded it, being bored with it. Carol is wearing a white dress—pioneer-like in cut and length, only cleaner and brighter. She's literally rolling up balls of yarn in an antiquated-looking wicker basket as she fields Joanna's questions about what she did when she was president—*president*, mind you—of the now-defunct Women's Club. She talks at length about how her husband's career and her children's well-being have improved since she's "always here" at home. "I'm sorry to disappoint you, but I'm happy," she affirms, in a soft, breathy, lilting voice that conveys no passion, no conviction, no substance, and no self.

This evacuation in the local women of any ambition, any sense of purpose or self, outside the domestic sphere is pervasive—and seemingly contagious. They visit another friend of theirs, Charmaine (Tina Louise), who had in earlier scenes been grumpy in her marriage, brash and opinionated like Joanna and Bobbie, and a huge lover of tennis. When Joanna and Bobbie arrive at Charmaine's house, they see that her precious tennis court is being ripped up, while Charmaine's husband surveys the scene, gloating. When they enter the house, Charmaine isn't wearing her usual brightly colored athletic causals but a white and floral pioneer dress—she looks as if she just stepped off the set for *Little House on the Prairie*. Her vocal patterns have changed to match all the other domestic goddess neighbors of Stepford: She's soft-spoken, mild-mannered, smiling, with a musicality to her voice that sounds false and hollow. Charmaine confirms that she's done loving tennis, and that all she wants to do now is please her husband. "I can't get my mind operating!" she notes, adding that she's "swamped with work" because she's fired their housekeeper and needs to focus on her husband. Bobbie and Joanna are scandalized, watching from above as Charmaine's husband guts the tennis court, their mouths literally hanging open in shock while Charmaine blithely smiles and waves down at her lord and master.

Joanna and Bobbie are increasingly convinced that something is seriously wrong with the women of Stepford, and that dark forces are somehow to blame. How could their town possibly be populated exclusively by beautiful, soft-voiced, ambitionless, vapid women, whose entire existence revolves—supposedly happily—around cooking, cleaning, raising children, and sexually satisfying their husbands? In 1975? Weren't they in the era of women's lib? Hadn't everyone read *The Feminine Mystique*? What the hell was going on? Truly, if you have ever spent time going down the algorithmic rabbit hole of Ballerina Farm or other influencers, simply channel those memories, then imagine those women moving into *every house in your neighborhood*, and you can intuit some of the vertigo Joanna and Bobbie are feeling by this point in the film. And for good reason: The walls of domestic horror are closing in on them faster than they know.

Joanna tries to assert herself throughout the film, to have a voice, to make images that are all her own. She tries to drum up more interest in her photography work; this effort succeeds, and she visits a gallery in Manhattan, where the gallerist tells her that her work has real potential. As he evaluates her, she appears nervous and insecure, watching him scrutinize the evocative shots of domestic life in Stepford that she's brought with her to show him. She pleads with him, "Don't say anything bad!" When he admires them, she responds, "You're not just telling me that because you're scared I might be a crazy lady?" Stepford, it's clear, has broken her confidence. When the gallerist asks her what she wants, she says that she wants someone, somewhere, to see a photograph and say, "That reminds me of an Ingalls." She goes on: "Ingalls was my maiden name." What she *wants*, then, isn't just fame but a durable individual identity that doesn't originate from her marital status. The movie offers up this scene as a shining possibility that Joanna will be able to break out of her town and make it on her own somehow—"to be remembered" as an Ingalls, not an Eberhart.

Meanwhile, Bobbie goes away for a weekend with her husband and returns transformed. Her breasts are larger; her hair is perfectly coiffed. She wears heavy makeup and a risibly frilled pioneer top and apron, a startling contrast to her previous uniform of shorts and T-shirts. Like Charmaine, Bobbie now confirms that she loves housework, wants to live for her husband, and is no longer worried about what's going on in Stepford. She says that her husband, after working hard all day, used to come home to "a slob," and she's not going to do that to him anymore, so she's wearing dresses and makeup full-time. Rather than swearing and huffing, Bobbie speaks in the same dulcet, singsong voice that Charmaine and Carol use. Joanna is horrified and tries to figure out how her brassy, sassy friend became this way overnight. She now is convinced that she herself is in danger of being transformed, like Bobbie, into a captive of domestic, suburban consumerism. She knows the Men's Association has something to do with it, though she doesn't know how, why, or what.

Soon thereafter, Joanna goes to see a female psychiatrist. Rather than dismissing or pathologizing Joanna's concerns, this psychiatrist empathizes with Joanna's feelings. She notes that any women with interests outside the family, upon moving from the city to the suburbs, would be rattled, saying the suburbs can "seem like a jaunt to Siberia." The psychiatrist then intuits that there's something Joanna's not telling her, and this is where Forbes's film builds on Levin's novel. Joanna admits, "I think the men are behind it . . . all of them. All of them in the association. My husband, everyone." She goes on to describe how she thinks the men somehow make the women change, noting that she sounds insane. She says, "They draw our pictures and they take our voices," recognizing the Men's Association's visit to her home as something dangerous, something she wishes hadn't happened. Joanna sounds *incredibly* paranoid, almost maniacal. But, shockingly, the doctor sympathizes with her and believes her. She kneels on the floor in front of Joanna and takes her hands in her own, urging her to leave: "I'll give you a prescription, which you'll fill, then you gather up your children, and you *get the hell away*! Don't tell your husband, don't tell anyone. Just go. Wherever you feel safe." She validates Joanna's reality as *reality*. With the chintzy 1970s décor of the doctor's office, Joanna's halting and emotional speech, and the psychiatrist's heartfelt advice, it's not a particularly artful scene, but I must tell you, it's the scene in the film that brought me to tears—because, for one hot second, Joanna wasn't *alone* with the horror closing in on her; someone was bearing witness to and confirming her reality. A reality in which women simply didn't deserve to be full people, a reality that women should run from like the death sentence it is.

Validated and empowered by her doctor, Joanna goes home to get her children and flee. She finds her house dark; the camera is trained tightly on her. We feel her anxiety, her claustrophobia, her sense that someone who poses danger to her lurks nearby. She soon sees that Walter is in the living room, so she sneaks up the stairs to find her children. We hear thunder booming outside. Walter creeps up on Joanna on the stairs, making her gasp. "They're not here," he says, realizing of course whom she's looking for. "They're fine," he keeps repeating, his voice slurred from drinking. Terror seizes Joanna's face, which we see from a steep camera angle looking down the stairs at her. Only her panicking face is illuminated. But, empowered by her shrink, she says that she's taking the children and leaving Walter. Now, the gloves are off as Walter shouts in her face, "Go upstairs and lie down! Now!" She refuses, and then we watch as Walter gets physically violent with Joanna. He throws a glass, and it shatters against the wall. He then battles her on the stairs, grabbing her by the wrists and trying to drag her back down. In this moment, the assaults on women that have been implied throughout the film become explicit and explicitly physically violent. In doing so, the film makes a quiet claim about the relationship between controlling behaviors—capturing women's voices, capturing their images, limiting their choices and freedoms—and frank physical abuse. Joanna screams, breaks away, and runs upstairs, locking herself in her bedroom as Walter tries to break through the door, screaming, "Joanna! Open this goddamn door!" Eventually, realizing he isn't strong enough to break the door down, Walter retreats back downstairs.

Joanna slips out. Now it's pouring rain outside, so she heads back to Bobbie's, thinking her children are likely there. Upon Joanna's arrival, we see Bobbie swanning around her home in a powder-blue-and-white pioneer dress and smock. Seemingly inured to Joanna's urgent pleas, she prattles on about making coffee. Joanna is stunned and horrified by Bobbie's transformation; her mouth open and her eyes wide, Joanna simply can't believe that her sassy, fun-loving, free-spirited, shorts-wearing friend is clad in pioneer frills and spouting platitudes about hot beverages. In her shocked desperation to remind Bobbie of who she is and of her own humanity, Joanna slices open her own hand to show that she's a human who bleeds. In the process, Bobbie gets stabbed with a kitchen knife, and then *fails* to bleed, instead spiraling into a massive system crash where she keeps repeating, "I was just going to give you coffee." Joanna's fears are confirmed: Bobbie is gone, replaced by a robot clad in almost absurdly traditional "female" garb. Joanna knows that unless she finds her children and escapes, she'll be next.

Joanna heads back to her house to find out where her kids are. The house is still dark, and Walter lies in wait, nursing another glass of liquor. He keeps stopping and listening, as if he hears something in the house. The camera is tightly trained on him until a flicker of light and shadow passes over his face, and we see that Joanna is coming up behind him, a fireplace poker held aloft in her hands. She brings it down hard on his head, screaming, "I want my children!" In a daze, Walter reveals that he has taken them and hidden them in the Men's Association building. Joanna is now in Walter's and the Men's Association's thrall because her children are on the line. Like *Rosemary's Baby* and *The Exorcist*, this film manifests a strong awareness that a woman's love for her children is part and parcel of her entrapment in the prison of violence that is her domestic life.

This is a crucial scene for the film's politics, and one that chimes loudly with *Rosemary's Baby*. It's Walter's wish to coercively control Joanna—to control her body, mind, and soul, to limit her whereabouts and determine what she wears and how she behaves—that puts her in gravest danger. Like the earlier movie—which, of course, is also based on a novel by Ira Levin—*The Stepford Wives* reminds viewers that denying women's rights, and specifically denying them the right to have a life and selfhood outside the home, is intimately connected to domestic abuse. It echoes and modifies the politics of *Rosemary's Baby*; there, we saw the connection made between coercive control and reproductive violence. Here, it's between coercive control and physical violence more broadly. Joanna, seeing the rapidity with which her husband's controlling behavior edges over into battery and seeing how far her husband and the Men's Association will go to literally dehumanize her, wants to get out of the domestic prison altogether. And she wants to bring her children with her.

At the Men's Association building, Joanna finds herself trapped in a dark Victorian mansion: inside, it's gloomy, archaic, labyrinthine. In the bowels of the house, she hears the voices of her children yet cannot find them—again, echoing *Rosemary's Baby*, when she hears the sound of her baby crying through the wall. The camera angles on Joanna are very steep, suggesting that she is being watched or spied on from above. She hears her children calling for her. They sound afraid, desperate. Her fear and desperation escalate: The camera pauses on her half-lit face, wet with a combination of rain and sweat, and her eyes, wide with fear. She follows the sound up the huge, dark staircase as thunder claps outside. When she finally throws open a door, she sees a recording device is the origin of her children's voices. She stops dead in her tracks, comprehending suddenly that she's been deceived. Technology has been used against her, again, this time as a tool of manipulation and coercion. When the head of the Men's Association, Dale Coba (Patrick O'Neal), who's been sitting there waiting for her, starts to chide her, she says, simply, "Where are my children?" The greatest power an abuser can wield over a woman is the power he wields over her children's physical safety. She is trapped by her love for them; she knows it, as does Dale.

He speaks to her calmly, confidently, telling her to ready herself for "another stage." "We've found a way of doing it that's just perfect. It's perfect for us, and it's perfect for you." Realizing her children are not there, Joanna tries to run, but all the doors are locked as Dale stalks her through the house. She finds herself, eventually, in a bedroom that uncannily resembles her bedroom at home. It becomes apparent to the viewer that this is some kind of staging area. In the room, she meets her counterfeit, the robot who will replace her: a creepily black-eyed, large-breasted replica of herself, brushing her hair and staring at herself vacantly in a mirror. The robot woman stands, and she carries a sash that she seems prepared to use to strangle Joanna. The scene fades to black; Joanna is no more.

In the final scene, we are in a grocery store. The scene is brightly lit and colorful. We hear an old-timey slow dance song playing in the background. The store is almost entirely populated by robot wives. We see Charmaine, clad in a huge sun hat, a prairie top, and a long floral skirt. She greets the other bot-women in the same exaggeratedly soft, lilting voice we've gotten used to by now as the lingua franca of the Stepford Wife. The Joanna-bot and the Bobbie-bot greet each other, and in their absent gazes, it is clear: Men's desire to control women has won out in Stepford. The real women are gone; the trad wife robots will have their day. It's a powerful, unsettling scene, the final touch on director Bryan Forbes's quiet but powerful commentary on women's rights under threat.

The Equal Rights Amendment: Reality and Spin

Forbes's commentary wasn't coming out of nowhere. Between the novel's publication in 1972 and Forbes's film's release in 1975, America had witnessed the bizarre, disorienting, and demoralizing trajectory of the Equal Rights Amendment, which had seemed poised to sail through Congress in 1971–72 but had fallen on hard times by 1974–75.

The Equal Rights Amendment to the Constitution is perhaps the single most important and most often forgotten aspect of American women's history in the 1970s. Readers who lived through the 1970s likely remember it; but many of my own undergraduate students have never even *heard* of the ERA and certainly have no concept that it was on the congressional docket for a decade and in American public discourse for the same period of time—from its rapid and almost uncontested passage through the two houses of the US legislature in March 1972 to its slow, death-by-a-thousand-cuts rejection by state legislatures in 1982.

The text of the Equal Rights Amendment is shockingly modest and short. It has one clause that is substantive, two that are logistical. In its entirety, it reads,

> 1. Equality of rights under the law shall not be denied or abridged by the United States or by any State on account of sex.
>
> 2. The Congress shall have the power to enforce, by appropriate legislation, the provisions of this article.
>
> 3. This amendment shall take effect two years after the date of ratification. (ERA, March 1972.)

That is the *whole thing*. As the renowned feminist scholar Jane Mansbridge has pointed out, the ERA guaranteed equal legal rights but did not guarantee any specific new rights or privileges to women. It did not challenge any specific traditional roles, practices, or social institutions. It was an extremely modest piece of legislation whose short-term effects would likely have been minimal.

Partially because it was a relatively modest rights bill, it sailed easily through the House of Representatives. On October 13, 1971, the front page of the *Times* ran an article announcing that the Equal Rights Amendment had passed in the House of Representatives by a vote of 354–23. A landslide, bipartisan victory. American women—and men—could see clearly and plainly that their government was in almost unanimous support of the equal legal rights of women and of amending the United States Constitution to reflect that support. But the very next day, buried on page 39 of the *Times*, was quite a comedown: because the Senate had a lot of urgent business to attend to, its own vote on the ERA would have to wait until 1972. Equal rights for women may have been a good idea, but it was just not, well, *urgent* in the minds of legislators. The article also noted that proponents of the ERA worried that trying to pass it in an election year (1972) rather than immediately after its landslide win in the House (late 1971), would significantly hurt its chances.

This pattern, in which women's rights seem to be going in a positive direction, making major, unambiguous strides, and then being curbed, limited, or threatened immediately thereafter, would continue throughout the early 1970s, producing a whiplash effect for Americans. To understand how this happened, we have to dig deeper into the controversies that surrounded the ERA, and the patterns and trajectories by which states approved or denied the legislation. First, we need to think about what women *thought* they might be getting (or losing) if the ERA passed. Obviously, they thought they would be getting equal rights under the law—and that would have been true. But between 1972 and 1975, the most public and politicized parts of the debate on the ERA were not focused per se on equal rights in the eyes of the law. They were focused instead on specific lifestyle issues—issues on which the ERA's eventual impact was hard to discern.

The element of the ERA that most threatened core American ideology was the idea that it would increase job opportunities for women outside the home. Even though other contemporaneous legislation rendered ERA's potential protection and expansion of women's jobs essentially irrelevant, the popular *perception* was that women had a great deal to gain (proponents of ERA) or lose (opponents) by the passing of the amendment. Many opponents who adhered to the traditional, patriarchal values that fetishized a man's right and responsibility to protect and provide for his wife found the idea of promoting women's status in the economy of extra-domestic work threatening and destabilizing—both to women's and men's gender roles.

That perception of threat wasn't entirely unfounded, considering the changing state of American domestic culture. According to censuses and polls from the 1970s, many fewer women chose to work exclusively in the home by the 1970s than had in the 1950s, and many fewer ranked housework as an occupation they enjoyed. This idea that housework was unfun and undesirable is reflected on nearly every page of Ira Levin's novel, and in nearly every scene of the *Stepford Wives* film. The devaluation of domestic work was a frightening and destabilizing notion for many women who valued homemaking as their exclusive work and saw it as the key to their social status. Jane Mansbridge has pointed out that part of the ERA's problem was that it seemed to differentially affect women of different educational classes: The more highly educated the woman, the likelier she was to want to work outside the home and the likelier she therefore was to benefit from what the ERA promised. By seeming to offer greater employment opportunities for women, however, the amendment seemed implicitly to devalue domestic labor. When the ERA rolled in, the implicit statement that it made was that women, now about to receive equal legal rights with men, would surely not *want* to make their lives in the domestic sphere anymore.

Both sides of the aisle jumped on the domestic lifestyle changes the ERA seemed poised to usher in. On the left, Bella Abzug penned a crackling op-ed in *The New York Times* in favor of enforcing equal employment opportunities, setting up federal childcare, and passing the ERA. In 1971, a *Times* article came out that a team of legal scholars supported the passage of the ERA and noted that these lawyers advocated women's participation in the military, education, and employment; these scholars also acknowledged that the ERA might change women's preferential treatment in family law. The article clearly both advocated for the ERA and saw it as powerful enough to quickly and substantively change traditional sex roles assigned to women, as well as women's position in the domestic sphere.

Meanwhile, right-wing opponents of the ERA were making noise in the press as well. On October 24, 1971, the *Times* ran a letter to the editor that attacked the ERA full force, seeing it as legislation that endangered "traditional roles in a family structure." The author of this letter, a doctor of neurology at Yale School of Medicine, pointed out that the weakening of the family would, in his view, lead to "increased rates of alcoholism, suicide, and, perhaps, sexual deviation." This doctor lampooned women's equality in the law as dangerous to mental health and what he saw as American sexual mores. Before the public's eyes, a rights bill was clearly and decisively being repackaged—not just by liberals but also by conservatives—as something much more exciting and much more threatening: a lifestyle bill.

Despite the ambivalence in the United States about the bill and about the lifestyle changes it seemed to promise and/or threaten, it flew through the US Senate. First, the Senate Judiciary Committee voted 15–1 on February 29, 1972, in support of the ERA. Then in mid-March, the Citizens Advisory Council on the Status of Women implored President Richard Nixon to voice his support for the ERA; their pleas seem to have had an effect, because Nixon spoke up in favor of the ERA the weekend before the Senate vote was to take place. Finally, on March 22, "the 49-year struggle of feminists to get the amendment through Congress ended at 4:38 p.m. when the 84-to-8 vote was announced." Eighty-four to eight: fewer than 10 percent opposition. It was another landslide.

As the ERA ratification shifted over to individual states, Hawai'i became the first to ratify. The *Times* noted a broad perception that the bill would achieve the ratification of the required thirty-eight states for its inclusion in the US Constitution. Within a week, five more states had ratified the amendment;

Kansas became the seventh on March 28. But that first heady week that envisioned a rapid-fire, landslide success for the ERA came to an end on March 29, when Oklahoma shot down the amendment, citing fears about changes to child welfare, marriage law, women's susceptibility to the draft, and their ability to take on jobs that would require them to lift heavy objects.

In the following week, a group of housewives spoke out in the *Times* against the ERA. The group's representative is quoted in the *Times* saying, "Our daughters are being taught in school that there is no joy or accomplishment in being a wife and mother . . . As real women, we want to defend our homes . . . [and] want to be loved and protected by our men." In the *Ladies' Home Journal* of 1975, a prominent opponent of the ERA named Phyllis Schlafly said, "The Equal Rights Amendment is the biggest fraud that has come down the pike since Charles Ponzi promised investors he would double their money every 90 days." The proto-Stepfordians were already taking center stage, shooting down the idea of equality because, somehow, it seemed to undercut women's importance in the home and their respectability and lovability in the eyes of their husbands.

Between 1972 and 1975, the ERA lurched painfully up and down in public sentiment, like an unending and senselessly volatile roller-coaster ride. In a 1975 Gallup poll, 58 percent of surveyed Americans favored the ERA. When broken down into categories, that 58 percent contained slightly more men than women (63 percent vs. 54 percent), more Easterners than Westerners, more Northerners than Southerners. That is, three years into the labored effort to pass the ERA, a significant majority of

American men and a slightly *less* significant majority of American women favored the passage of the ERA. And yet, somehow, it just wasn't passing—at least not by 1974. Which was the year in which Bryan Forbes began shooting *The Stepford Wives* in Connecticut.

That "somehow" had quite a lot to do with the aforementioned Phyllis Schlafly. Although my undergraduate students very rarely even recognize her name, Phyllis Schlafly is the ultimate, original, and most influential trad wife in American history, having initially come to prominence in 1964, when she published a conservative book called *A Choice Not an Echo*, and then running an unsuccessful but highly visible campaign to be president of the National Federation of Republican Women in 1967. An article from *The New York Times* in December 1975 opens "Phyllis Schlafly, the 50-year-old conservative Republication who heads the nationwide crusade against the Equal Rights Amendment," and goes on to describe her as "immaculately groomed . . . with streaked blonde upswept curls who stands 5 feet 7 inches and weighs 135 pounds—'the same I weighed before my six children were born.'"

At the head of her "troops" of 1970s trad wives, Schlafly urged them to deploy "femininity tactics" on lawmakers as well as on the American public: "Her supporters wear long dresses and hand out such things as homemade bread, apple pies, and jam to legislators." She weaponized traditional femininity and, perhaps unsurprisingly given the entrenched gender conservatism of mainstream American culture, it worked like a charm. Schlafly characterized feminism as an "antifamily movement" that refused to see that "most women find their major fulfillment in the home." By far her most famous "contribution" to American politics, however, came in her successful grassroots dismantling of the ERA.

In large part through the action of Schlafly and her "troops," the momentum that had made the ERA seem like a legislative slam dunk in 1971–72 simply died. By 1975, American women had come to grips with the very painful reality that not all Americans—and in fact, not all American *women*—wanted equal rights for women. By the time *The Stepford Wives* hit theaters, moviegoers were well aware that there was a very real chance that the liberated and often urban women of American might very well be stopped in their tracks by the domestic goddess suburban "hausfraus," who were painfully successful at keeping their men satisfied, happy, and secure in their status as heads of household. So, even though *The Stepford Wives* was and is a horror movie, and a horror classic at that, it also hit theaters and communities very much as a sociopolitical satire.

Afterlives of *The Stepford Wives*

The reception of the horror-satire of *The Stepford Wives* in 1975 was mixed, to say the least. Betty Friedan herself—whose ideas about the dangers to women of suburban life in *The Feminine Mystique* clearly inspired both the novel and the film—roundly condemned the film, seeing it as a mockery of feminism. Apparently, she stormed angrily out of the screening room when she saw it. Feminist Lois Gould called the movie "junk" but said flippantly that she'd be happy to have a robot housekeeper. But not all 1970s feminists had the same reaction. Feminist critics Gael Greene and Eleanor Perry praised the film for what they judged to be its obvious feminism. To them, it satirized and villainized men for wanting women to be automatons who served them snacks and sex. Mainstream critics like Roger Ebert also saw it as a feminist triumph, noting that "[The actresses] have absorbed enough TV, or have such an instinctive feeling for those phony, perfect women in the ads, that they manage all by themselves to bring a certain comic edge to their cooking, their cleaning, their gossiping, and their living deaths." Even the film's crew insisted the film was, if anything, "anti-men" and not "anti-women."

The Stepford Wives is a story set in a town where women not only lack equal rights, but any rights at all. They have no autonomy over their bodies, no choices, no nothing, because they are *dead and replaced by robots*. By devising a world in which women are stripped of their rights entirely and replaced by robots, *Stepford Wives* takes the fantasy that the anti-ERA proponents seemed to believe in—women were wholly satisfied by domestic life and labor, satisfied to live at the pleasure of their husbands—and makes it horrifying and dehumanizing.

Alas, the horror of *Stepford*, both novel and film, was prophetic. It presaged the ultimate failure of the ERA in 1982. By then, even with a three-year extension on the original timeline to ratify, a group of states stood firm in their opposition: Alabama, Arizona, Arkansas, Florida, Georgia, Illinois, Louisiana, Mississippi, Missouri, Nevada, North Carolina, Oklahoma, Utah, and

Virginia. Despite its wildfire approval in the heady early days of 1971–73, the ERA withered on the vine and died. It withered and died in part because Americans just couldn't get comfortable with how women's equal rights might change how we live our lives, might change the role of women in the home, and might undermine the power that men have over women. Better a bot than an equal citizen before the law.

If that doesn't strike you as horror, you need to look around, because this retrograde mania is ongoing. It took until 2020 for the required thirty-eighth state to ratify the Equal Rights Amendment, but as of early 2025, the American Congress has *still not made the amendment into law*. The reasons? First, the original deadline for ratification had lapsed years before. Second, several states have moved to rescind their own prior approval. We are still living in the aftermath of 1970s feminism, however much we might want to believe we have moved beyond it. We are still living in a culture that is profoundly ambivalent about the fundamental question of whether to grant women equal rights under the law. We are still living in Stepford. 2025 is looking a whole lot like 1975.

Now, again, in the third decade of the twenty-first century, the trad wife phenomenon speaks hauntingly to that truth. Honestly, when I see trad wife content on TikTok or YouTube, I often think they must have studied Bryan Forbes's film in order to cultivate the vocal traits they exhibit in their voice-overs. It's uncanny. Trad wife influencers speak in dulcet and strangely robotic tones to narrate their processes of making jam or breakfast cereal from scratch, just like the women of Stepford. Also like them, the trad wives lionize and fetishize domestic labor as the be-all and end-all of what it is to be a woman. Trad wife media also fetishize female sexual pliancy and physical beauty as things that married women owe to their men, as a constitutive part of their contribution to the functioning of the family. On top of that, they often dress in pioneer-chic clothing, looking very similar to Bobbie or Charmaine after they are roboticized. By trying to seem like the ideal, peaceful, beatific, and perfectly coiffed wives and mothers, these influencers have found a way to market a vision of a "lost" family culture now newly resurrected in a modern America that is aching for moral absolutes. They sell wholesomeness and homespun lifestyles by packaging those ideas every bit as prettily and tidily as the Men's Association packaged its renovated "women." Eerily, these influencers often have hundreds of thousands—and sometimes millions—of views and likes.

Trad wives are creating a culture of spectacle around the domestic sphere and around old-fashioned modes of cooking and living. Trad wives don't want equal rights. They want only those privileges that are attendant upon being the helpmate and servant of the heads of their households. They want to embody the values of the Men's Association in *Stepford*. And they are gaining popularity day by day, inaugurating a new pioneer frontier for women's rights, which is the right to have no rights beyond what rights are offered up through the generosity of the male head of household. We are living, right now, in a social media deluge of regression—which, in itself, reflects the very real political regressions we're living through simultaneously. And we, like Joanna, should be screaming and trying to get out. Because it is absolutely the case that, when the domestic sphere is radically divided according to sex and gender like this, the rates of gender-based domestic violence and sexual assault in the home skyrocket—as the film makes plain with Walter's assault on Joanna on the stairs.

In fact, throughout most of American history, the idea that a woman lived under the rule and rod of her husband entailed the idea that she owed him sex on demand. This idea was so utterly baked into American social and legal culture that it was not possible to convict a man for raping his own wife. Instead, the going assumption in culture and at law was that a man had a right to sex from his wife, and that if he had to extract sex from her by force, that was unproblematic. This "marital exemption" for the husband from being prosecuted for rape remained on statutes books in the United States until 1993, although individual states started revoking the marital exemption as early as about 1980.

If we really want to fetishize an old-timey domestic power dynamic, in which the wife is subordinate to the husband and obedient to him, we need to be very clear about what we're endorsing. We're endorsing the sexual and domestic automatism of *Stepford*, and we run the risk of returning to a world in which a women couldn't even bring a suit for sexual violence against her husband, let alone have a prayer of winning it. Making jam from scratch may seem a far cry from sanctioning marital rape—and, on its own, it is. But when the making of jam gets conflated and confused with a sexual subordination ideology about what a woman owes a man in the domestic sphere, well, at that point, the distinctions start to get a little blurry. And that's what Ira

Levin knew in his novel, and what Bryan Forbes amplified in his popular film: Making the jam and keeping house are fine and good so long as they don't come with a rider about being an automaton who exists only for the pleasure and satisfaction of a man. Once that starts happening, you're living—again—in the dystopian domestic horror of *Stepford*.

CHAPTER 4

Benign Patriarchy Turns Malignant: *The Omen*

Of all the 1970s horror films in this book, *The Omen* is the least obviously engaged with women's rights. Widely received in its own time as a slightly campy reboot of *Rosemary's Baby*, the film centers on the Thorn family, who move to the UK so that its patriarch, Robert Thorn, can be the US ambassador to Britain. Once there, however, strange things start to happen around their young son, Damien. It eventually comes out that Damien is the son of Satan and has come to wreak havoc on the world as the Antichrist. This is a fair summary of the film, but it leaves behind *The Omen*'s powerful commentaries on the women's rights movements. Because, en route to his wreaking havoc on the world—which we actually never see in this film—what we're actually watching all throughout is Damien, unwittingly abetted by his father, wreaking havoc on his mother. To highlight how this film is domestic horror, we'll spend some time thinking through the opening scene of the film, in which Mrs. Robert Thorn—Kathy—is made to raise a child that is not her own.

But before we do that, I want to set the stage by laying out how reproductive rights in the United States had evolved by the middle of the 1970s. In the years following the *Roe v. Wade* decision in 1973, American women's reproductive rights faced tremendous opposition. That opposition came primarily from two corners: the Catholic Church and a grassroots antiabortion movement of American citizens. The Catholic Church came charging out first, with the Vatican condemning the Supreme Court ruling just two days after *Roe* was decided. Then Catholic leaders announced that anyone who participated in abortion would be excommunicated. A few months later, Cardinal Terence Cooke, archbishop of New York, stated that any Catholic who had *any* involvement of *any* kind with abortion would be excommunicated.

Meanwhile, the grassroots antiabortion movement gained momentum that summer. In June 1973, antiabortionists rallied in Detroit, calling for a revision to the Constitution that would make abortion illegal. Ten thousand people in Providence gathered for the March for Life event on October 7, 1973. One year after the *Roe v. Wade* decision, in January 1974, six thousand antiabortion representatives converged on Washington to press their case. Across the country in 1974, pro-life constituencies sought to prohibit abortion on any grounds other than when the life of the mother was at grave risk.

In 1975 and 1976, federal and state government officials

started feeling the pressure. Many states reinstated the mandate on spousal consent for abortions (or parental consent for abortions if a woman was under eighteen). On February 3, 1976, President Gerald Ford announced that he felt the Supreme Court had gone too far with *Roe*, and that he supported a scenario in which federal law only protected abortion when a woman's life was in danger or she had been raped, and that any other abortion rules should be made at the state level. Then the Hyde Amendment passed, which forbade the use of Medicaid funding for abortions unless the life of the mother was in danger or she was the victim of rape or incest. Bear in mind, of course, that since rape was not illegal in marriage in the 1970s, a woman couldn't claim the right to an abortion if her pregnancy resulted from rape by her husband. By 1976, access to abortion was not anywhere near as secure or protected as *Roe*'s proponents wanted it to be nor as many American women had assumed it would be.

At the same time that reproductive rights in the United States came under heavy fire, public awareness of and outrage at domestic violence was skyrocketing. Even mainstream, traditional women's magazines started running pieces on wife battery regularly. An article in *Ladies' Home Journal*, published in June 1974, described in detail the pattern of violence in the life of a fifty-year-old, educated, white woman, who had ultimately tried to divorce her husband shortly before he killed himself with a rifle. The article pointed out that, contrary to then-current stereotypes about wife beaters as drunk, poor, and undereducated, wife battery was a problem afflicting all women, of all socioeconomic classes, and was not necessarily even tied to alcohol consumption. The battery of wives, the article implies, could be happening close at hand, behind a neighbor's door—even behind the door of a neighbor who seemed smart, nice, sober, and responsible as a husband and provider. Batterers, these writings emphasized, wouldn't necessarily look like the kind of man who might beat a woman. Batterers could look like nice guys. They could be educated. They could be rich. They could appear to be doting and devoted.

The Omen (1976) picks up on this agitation around women's rights and goes somewhere radical, to say things that *no one* was saying—not researchers on wife battery and not women's magazines. First, *The Omen* draws a line connecting reproductive coercion to the frank physical battery of women. Second, *The Omen* makes clear that abusers do not always look like abusers *even in their own minds*. That is, some of the doting, devoted married men out there, who would never think of themselves as abusers and might not ever raise a hand to hit their wives, might nevertheless be capable of life-threatening or even fatal conduct toward them. Just as some abusers look like nice guys, so some forms of abuse look like relatively benign conduct when viewed from a distance. *The Omen* braids together these issues—the connection between reproductive coercion and physical battery and the debunking of the idea that only obviously cruel men who hit women are abusers—with a scorching feminist critique of Catholic dogma. As a package, *The Omen* offers one of the most subtle but trenchant takes on domestic horror in the 1970s.

Priests and Well-Meaning Husbands: Agents of Satan in *The Omen*

In its opening scenes, *The Omen* shows a man named Robert Thorn (Gregory Peck) rushing to a Catholic-run hospital at night in Rome and then coming to grips with the news that his newborn son has died at birth. We see Robert, who looks to be about fifty-five or sixty years old, from a very steep camera angle, talking conspiratorially with a priest, who is also the head of the hospital. Grief-stricken, Robert wonders aloud what he will say to his wife, who had been unconscious during the birth. The priest mentions that another baby boy was born right when Robert's own child died and encourages Robert to deceive his wife into believing that this other child—whose mother died in childbirth—is her child. Robert hesitates, stating that he knows that Kathy wanted her children to be biologically her own. The priest pushes hard, animated by a little *too* much personal investment in the Thorn family's woes. Addled by grief and worry for his wife's mental health, Robert capitulates.

In the next scene, he brings the baby boy to her bedside. We see that Kathy (Lee Remick) looks to be in her thirties, substantially younger than her husband. The energy in the room is happy, peaceful, contented. Smiling at his wife, Robert allows her to believe this is the child she gave birth to. In their interactions in this scene, it's evident that he loves her. He treats her with great affection and care and smiles adoringly at her when he hands her the baby. We are encouraged even by the soundtrack to approve of the new family unit: The score is upbeat, written in a major key, and very soothing. The camera dwells on Kathy's beatific and joyful face. Watching this new, happy family and hearing the mellifluous soundtrack, we begin to think that Robert has made a reasonable decision in his lie. Look how happy Kathy appears when her newborn son is put in her arms! The scene reads like the opening to a happy family film, centering on a besotted older husband and his beautiful young wife, bringing their child into the world.

Except, of course, we know this husband has lied to his wife about the identity of the baby. This *should* be a bone-chilling scene, but the movie encourages us to sympathize with Robert and to support his decision. In *Rosemary's Baby*, we knew all along that something was wrong with Guy. We knew he facilitated his wife's being Satanically raped. We knew he treated Rosemary badly in general. We knew he had been loath to start a family with her and only changed his mind when leaned on by the Castevets. Guy was, beyond question, a bad husband. *The Omen*'s presentation of Robert, by sharp contrast, encourages us to see him as a kind, doting husband, focused on his wife's feelings. With Robert's lie, and the film's insistence that we should like him anyway, the film becomes political—very subtly.

This seemingly adoring man deceived his beloved wife about the fate of their own child and in the process, denied her some very basic human rights: the right to grieve her dead child, the right to choose whether to adopt this orphaned child, the right to know her own reality, the right to manage her own reproductive life. All this despite the fact Robert knew that Kathy had not wanted to adopt: "She wanted her own," he had told the priest.

Yet he chose, ostensibly on her behalf yet knowingly *against her wishes*, to foist this child upon her secretly. However doting Robert may seem, and however beneficent his conscious intentions, he has taken on a role that is acutely and troublingly patriarchal, deciding to control the reproductive life of his wife without her consent and without her knowledge.

Not just troublingly patriarchal but also troublingly Catholic. Remember that Robert has taken his stance on Kathy's reproductive life only through the intercession of and pressure from a Catholic priest, in a Catholic-run hospital—in Rome, no less. The film was released three years after *Roe v. Wade*, in the heat of the Catholic Church's sustained efforts to reverse the *Roe* decision. The film, then, is asking the viewer to consider the importance of women's agency over their reproductive lives and forcing American audiences to recognize how the Catholic Church in the '70s lined up to impede that agency. In its first few scenes, *The Omen* isn't yet asking—although it will ask explicitly later—whether women should be allowed to terminate pregnancies. In its opening, it's asking whether anyone *other* than a woman should be able to force her to have a child she does not want. In particular, it's asking us to consider the extent to which a husband or the Church should be able to force a woman to have or raise a child she doesn't want.

The boy, whom Robert and Kathy name Damien (an obvious nod to Father Damien Karras from *The Exorcist*; this Damien is played by Harvey Stephens) grows up normally at first. When he is about four, the family relocates to England so that Robert can become the US ambassador to the UK. Rather than discussing this promotion with Kathy, Robert presents it to her as a fait accompli, deepening our sense that, however affectionate Robert is, he doesn't really see Kathy as an equal partner, but more of a ward, who can and must accept his decisions as law.

When Robert tells Kathy about the promotion and relocation, she is happy, wrapping her arms around him and squealing girlishly over his success. After the move to England, we see numerous brief scenes and still shots, a carousel of slides of the family's day-to-day life in England showing the three of them laughing together, holding hands, smiling brightly for the camera. Kathy pulls Damien's little toy dog on a leash across a lawn while Robert carries Damien in his arms; Kathy and Robert stroll at sunset, arm in arm; the family feeds ducks at a pond; they ride in canoes together; they grin at one another while taking taxis around town. They are clearly a loving, close, happy family, and the film encourages us to approve of them, to like them, to admire them.

Until, ominously, the still photographs start to show Damien at his fifth birthday party, and the soundtrack shifts to a creepily tinkling rendition of "Happy Birthday to You." The stills stop, and the camera rolls again just as Damien blows out the candle on his cake, leaning happily into the arms of his pretty young nanny. Soon, when the nanny is alone at the party, she makes eye contact with a fierce looking mastiff that's unaccountably appeared at the edge of the party. The soundtrack shifts to an eerie, discordant, amelodic, pulsating piece of music as we zoom in close on the nanny's eyes, intercut with the eyes of the dog. Something happens to the nanny. She looks bewitched. A few seconds later, we hear the nanny shout,

"Damien! Look at me! Over here! Damien, I love you!" We don't know where she is at first, but the camera finds her, standing toward the top of the Thorn mansion, in a windowsill. Zooming in close, we can see that she has a noose around her neck. She shouts down at the partygoers, "Look at me, Damien! It's all for you." Everyone watches her as she leaps from a window ledge and hangs herself. Kathy and Robert are appropriately horrified at her death, as are all the screaming children. Damien, however, cradled over his mother's shoulder, seems unfazed or maybe even mildly pleased. Soon, his eyes, too, lock with the mastiff hellhound's; a flicker of recognition passes over Damien's face, and he waves at the dog, while the chilling amelodic song pipes back up. Looks like the good times for the happy little family may be coming to an abrupt close.

Soon after, a replacement nanny arrives, a strange woman named Mrs. Baylock (Billie Whitelaw). As soon as the new nanny is alone with Damien, she calms him and says, "I'm here to protect thee," switching to the now-defunct second-person singular pronoun (thou/thee/thy), which tells the audience that there is something sinister and archaic about her and about her relation to Damien. She clearly knows something about who this child *really* is, even if we as viewers don't yet.

The sinister vibe escalates and gains anti-Christian specificity when, on approach to a church for a wedding, Damien flies into a rage in the car, tearing Kathy's blue turban off, ripping out her hair, and hitting her in the face. The family is forced to return home. Later, we see Kathy and Robert in their room, with Kathy carefully treating her facial bruising. It looks *very* much like a scene of a woman treating herself after an incident of domestic violence, but of course, here it's her own child, and not her husband, who beats her. Again, echoes of *The Exorcist*: A child beats a mother through the malign agency of a demonic force that lies within the child. But the context here is importantly different, because we also have Robert—the supposedly kind, loving, doting man—who has contributed to or even caused Kathy's lack of safety. Robert, who loves Kathy very much, talks about his love constantly, and would never directly hurt her himself, has nevertheless put her in harm's way by denying her reproductive agency and inviting in chaos. Robert flung her into Satan's clutches, even if he's not yet aware of it and never meant to do so.

Let's pause on the scene in the car and think about how that scene speaks to the film's larger concerns and, in particular, to its critique of Catholic stances on abortion. In the car, Kathy is wearing a beautiful blue suit. She wears blue frequently in the film, but it's conspicuous here because she's clad *entirely* in blue, including the turban that covers her hair. Remember that she is a lovely younger woman married to a doting older man. They have a son who is not the biological child of the father and who is given to the mother without her physical participation in a sexual act that would create a baby. Another family works in a hauntingly similar way: the Holy Family. Mary is young; Joseph is old; Jesus is not Joseph's biological son, and Mary did not have sex to produce this baby. The Virgin Mary's iconographic color is blue. *The Omen* leverages the archetype *Rosemary's Baby* deployed—we have a monstrous child raised by a mother who invokes the Virgin Mary. Like its demon-child predecessor, *The Omen* hinges on a dark reinvention of the Holy Family.

That dark reinvention dynamic carries through the film. Kathy and Damien drive through a zoological park in which the prey animals run from Damien and the predators run toward him, to attack. The baboons, in particular, rage all over their car, roaring and biting. Kathy is petrified and drives off, deeply shaken and increasingly convinced that something may be wrong either with her or with Damien. Kathy may be in a position analogous to that of the Virgin Mary, but whereas Mary always knows that her child is the child of God, Kathy is clueless about the identity of her child as a child of Satan. The birth of Christ emerged from a miraculous agreement between God and Mary—her joyful, fully informed accession to His will. The raising of Damien is built on an under-the-table baby-switch deal between a priest and Robert. Much less auspicious, both for the mother and for humanity.

In reimagining the Holy Family as an Unholy one, the film takes a step in its critique of Catholic pro-lifers and their position. People who oppose abortion, since the 1970s, have routinely used the argument against abortion that one could never know what a terminated pregnancy might have grown up into, had it been allowed to be born as a person. Opponents of reproductive freedom asserted that every pregnancy could end up being a miracle child of some kind. An aborted fetus could be the next Einstein, Marie Curie, Gandhi, Martin Luther King Jr., or Malala. Underpinning this conviction is the belief in the Virgin Birth and the birth of Jesus as the ultimate miracle baby. Had

Mary terminated her pregnancy, God could never have taken human form. Human salvation would have stopped. Christian belief is predicated on the idea that all humanity is saved by the birth of one special child—fully human, and fully divine. Of course, from the vantage point of a religion so tightly pinned to that idea, where terminating a pregnancy runs the risk of being catastrophic for humanity, the idea of allowing women to choose to terminate pregnancies of their own volition seems insane.

The film's powerful move, from a theological standpoint, is to remind viewers that babies aren't always good and virtuous, miraculous and salvific. There's no guarantee when a child is born that it won't be a murderer or a sociopath. All parents roll the dice. Now, I'll freely and enthusiastically admit, as a committed adorer of babies and children, I think human children are delightful and wonderful. But the movie isn't picking a fight with babies; instead, it's picking a fight with *the idea of salvific children*, because it's that idea that quietly motivates a lot of pro-life ideology and that tends toward the dehumanization of women as mere vessels for babies.

Kathy returns home from the wild animal park to Robert and confesses that she is preoccupied with anxiety about Damien. She says, "I need to see a psychiatrist. I have such fears." She's afraid Robert will put her in an asylum, which he has the legal right to do at that time, as the *paterfamilias*. Instead, he affirms repeatedly that he loves her, to which she responds simply that she wants him to find her a doctor. This moment in the film reminds us that Kathy's freedom and personhood are circumscribed by

Robert, however tender and loving he may appear or even intend to be. She cannot even seek psychotherapy without his consent and facilitation. It also conveys to viewers that Kathy is having doubts about her child but that Robert feels no compulsion to reveal his misconduct.

Those doubts come into focus soon thereafter, where Kathy sits in the huge, wood-paneled parlor of their mansion while Damien makes noise in the background. She is holding her head in her hand, as if she has a migraine, but her facial expression reads much more as fear or anxiety than physical pain. When Robert enters the room and asks if she's all right, we see her flinch and try to twist her face into an expression of simple physical pain. When she complains that she can't stand Damien's noise anymore, Robert minimizes her concern, and he tries to lighten the mood by playing with Damien, but Kathy calls angrily for Mrs. Baylock and commands her to take Damien out of the room. Robert tries to soothe Kathy, but she shouts at Mrs. Baylock to get Damien out immediately. After her outburst, the camera reveals that Kathy's facial expression has settled back into intense anxiety. This is no longer the sweet-tempered Kathy, the soft-voiced, dedicated mother. Realizing she has to account for her outburst, Kathy tells Robert, "Darling, I don't know what's the matter with me . . . I don't seem to be able to . . . I don't know." She doesn't say it outright, but the scene makes clear that what she doesn't seem able to do is tolerate their son.

Robert reconfirms his love for Kathy but expresses skepticism about her psychotherapy, suggesting that "this is what the doctor's doing" to her. He offers to speak with her psychiatrist, which she encourages, saying the doctor has something to discuss with Robert. With somber classical music playing as the two hold each other and stare out the window into an eerie night, Kathy haltingly informs Robert that she never wants any more children. Clearly taken aback, Robert haltingly consents to her wish. But then Kathy plangently begs him, "Then you'll agree to an abortion? I'm pregnant, Robert, I just found out this morning." This time, Robert doesn't reply, thereby locking in the same ostensibly loving reproductive coercion with which the film opened. Kathy's reproductive agency and autonomy are contingent upon *him*, upon his approval. However much he may love her, she cannot choose to have an abortion without his consent any more than she was allowed to choose whether to raise this child. This moment reflects a legal reality that many American women faced in the mid- to late '70s: Even though federal law protected the right to abortion, in many states, women had to seek their husband's consent before terminating a pregnancy.

Without consenting to the abortion Kathy desperately wants, Robert goes to speak with her psychiatrist, who tells Robert that Kathy has fantasies that Damien is evil and not her own child. Though Robert knows that these are *not* fantasies, but rather evidence that Kathy is picking up on his lie about Damien's parentage, he looks away from the psychiatrist in shame and says nothing. The scene is understated but crushingly powerful: In this moment, Robert has the chance to exonerate Kathy of any serious mental disorders. He has the chance to tell the psychiatrist that Kathy is *right*, that the child is not hers. In so doing, Robert could release Kathy from her own fears about her mental health, as well. He chooses instead to protect his honor and integrity, keeping the baby switch back in Rome secret.

Even so, the psychiatrist perseveres in his advocacy for Kathy, urging Robert to agree to an abortion. For the first time in the film, Robert loses his cool, shouting brusquely at the doctor with one sharp "No!" The *paterfamilias*, however kind-hearted he may seem, does not brook anyone else—not his wife, not her doctor—telling him how and whether he can bring more children into his family. That will be *his* call, and his alone. He will, once again, deny Kathy her reproductive agency, even though he now understands that something may be seriously wrong with Damien and that his deceit of Kathy has been psychologically harmful to her. Moreover, he will deny the truth to her psychiatrist, allowing him to continue to believe that Kathy lives in a "fantasy," while knowing that Kathy's seemingly delusional belief is actually *the reality that he has constructed for her without her consent.*

In doing this, *The Omen*, a film with no ostensible gender politics to it, a popular but second-tier film that is rarely read seriously even by film critics and scholars who focus on horror, takes a big step toward indicting *patriarchy itself*, through the seemingly well-meaning Robert Thorn. Robert isn't selfish or egomaniacal; he isn't mean, cruel, or belittling to Kathy. He doesn't physically abuse her; he certainly doesn't bawd her out to Satan. Even so, he construes his status as the patriarch as a more than ample mandate for his deception of his wife about her own mental and reproductive reality—and he does so out of a belief that he is looking out for the *best interests* of his wife and family. *The Omen* shows us an insidious form of abuse and control, insidious because it is not *intended* as abuse or control, but as beneficence and care—from the point of view of a man completely confident in his own absolute authority over his wife, her body, and her choices.

What's yet more sophisticated is how the film clearly understands that ostensibly beneficent patriarchal control as a portal toward more overt, brutal, and even lethal forms of domestic violence. In the next scene, we see Robert speeding home from Kathy's psychiatrist's office in his sporty convertible, which then cuts to Damien—imitating a raging car vrooming along a highway as his father is currently doing—riding in circles on a tricycle in the family home upstairs. The sound of a spooky Latin choir starts bleeding into the scene as Kathy stands by the upstairs balcony, tending to her flowers. If you listen *very* closely, you can make out the sopranos singing "*Ave Satani!*" or "Hail Satan!" Kathy pushes an unsteady table under a hanging plant and climbs up, perched terrifyingly close to the banister that separates her from a twenty-foot drop to the wooden floor below. Damien, maniacally peddling around his room in circles, is sent out by Mrs. Baylock and goes peeling down the hallway toward Kathy. The Satanic choir stops; all we hear is the squeaking of Damien's pedals. He deliberately rams into the table Kathy is perched on at full speed; she goes careening off the balcony, though she catches two balustrade posts and dangles there for a moment, panicking. She fights for her life, holding on tightly and swinging her left leg up to the balcony, hoping to hoist herself back up. Damien crouches down to look at her through the posts of the banister while she pleads for his help. Inevitably, she slowly loses her grip, and, screaming, "No, no, no, no!" she plunges to the floor, landing belly first. Damien doesn't flinch or try to help her. Instead, he peers down at her from between the posts, calm and collected, while drops of blood flow from her mouth.

The film uses all its cinematic resources to dial us right in on the horror that has befallen beautiful, young, innocent, deceived Kathy. We, the viewers, see Kathy's face in an extreme close-up, so that her unconscious—and possibly dead, we don't know yet—face takes up almost the entire screen. We are invited by the film to wonder if she's survived, to try to detect her breathing, even just a hint of life in her, as the blood drips onto the floor. Damien's face, as he stares down at her, is devoid of pity, devoid of concern. When the camera flashes back from Damien to Kathy, this time at a distance of perhaps ten feet, we can tell by the positioning of her body on the floor that at least one of her arms is broken. The image is arresting and horrifying. This is a woman who has become the victim of domestic violence in her own home but at the hands of a small child—a small child who, let's never forget, is not her own child but one her ostensibly loving husband foisted on her against her wishes and without her knowledge. So who, the film asks, is ultimately to blame for Kathy's fall? Is it Damien, or is it Robert?

Miraculously, Kathy survives the fall. From Robert's point of view, we enter the hospital, where we see a crowd of reporters waiting to get his comment on his wife's status. Pulling away from them, Robert joins Kathy's doctor, who reveals that Kathy has suffered a concussion, a broken arm, and "internal bleeding." In horror, Robert reveals Kathy's pregnancy to the doctor, who makes clear that he already knew that, and that Kathy lost the baby as a result of the fall. What Damien accomplished when he rammed her off the balcony was an at-home, nonmedical abortion. And, as has been the case far, far too often in American history, that at-home, nonmedical abortion nearly killed the woman who endured it. As a well-meaning priest named Father Brennan (Patrick Troughton) had warned Robert earlier in the film, Damien wouldn't tolerate a competitor for his status as sole child. He needed to be the lone heir to the Thorn family's wealth and power. The fetus had to go. Father Brennan also had to go, for having had the temerity to interfere with Damien's plan to be Thorn's sole heir: While trying to take shelter at a church from a sudden diabolical windstorm, Brennan is summarily impaled by a falling pole knocked off the church roof.

It turns out that Kathy has to go, too, eventually. Despite his inability to believe Brennan's warnings, Robert Thorn gradually gets wise to the true situation with Damien—that he has some kind of unnatural imprimatur on him. He begins standing up to Mrs. Baylock, yelling at her when she fails to do as he asks around the house, insisting she get rid of the demonic mastiff she had brought into the house ostensibly to protect the family. Despite his attempts, however, it's clear that the Thorn household is under her thumb entirely and that she is colluding with Damien to bring about Kathy's death.

While Kathy is still recuperating in the hospital, Robert goes on a quest to figure out Damien's origins. What he learns panics him: His own son hadn't died in childbirth but had been brutally murdered by the priest-doctors in the Roman hospital. Damien hadn't been born to normal, mortal human parents but to a woman and some kind of jackal. Once he learns this, Robert realizes the danger Kathy is in, and he calls her to urge her to flee the hospital for her own safety. But it's too late: Mrs. Baylock is on the way to the hospital to finish what Damien had started.

In that scene, Kathy is again clad entirely in blue. She is trying to change clothes, preparing to flee the hospital, but it's hard for her because her arm is in a cast. She pulls her thin, vapory, blue robe backward over her head, so that it covers her face like a veil—more Marian imagery—and through the veil, she sees the sardonic, smiling face of Mrs. Baylock approaching her. Suddenly, the scene fills with loud, dramatic (and grammatically inaccurate) Latin chanting. It is meant to sound like some kind of Black Mass: "*Sanguis bibimus, corpus edimus; sanguis bibimus, corpus edimus. Tolle corpus Satani! Ave, ave versus Christus! Ave Satani!*" ("We drink the blood, we eat the body; we drink the blood, we eat the body. Lift up the body of Satan! Hail, hail, against-Christ! Hail Satan!") It is confirmed: Damien is the son of Satan, Mrs. Baylock is a Satanist sent to keep Damien safe and guarantee his access to Robert Thorn's political capital, and Kathy must go. She has made her dislike of Damien evident and, as far as Damien and Mrs. Baylock know, she may still be pregnant.

Mrs. Baylock attacks Kathy, aiming to push her out a high window. As she is pushed, clad in diaphanous blue, we hear the chant "*Ave Satani*," which, of course, is a direct substitution for the traditional "*Ave Maria.*" This scene instructs us that, in this unholy, inverted family, the mother has to be sacrificed for the son to be saved. This, of course, reverses the traditional logic of Christianity: Jesus's self-sacrifice on the cross brings salvation to all humanity—including his mother, the Virgin Mary. With her blue robes fluttering angelically around her, Kathy falls all the way down through the roof of an ambulance. The door to the ambulance swings open, and we see Kathy, dead and bloody, lying on a hospital gurney.

This moment—about three-quarters into the film—is the most explicitly political scene so far, providing a visual of how women had sacrificed their medical safety for *years* as a result of laws protecting unborn fetuses. The image of a woman, bloody and dead, lying on a gurney outside the hospital was one the American public had had occasion to imagine all too often, well into the 1970s. Women who had terminated pregnancies in basements, in dry cleaning stores, or in private offices and had died in the process—they, too, were rushed to hospitals, too late to save their lives. Like thousands and thousands of pregnant American women before her, Kathy has been sacrificed by a patriarchy that wanted to keep her pregnant more than it wanted to keep her alive. Remember, Damien kills her through Mrs. Baylock, both believing that she may still be pregnant with Robert's unborn true heir. Mrs. Baylock's hands may be the bloodiest, but it's Robert's prohibition against abortion that caused Mrs. Baylock to push Kathy out the window. Kathy dies because Robert wouldn't let her terminate her pregnancy.

When Robert finds out that Kathy has died, he is still in

Italy, preparing to return home and reveal everything to Kathy. Suddenly, the phone rings, and he picks up the receiver. We watch his face register shock, worry, and grief in quick succession. He hangs up the phone and buries his face in the bedspread at his hotel, clutching the edge of the bed in agony. His agony, of course, is both that Kathy has died and that he knows *he* is the one whose pattern of lying brought about her death. If he hadn't lied to her about Damien and denied her an abortion, she'd still be alive. He knows it; we know it.

In the wake of the revelation that Kathy has died, Robert finally accepts that Damien is evil, and that it's up to him to right the system that he threw out of whack with his coercion years before, when he forced Kathy to raise an adopted child against her will. In the heat of his grief and remorse, Robert resolves to slaughter Damien. Robert and a photographer named Keith Jennings (David Warner), who had been present at Damien's calamitous fifth birthday party and is now entangled in the Satanic mystery, travel to the city of Jezreel to meet an archaeologist named Carl Bugenhagen (Leo McKern), who studies ancient religious arcana. The three of them descend into ill-lit subterranean passages in which Bugenhagen apparently does his research on ancient religions. In a massive cavern of archaeological tools and artifacts, Bugenhagen reveals that Robert must kill Damien using a set of special knives and on hallowed ground in a church. We see Robert hold a ritual knife downward, as if imagining stabbing it into Damien; the dim lights of the cavern glint on his gold wedding band, reminding viewers that this act of infanticide is revenge for Robert's brutally murdered wife. Bugenhagen urges Robert, "This is not a human child. Make no mistake . . . you must be devoid of pity." Robert heads out of Bugenhagen's archaeological site with the set of knives wrapped up in cloth. He will now return to England, ceremonial murder tools in hand, to destroy the son of Satan, who has been living under his roof, as his son, through his own coercive choices.

One of the most powerful and troubling aspects of this film's representation of reproductive coercion and domestic violence, however, is that it situates its point of view not in Kathy but in her husband, Robert Thorn. We see a few scenes squarely from Kathy's perspective—the scenes of violence in the car, at the balcony railing, and in the hospital. But for the rest of the film, we experience this story from Robert's perspective. By situating our perspective largely with Robert, *The Omen* urges us to feel sympathy for him. The viewer's alignment with Robert would seem to say that, sure, he lied to Kathy for years, in a way that resulted in her being brutally assaulted by her son and eventually killed by their nanny, but he's not a *bad guy*. It's no accident that the filmmakers cast in this role Gregory Peck, who by 1976 was familiar to and beloved by Americans as Atticus Finch in *To Kill a Mockingbird*. Here, viewers of this film would have a hard time concluding Robert was the villain not only because the film is shot from his POV but also because Atticus Finch is pretty much the anti-villain of mid-twentieth-century film.

Part of the feminism of *The Omen* lies precisely in the fact that it shows how a well-meaning and likable husband can *still be a perpetrator of domestic violence*, however unintentionally.

In *Rosemary's Baby*, *The Exorcist*, and *The Stepford Wives*, the male malefactors were deliberate and malicious toward the women they tormented. They were strategically manipulative, verbally assaultive, physically cruel, and sexually abusive. They consciously sought to do something they *knew* was bad, hurtful, controlling, and dehumanizing. Robert, by contrast, is uxorious, lying to Kathy *because he genuinely believes it will be best for her*. By extension, the film warns that any man, thinking he is doing right for his wife, may do violence to her simply by denying her agency, knowledge, and choice.

Part of the horror hangover in this film is that one feels gross at the end. Viewers know they are supposed to feel compassion for Robert, but they are troubled by him. He sacrificed his wife, though unintentionally, and he raised the Antichrist, all through his conviction that he should be in charge of Kathy's reproductive life. It's very disquieting, this idea that a kind, loving, well-meaning husband might be complicit in Kathy's horrific suffering and death. And it stays with you all the way home. Why didn't Robert just *tell her*?

The final feminist critique made by this film, in my view, is of what we now call *benign patriarchalism*. Robert keeps Kathy in the dark not because he hates her but because he loves her. He tricks her not in order to get something for himself but in an attempt to spare her from pain. Her body is broken, battered, and ultimately destroyed not through intentional malice but through Robert's overconfidence in his own decision-making abilities. It starts with the presumption that Kathy cannot cope with the reality of their son's having died at birth. By deciding to spare her from that reality, Robert puts Kathy into a place of fundamental vulnerability and unreality. At his core, Robert's trouble is that, as a benign patriarch, he doesn't trust Kathy to be able to tolerate the truth. He doesn't entrust her with reality or with the right to knowledge and autonomy.

This is something contemporary domestic violence therapists, lawyers, activists, survivors, and scholars talk about all the time. Abusers create fictions around their victims so as to keep victims in a state of unreality, so that they cannot extricate themselves or make choices that benefit themselves. Although Robert isn't a deliberate, malevolent abuser, he nevertheless forces Kathy to live in unreality. Fundamentally, that enforced sequestration in unreality is what puts her most at risk from Damien. That element reveals the film to be *years* ahead of its time in how it theorizes reproductive violence and even femicide in relation to ostensibly well-meaning patriarchalism.

The Omen did not win the same kinds of contemporaneous accolades that laureled *Rosemary's Baby* or *The Exorcist*. Quite the contrary: many contemporary viewers who had loved those two prior films—like Roger Ebert—gently panned *The Omen*, seeing it as little more than a knockoff of *Rosemary's Baby*, and a far less bewitching one at that. Richard Eder, the reviewer for *The New York Times*, claimed the film as being directly in lineage with *The Exorcist*, but noted that there was precious little to recommend *The Omen*, which he saw as both "dreadfully silly" and "terribly solemn," rather than exhilarating or terrifying like its predecessors.

Despite the critics' generally negative response, the film was a huge commercial success, grossing more than $60 million in its initial release, making it one of the highest-grossing films of 1976—a year that also saw massive moneymakers like *Rocky* in theaters. *The Omen* may have missed the mark for reviewers, but evidently it hit a nerve with the American public. In the final scene of the film, after Robert has died, Damien is shown being raised by the seated president of the United States, who was a close friend of Thorn's during his life. The notion of a dangerous, demonic figure close to the Oval Office resonated with an American public that was still reeling from the Watergate revelations, only a few years earlier, and the correlative idea that the highest offices in the land were corrupt and broken.

But part of the reason for the film's popularity, both then and now, was Lee Remick. Roger Ebert acknowledged her as one of the best things about the film, for her "realization-of-dawning-horror" scenes. When she's stuck in the car with Damien, we feel her panic; when Damien assaults her in the car, we feel her shock; when Damien lets her dangle and fall from the balustrade, we feel her horror. It is through her embodied experience of pain, fear, and confusion that the horror of *The Omen* ultimately lands. As she falls to the floor or falls from the hospital window, screaming both times, we want to scream with her.

I haven't found reviews like Kathleen Carroll's review of *Rosemary's Baby*, clearly linking female entrapment to the soul of the horrific in the film. But the critique of the benign patriarch as the motivating force behind a woman's suffering and death was right there to see, right out in the open. And, of course, Gregory Peck conveys it through the profound guilt and vengefulness that

Robert Thorn feels when he finds out Kathy has died. He knows this debacle was his own doing and through him, we know it, too. In the end, *The Omen* advances a theory of domestic horror that is much more capacious and, in some ways, more frightening than what we saw in *Rosemary's Baby* or *The Exorcist.* There, the bedeviled women are facing obviously malign forces. For Kathy, the domestic danger originated not in Damien, but in her loving husband, Robert Thorn. Watching a woman suffer reproductive coercion, reproductive disempowerment, physical battery, and death indirectly but incontestably at the hands of a man who loved her very much added a new layer to the feminist critiques of the 1970s. Even if your heart is "in the right place," anytime you deny a woman agency, knowledge, or autonomy, you put her life in danger, and you make her life a horror.

CHAPTER 5

Reproductive Violence in Outer Space: *Alien*

In late June 1979, eleven years after the release of *Rosemary's Baby*, six years after *The Exorcist* and the *Roe* decision, and three years after *The Omen* hit theaters, Ridley Scott released one of the most important feminist films of the 1970s: *Alien*. In the film, Ellen Ripley (Sigourney Weaver) and her shipmates find themselves under siege by a malevolent, ferocious, and nearly indestructible alien that they bring back to their interstellar freighter, the *Nostromo*, while exploring a desolate planet called LV-426. With its iconic visual and sound design, Ridley Scott's nimble and experimental direction, and a staggeringly simple but compelling storyline, this film was, like the others in this book, immensely successful in its theatrical release. The film cost a reported $11 million to make but grossed nearly $80 million in the US and an additional £8 million in the UK. People loved this movie in 1979, and they have loved it ever since.

The core reasons for its enduring popularity, however, aren't about the design or the direction so much as they are about the blazing feminism of the film. On the *Nostromo*, Lieutenant Ellen Ripley winds up being the sole crewmate to survive the alien's attack, and she survives by a combination of physical strength, strategic cunning, and technical know-how. She's no shrinking violet, and she's no victim. She's a powerhouse, a fighter, a survivor. She is helped by her crewmates at various points, but, in the end, Ripley makes it through of her own sheer willpower, resourcefulness, and bravery. For all these reasons, *Alien* has gone down in history as the apotheosis of feminist horror. As well it should.

Though no one who has seen the film would ever contest that the film is feminist in nature, its signal contribution to the feminism of the domestic horror genre has not been fully explored. Like *Rosemary's Baby*, *The Exorcist*, *The Stepford Wives*, and *The Omen*, *Alien* speaks to—or, better, screams about—the horror of reproductive coercion, domestic violence, and women's lack of equality in American law and society. To be more specific, *Alien* imagines a world in which (1) reproductive violence is the point of origin for horror, (2) the people you live with seek to abuse and brutalize your body and hijack your reproductive agency, and (3) the only path out is to become a warrior.

That last element—the image of the warrior-woman for which Sigourney Weaver as Ripley is so rightly renowned—feels particularly powerful when we consider the social fears of that time. When the film was released, America was still in the throes of its debate around the ERA and *Roe v. Wade*. So, before we drill into the film, I want to set the stage culturally, by reminding us what was going on at the end of the 1970s.

By 1979, when *Alien* was released, *Roe v. Wade* was on the rocks. Two potential presidential candidates for the 1980 elections were openly antiabortion: Republican Ronald Reagan and Democrat Morton Downey Jr. Gallup polls conducted in 1979 revealed that, even with the legalization of abortion and the concomitant massive reduction in maternal mortality, only 22 percent of the American population thought abortion should be legal in all circumstances, 54 percent thought it should be legal in some circumstances, and 19 percent thought it should be illegal. For the second half of the '70s, then, only about 80 percent of Americans thought abortion should *ever* be legal, and the large majority of those believed it should be legal only in specific circumstances. Going deeper into Americans' feelings on abortion, the 1979 Gallup poll showed that, whereas 78 percent of Americans believed abortion should be legal when the mother's life was in danger during the first three months of pregnancy, only 59 percent believed it should be legal when the mother's life was in danger in the last three months. In the year *Alien* was released, then, 41 percent of polled Americans thought that, starting at six months of gestation, the fetus's life outweighed the mother's, full stop.

These polls make clear the American public's deeply divided views on abortion at that time. On the sixth anniversary of the *Roe* decision, January 22, 1979, sixty thousand antiabortionists marched on Washington, chanting "Life, life, life!" An abortion clinic on Long Island was demonstrated at by antiabortionists numerous times in 1978 alone; in 1979, seeing that the demonstrations had done very little to shut down the clinic, a man simply set the clinic on fire. Democratic President Jimmy Carter looked to hire health advisors who were known to be antiabortion. 1979 saw increasing conflicts even in very liberal states, like New York, about the use of public funds to support abortion. Federal financial support for abortions was virtually nonexistent, creating a severe access problem for poor women who sought to terminate pregnancies. Abortion may have been federally legalized, but its status as a "right" available to all American women, regardless of status, income, or profession, was far from settled.

Alien begins to signal its affiliation with and interest in the women's reproductive rights movement subtly but early on in the film. After a long opening sequence in which the camera slowly surveys a silent, sleeping interstellar freighter, we see the main computer chirp to life. After that, the camera continues its survey and finally stops with a shot of a crew of people asleep in hypersleep beds. They are awakened because the computer has received an order from Earth directing them to explore the nearby planet LV-426. As the crew awakens, we see that the shipmates have a warm collegiality about them, functioning much like a family, with Captain Dallas (Tom Skerritt) as the de facto dad of a bunch of rambunctious siblings, and the ship computer functioning as the mother. The ship computer, in fact, is *called* Mother. Despite being way, way out in deep space, then, the *Nostromo* is cast as a domestic space.

When the sortie ship detaches from the *Nostromo* so that the exploring crew can check out the alien world beneath, Ripley, a lieutenant on the *Nostromo*, says "Umbilicus clear," immediately invoking an idea of gestation and parturition. When the team then lands on the surface of the alien world, to do the salvage mission that Mother has set them on course for, they arrive at a structure that appears to be at least in part organic. They enter into a space that feminist scholar Barbara Creed rightly describes as a "gigantic, cavernous, malevolent womb." The search party lowers crewman Kane (John Hurt) into a cave where it's as hot "as the goddamn tropics." Like the body temperature inside a birth canal, perhaps? And then, voilà, Kane finds a trove of eggs and falls down among them. While on the floor, he examines an egg. He sees something alive and moving inside of it. It looks fetal. The egg opens. Kane leans over it, curious, and the egg ejects an organism that pierces Kane's helmet and appears to attach to his face. Not good news for Kane.

The sortie party drags Kane back to the ship, but Lieutenant Ripley, who is the commanding officer while Captain Dallas is in the away party, insists that they follow quarantine protocols. Kane, she avers, should not be allowed back on the ship; none of them know what the organism is or whether it's contagious. Even when Dallas—again, the ship's captain—orders her from the entry bay to let him and the others bring Kane in, she stands her ground and decisively tells him no. Our Ripley is one seriously rule-abiding officer. Unfortunately for everyone, Ash—the chief science officer aboard the ship—is not so rule-abiding. He opens the bay door and allows the away party and the alien that's affixed itself to Kane's face free entry into the ship.

Once Kane has been taken back inside the *Nostromo* and his helmet is removed, we see a crablike creature attached to his face. The crew members, led by science officer Ash, scan Kane, producing a series of images that look like a sonogram, showing a system of organs running down Kane's throat. Ash warns Dallas that removing it might kill Kane, but Dallas wants to remove it anyway. "You'll take responsibility?" asks Ash. "Yes, yes, I'll take responsibility," replies Dallas. This language of "taking responsibility" clearly invokes the discourse around pregnancy and abortion from the vantage point of the man who impregnates the woman. Of course, in the explicit logic of the narrative, what Dallas means is that he'll take responsibility if Kane dies; he'll be the one to make an account of things to anyone back on Earth, such as his employer, or Kane's family. But symbolically, we now realize what has happened here: Kane has been raped by an alien life-form that has impregnated him. Dallas is trying to make an abortion happen and is willing to accept the consequences if something goes wrong.

Perhaps not surprisingly, problems arise immediately when they try to remove the crablike alien and fail; it has "concentrated acid for blood" and tightens its tendrils' grip around Kane's throat so they can't cut it off. They have no choice but to wait and see how this alien pregnancy will proceed, and whether Kane will survive. Though set in outer space in the year 2122, the film offers up a fascinating and very timely meditation—both for 1979 and in our current era—on the dangers of forced pregnancy and forced birth.

Soon, however, it looks like things will work out for Kane. Overnight, of its own volition, the crab-alien creature releases him, dropping off and dying in a corner of the room. Kane revives, gets his bearings, and rejoins his compatriots. The crew returns to the center of their interstellar home, the kitchen and mess hall, happy that Kane has woken up with an appetite. While they all eat together, the fraternal energy returns; everyone is chatting and laughing. During this scene, our eye is focused not on Ripley but squarely on Kane. In fact, by this point in the film, it's not yet clear who the film's hero and the focus of our empathy is supposed to be: could be Captain Dallas, could be Lieutenant Ripley, could be Kane. We watch Kane eating and smiling in relief. But something changes. Suddenly, he looks surprised, then very afraid. Quickly, his expression turns to agony, and his body starts twisting and contorting as something tries to push its way through his abdomen.

The camera position shifts. We are watching him from behind, suddenly, just over his shoulder—very much the position from which many people watch their wives, girlfriends, or partners deliver a baby. Then Kane is shifted so that he's lying on the table—again, an iconographic reference to labor and delivery: Women often sit partially upright during delivery, up until the point that it becomes clear that they need surgical intervention and they are moved to the operating table. As we watch Kane, lying face up on the dinner table, get torn apart from the inside by his alien baby, he is the center of our field of vision; he is the locus of our empathy and of our horror. The spidery alien's offspring pushes out of him, much as a human baby pushes its way out of its mother.

The scene is often referred to as the "chest-burster scene," but it should properly be called the "abdomen-burster scene" because the alien baby clearly comes through the soft tissue of Kane's body, not through his sternum or ribs.

Throughout Kane's agonizing and lethal delivery of the alien baby, Ripley is visually sidelined, located in the background of the shot, in parallel depth of field with other crew members. The scene is entirely focused on Kane, his body, and how it gets torn to pieces. Throughout the scene viewers are painfully aware that whatever is in him has no way out, except right through his abdominal wall. The alien baby looks horrifying: yellowish, but covered in blood, with a small round skull, two black eyes positioned on the side of its head, atop a gaping mouth set with razor-sharp teeth.

Unsurprisingly, the alien baby's allegorical meaning has been discussed widely since the film's release. Members of the film's cast describe it as "a penis with teeth." Similarly, scholar James Kavanagh said in 1980, "Kane dies in agony enduring the forced 'birth' of the razor-toothed phallic monster that gnaws its way through his stomach into the light—a kind of science-fiction *phallus dentatus*." Without a huge amount of visual justification, the scholar Barbara Creed posits the alien baby represents the Freudian *vagina dentata*. That's fine, to go all Freudian on it, but both the phallus and vagina readings miss the forest for the teeth. *Apart* from the teeth, the creature looks more like an early-stage human fetus than anything else. It's clearly not human, but it is more than a little bit anthropoid.

The alien baby has a rounded head at the top of its body. Its flesh is slightly yellowish but recognizably within the realm of imaginable human skin colors. It has a mouth with a horizontal jaw in two parts, two eyes on either side of its head, two short arm structures. We are dealing with *aliens*, here, let's not forget. It would be reasonable for them to have no arms and no legs, no head and no eyes. But this little alien baby is bipedal, like a person—when it runs off the table, it runs on its hind legs. It does also have a bony-looking tail, but that needn't disqualify the comparison to a human fetus, since human fetuses have tails for a period of time in the womb, early in gestation. In fact, some human babies are born with the fetal tail still attached. Honestly, the alien looks like a human fetus that is somehow arrested in its development, but makes it out of the host's body alive anyway. And has teeth. The alien baby is an uncanny little fetus monster. Ash later recognizes this explicitly, referring to the offspring as "Kane's son," an obvious pun on the sin-riddled biblical Cain, from whom sinful peoples issue forth in Genesis. The idea here is that this brutal alien baby will augur in a new race of evil, wicked beings if it's allowed to reach Earth onboard the *Nostromo*.

In staging Kane's rape, pregnancy, and lethal birth, the film allegorizes the sociopolitical issues surrounding abortion legislation in the United States in the 1970s. Remember, early attempts to change abortion laws focused on the idea that rape victims should be allowed to terminate pregnancies, even if other women could not. Although male, Kane is a rape victim, and he dies from his alien impregnation. The extraterrestrial impregnation of Kane and his subsequent death lay bare a fundamental inequality back on Earth: men are not asked to carry unwanted pregnancies nor to risk their lives in order to give birth. But in *Alien*, we bear witness to a reality in which a *man* gets raped and impregnated and then dies during birth. The horror of this film isn't just about women's bodies but about men's, too, asking male viewers to imagine a world in which they had no agency over their reproductive lives, even when their lives were, in point of fact, on the line. Unthinkable! Unless you were, of course, a woman.

Many scholars who study this film, even from the vantage point of feminism, assume Ripley is the epicenter of the audience's empathic allegiances. And that is generally true, and is *certainly* true toward the end of the film. But in the scene where Kane gives birth to the alien, we identify not with Ripley but with Kane himself. *Alien* urges viewers to imagine a world in which reproductive violence could be committed against men and could be lethal. Indeed, after Kane dies, two other male crew members follow him: Captain Dallas and Brett (Harry Dean Stanton). This violent alien species isn't just targeting women—in fact, it doesn't seem to be targeting women at all. It doesn't care about the sex or gender of the body it penetrates. All it needs is a warm, safe abdomen to gestate in.

Adding depth and nuance to its interstellar assault on the antiabortion movement, *Alien* has its own take on and treatment of domestic violence and how it relates to forced pregnancy. Ripley soon finds out that Ash, the science officer, is somehow colluding with the company that funds their voyage to bring the alien back, with or without the crew alive. Typing furiously into

Mother, she discovers that the ship was rerouted deliberately to the planet where the alien species was found, so that Ash could bring back a specimen of this new life-form. "Priority one," Mother informs Ripley, is to "insure return of organism for analysis. All other considerations secondary. Crew expendable." *Expendable.* That's a painfully on-the-nose way of talking about 41 percent of Americans' attitudes toward women late in pregnancy in 1979. The deaths of Kane, Dallas, and Brett had all been costs the company was happy to incur in order to bring this infinitely valuable alien fetus to life safely. Raging against the literal and metaphorical machine that she realizes has condemned them all to be vessels for violent and lethal reproduction, Ripley demands an explanation from Ash. Realizing she won't be satisfied by anything he says, she stalks off to find the other two surviving crew members, hoping to warn them.

But Ash isn't going to let her. He seals her into a section of the ship with him, locking her into a small corner of their shared domestic space. He stands in the doorway, still as a stone, with a terrifyingly impassive face, which we see in extreme close-up. Eventually, Ripley sees what we see: He has a laceration along his hairline, and white fluid is slowly leaking from it. Ash isn't human; he's an android, a machine, like Mother, in thrall to the larger machine of the corporation that would gladly sacrifice the entire crew in order to bring home an alien baby.

His expression still cold and hard, Ash starts brutally beating Ripley, ripping her hair out in huge clumps. He throws her to the ground; he slams her into furniture. She tries to escape by crawling across the floor, the camera zoomed in on her panicking, pain-stricken face. Next, Ash grabs her by her clothes and throws her across the room into a wall. She loses consciousness for a second; during that time, the camera rotates around Ash's face, and we see how unmoved he is, unremorseful, unfeeling. As she starts to come to, he throws her again. She screams as she hits the wall and then loses consciousness again as she collapses to the floor.

This is a scene of frank domestic battery: Ash has shifted from being chief science and medical officer to being a domestic abuser, violently assaulting a woman whom he, until this moment, has lived with in relative peace on board the *Nostromo*. He assaults her because he wants to use her as a host for another alien spawn. Through this scene, *Alien* recognizes that the desire to control women's reproductive lives can—and does, all too often—result in other forms of domestic abuse, much as it had in *Rosemary's Baby* and *The Omen*.

Fundamentally, what *all* domestic horror films understand is that the dehumanization of women is the problem, the source of the Horrific. Rape, forced pregnancy, forced birth, domestic violence, coercion—these are all social practices predicated on the notion that the victim is not fully human and is not, therefore, deserving of the full rights and privileges of safety and self-determination. Ash doesn't see Ripley as deserving of basic human rights; he sees her as a vehicle for transporting the aliens back to Earth. Ash represents, then, another layer in the structures of power that support the sexual and physical oppression of women. Ash has neither interest in nor capacity to understand Ripley's—or Kane's, for that matter—humanity, because he is programmed simply to support the directives that come into Mother from the human companies and industries back home.

All these horrific dynamics come into sharp relief when Ash tries to stuff a rolled-up newspaper down Ripley's throat while she's passed out from the savagery of his beatings. At first, it seems he may simply be trying to kill her. But remember that it's via the throat that the embryos are implanted, and that it's Ash's job is to bring the aliens back to Earth. Through this penetration of her mouth by the newspaper, he's trying to prep her for forcible impregnation by an alien. He's trying to force Ripley to carry a pregnancy she does not want, a pregnancy that will kill her.

The fact that he shoves a rolled-up *periodical* down her throat deserves extra scrutiny. In deep space, the crew of the *Nostromo* is ten months from home, which means they've been away from home for *at least* that long already. So what good is a periodical? Who reads magazines and newspapers that are almost two years old other than archivists, scholars, and hoarders? But it makes sense symbolically. The news was where the war about reproductive freedom and violence was largely fought. Ash is trying to silence Ripley by forcing media down her throat. The scene is an absolute triumph of allegorical sophistication about the precarity of women's reproductive status in the US and about the role of the media in determining that status.

Amidst this violence, two of Ripley's shipmates, Parker (Yaphet Kotto) and Lambert (Veronica Cartwright), the only other surviving members of the crew, band together to defeat and destroy Ash. Over the course of the battle scene, Ash is ripped to pieces but continues to fight back, at one point pinning Parker—a large man—to the ground, with his own groin jammed up against Parker's. Visually, what we're seeing here is a male robot appearing to attempt to rape a male human. Parker is saved when Lambert grabs a highly phallic looking metal pipe and rams it into Ash. Again, the film asks viewers to imagine a world in which men are equally vulnerable to sexual violence and forced pregnancy, to chilling effect. The catch line from trailers of the film in 1979 was "In space, no one can hear you scream." That's right: exactly like screaming in your own home. But this time, the men are screaming, too, right along with Ripley and Lambert.

Together, the three remaining human survivors attempt to outwit the aliens but to no avail: Parker and Lambert soon get killed by the now-giant alien baby (evidently, its rate of growth *far* outpaces that of humans). Ripley realizes she must survive and escape the alien on her own. To do this, she transforms herself into a warrior. She ties back her luscious, curly hair into a ponytail. She carries a huge flame-throwing weapon under her arm. She sneaks around the ship like some kind of futuristic Navy SEAL, attempting to be silent as she moves through the mostly dark ship—availing herself of her slender build to maneuver around dark corners in murky passages. When she has to move fast, she runs hard, not gracefully, grunting and grasping. Ripley's not trying to look pretty; she's trying to survive.

She soon realizes that the ship itself may be her best weapon—perhaps she can set it to self-destruct and propel herself toward home in an escape pod. To do this, she engages the ship's self-destruct mechanism to detonate and destroy Mother and the entire *Nostromo*. Ripley's transformation from cautious, rule-abiding officer to bold, rule-breaking warrior over the course of the film, coupled with her symbolic decision, at the end, to destroy Mother, points to the final profound feminist critique that the film makes. And that critique has everything to do with the ERA and with what the ERA promised (or threatened) to do for women by 1979.

Women Warriors in the United States and in Outer Space

The late 1970s were a dark time for women's efforts to secure equal rights in the United States. After the ERA zoomed through federal channels of approval, it had stalled in a small but intractable group of states. And there it withered, until 1979, when it had to either pass or be killed. Jimmy Carter would give the ERA an extension of three years—a sort of Hail Mary that somehow, someone might convince a few states to endorse women's having equal rights under the law—until 1982. Significantly, *Alien* was made before Carter granted the extension, in a sociopolitical environment in which the collapse of the ERA seemed not only probable but imminent. In fact, *Alien* wrapped about the same time as the ERA's first drop-dead date, which was March 22, 1979.

The popular perception, endorsed by both the right and the left, was that the ERA could do three signal things to change American ways of life. First, it could protect women's reproductive freedoms. Second, it could change the structure and function of the American nuclear family. The third powerful lifestyle change the ERA portended was to *expand the role and participation of women in the US military*. Specifically, the ERA was understood as a bill that could result in women being eligible for active combat situations in military service. The ERA promised—or threatened, depending on your perspective—the idea of an American armed forces staffed in part by women warriors.

It's the third lifestyle element of the ERA that I want to focus on now—the military part—and how that element was operationalized in American news media by 1979. Mainstream newspaper coverage during the '70s noted that "the E.R.A. would require that the full range of military activities, including combat duty, be open to women." Proponents of the ERA pointed out that, since women had historically been banned from combat situations, they were also, in practice, debarred from promotions to the higher-ranking offices in the US military. There was a glass ceiling, in terms of both pay and rank, because they couldn't be in active combat. Proponents argued that the ERA would make it easier for women to enter into combat situations and prove themselves as warriors so that they could climb the professional ladder. Opponents of the ERA emphasized that women would be in combat situations, on the front lines, and would be coming home in body bags. Opponents didn't feel comfortable entrusting the safety of fellow soldiers to women, who they claimed could not hoist an injured fellow across a battlefield nor manage a heavy modern gun with sufficient skill to kill an enemy combatant. In 1975, states started to reject the ERA because of fears that it would make women eligible for the draft. In fact, in 1978, when

Alien was being planned and shot, women were still restricted in the Air Force and barred from most naval vessels.

A 1979 op-ed entitled "The Case Against Women in Combat," ran in the *Times* only months before *Alien* hit theaters. The article opens with deliberately acerbic images of "Marine coeds bunking down in bivouacs in combat zones" and teenage girls in helmets "charging over beaches under fire with bayonets fixed." The article goes on to say, "Such images may seem sheer fantasy—the farthest shores of radical feminism or an arresting montage for a futuristic film. Until recently, in fact, the military services and some factions of the women's liberation movement have dismissed the idea of warrior roles for women as 'unthinkable.'" The article went on to talk about how one argument in favor of allowing women into combat roles lay in the changing nature of military technology: If "combat will no longer depend on bayonets and physical force—rather on lasers, microprocessors, and other sophisticated devices that render obsolete the conventional images of battle," then maybe, maybe there would be no problem with women in combat, because "in the future, there will be no front lines." But, the piece goes on, to think in these ways is naive and dangerous to national security. Favoring women with higher school test scores over men with higher baseline aggression and physical strength is to undervalue the qualities necessary for battle success. And, really, for success in general: "Almost every study of productivity in American industry or of success in the economy, as well as of courage in combat, has shown that the intangibles of character—enterprise, aggression, drive, willingness to risk are much more important than the measurable quotients of classroom ability." So, smart women should step right on back, because undereducated, aggressive men really *are* better suited to military action. The *Times* article concludes by pointing out that "the ancient tradition against the use of women in combat embodies the deepest wisdom of the human race." *The deepest wisdom of the human race*. Well, released six months after that article ran in the *Times*, *Alien* would hotly contest that deepest wisdom.

Ripley is the only character who keeps her head clear throughout the entire film. She was in fact the only one who tried to *prevent* Kane from reentering the *Nostromo* once he had been in contact with the unknown life-form on LV-426. She ordered the away team to stay outside and follow twenty-four-hour quarantining procedure. It was Ash—the traitorous, violent corporate android—who overrode her orders and let Kane back on board the ship. Put otherwise, it was Ripley's level-headed respect for rules and honoring of rank—as she says, when Dallas is off-ship, *she* is the highest-ranking person on the ship, and makes the decisions—that could have protected the crew. Ripley is the one who later devises a plan to leave the *Nostromo* via the shuttle and detonate and destroy the ship with the alien inside it. It is Ripley who single-handedly keeps the alien at bay with a flamethrower and makes it onto her shuttle. It is Ripley who fights the thing, cleverly squeezing herself into a space suit so that she can blast the alien out of the air lock without depriving herself of oxygen in the process. Ripley is the best warrior in the film, and it's not because she's the strongest, the most aggressive, or the most willing to tolerate risk; it's because she's the *smartest*.

Throughout the film, Ridley Scott showcases Ripley's suitedness to military service. We see her wielding guns, managing a complex starship's self-destruct controls, piloting a small getaway ship, and obliterating an alien invader. She's doing exactly what anti-ERA advocates in the 1970s said women couldn't be expected to do in the armed forces. She *is* the armed forces. Ripley stands as proof that women could not only perform active combat service but think more clearly and execute complex battle plans more successfully than their fellows.

Alien is a parable about the dangers of dehumanizing women, a parable that suggests, ultimately, that a society that seeks to oppress women has something to be afraid of. And it's not (just) the alien. It's Ellen Ripley that society needs to fear. Because Ellen Ripley is going to turn around and detonate not only the alien but *Mother*, the ship that symbolizes dehumanization and entrapment in the home, the ship that embodies the imprisonment of women in a complex web of power and patriarchy from which they themselves are largely excluded. Ripley would rather float in an escape pod through the blackness of space, hoping to get picked up, than be trapped in the hell of domestic violence and reproductive abuse.

Interestingly, some mainstream reviewers completely missed the point of the film upon its release. Janet Maslin, in an unusually tone-deaf review, complained that *Alien* wasn't "fun." That's fair enough, but *Alien* isn't trying to be "fun." It's a radical feminist film trying to make all viewers—male and female—feel the kind of profound sexual and physical vulnerability to assault that hundreds of thousands of American women were subjected to in their own homes every year. Derek Malcolm wrote in *The Guardian* that the "values" of *Alien* weren't very "enlightening." Malcolm was perhaps not ready to grasp the magnitude of this film's feminist ambition.

One very prominent and influential person very clearly *did* grasp it—all of it. That was filmmaker James Cameron, who directed the sequel to *Alien* seven years later. As horror sequels go, this film is exemplary. Its central strength is that Cameron is an excellent reader of Scott's film, reenacting and accentuating some of its most important conceptual dynamics. *Aliens* opens with Ripley, again in hypersleep, being found by a deep salvage team. When she comes to, it's revealed that she's been floating in space for fifty-seven years. Everyone she knows on Earth is gone, so she is desperately alone. She can't get a job because she blew up the *Nostromo*, and there's no physical evidence of the alien that she says necessitated that decision. Quite the contrary, as she learns, there now is a colony of "sixty or seventy families" terraforming the planet (LV-426) that the derelict alien vessel was on; no complaints of a violent alien. She tells a corporate tribunal about the nature of the alien, and the members don't believe her, instead mocking her story that the alien is "a creature that gestates inside a living human host." Ripley, in her narrative to them, amplified the maternity of the creature, the idea of *gestation*. And no one believed her. How shocking: a woman reports rape and forcible impregnation and is not believed by those in power to help her.

But suddenly, soon after Ripley has told her story to the corporate tribunal that's assessing her actions, the colonists on the planet become uncontactable. Ripley is asked by a corporate agent to return as a consultant for what will now be a purely seek-and-destroy mission, headed by an elite squad of soldiers. Ripley will be safely removed from any combat situations, they assure her, since she'll be surrounded by professional soldiers, rather than by her old shipmates, who were soldiers of necessity on the *Nostromo*. Ripley is terrified to go, altogether too familiar with what the alien species is capable of. Plus, she is well aware that the alien egg Kane was forcibly impregnated by was one of dozens of eggs on LV-426. What ultimately convinces her to return is that, since she awoke from her long hypersleep, she has suffered from night terrors she can't shake. She decides that confronting the aliens and destroying all of them is the only way for her to heal, so she joins the expedition.

Since this is the future, where women presumably *do* have equal rights, including rights to be military combatants, two of the soldiers that will accompany Ripley are women: Vasquez and Ferro. Vasquez (Jenette Goldstein) is a muscular and fierce woman, styled to appear masculine by 1980s standards. Early on, in fact, one of her male colleagues says, "Hey, Vasquez. Have you ever been mistaken for a man?" And she replies, without missing a beat, "No, have you?" Burn. So, well before we see any actual combat, the film has called attention to Vasquez's status as female, and she has changed the terms of the conversation by insisting that only a man deficient in and insecure about his masculinity would ask a woman warrior whether she was mistaken for a man. Seeing that she is extremely good at verbal battle, we are immediately eager to see how Vasquez will do in combat situations, which she is amped and ready for. The other woman soldier, Corporal Ferro (Colette Hiller), is a combat pilot. So, we have two women who fulfill two functions that opponents to the ERA had been most concerned about women being allowed to fulfill: active combat and flight. Clearly, this film is going to make certain claims about the suitedness to having women in the military.

Cameron doesn't just amplify the women-in-the-military aspect from the first film. He also amplifies the forced pregnancy dynamic. After Ripley, the soldiers, and the corporate liaison Burke (Paul Reiser) have landed on LV-426, they encounter a huge number of aliens, as well as a very young girl named Newt who survived the carnage among the settlers. Burke, hoping to bring an alien specimen back to Earth for study, tries to entrap Ripley and Newt into being impregnated by an alien. Ripley reveals his treachery to the soldiers, saying, "He figured that he could get an alien back through quarantine if one of us was impregnated . . . nobody would know about the embryos we were carrying." *Impregnated. Embryos we were carrying.* The gender politics of the second film are less subtle than in *Alien*—in this film, a human male explicitly tries to force two human females to become "impregnated."

Now that the aliens have found the humans on the ship, the soldiers are picked off one by one. The hypermasculine Hudson, who had earlier cast aspersions on Vasquez's femaleness, ends up getting pulled through a floor panel by the aliens, screaming "Fuck you!" all the while. Immediately after that, Vasquez helps rescue a fellow soldier and then single-handedly takes out half a dozen aliens before retreating. Then, as the survivors try to escape through the ventilation system, Vasquez—again single-handedly—holds off the alien horde, giving the others some extra time to flee. Eventually, as she retreats into the vent system, Vasquez gets alien acid blood on her leg, incapacitating her. One of her teammates tries to help her, but they both get trapped together and decide to blow themselves up with a grenade so that their deaths will at least also involve taking out another wave of aliens. Vasquez is the bravest, most tactical, strongest, and most self-sacrificing of the soldiers. Take that, ERA opponents.

By the final scenes, only Ripley, Newt, a benign android named Bishop, and Ripley's love interest, Hicks (Michael Biehn), survive—though Hicks is badly wounded. Newt gets separated from the rest and is trapped and cocooned by one of the aliens. Ripley gets Hicks to Bishop and returns to find Newt on her own. Like Vasquez, Ripley is shown to be braver, more team-oriented, more tactical, and more self-sacrificing than any of the men around her. Once again, take that, ERA opponents. Ripley finds and rescues Newt, only to encounter the alien progenitrix alone. When this happens, Ripley realizes that she needs some technological advantage, so she straps herself into a heavy-machinery loading device, which functions essentially as an exoskeleton for her. She battles the alien progenitrix in hand-to-hand combat, again proving her worth as a soldier and combat tactician. Ripley knows she has to become more than human in order to defeat the alien progenitrix, and she does that. In the end, however, it's not her exoskeleton but her intelligence that wins out. She defeats the mother alien—again—by blowing her out the air lock.

As I said, James Cameron was an excellent reader of Ridley Scott's film. Even so, Cameron does dampen some of Scott's feminist critiques. First, even though Ripley is still unquestionably a righteous warrior in this film, *Aliens* makes Ripley's military exceptionalism a tiny bit less exceptional than it was in *Alien*—she requires her massive metal exoskeleton and a team, including Hicks, Vasquez, and Bishop. To be sure, in the original film, Lambert and Parker were there to help her, but not through to the end. She had to figure out her ultimate exit strategy entirely on her own. In *Aliens*, she's got a little girl, a new boyfriend, and a supportive (if severely damaged) android egging her on and helping her survive. Indeed, in the final part of the fight sequence between Ripley and the Queen Alien, it's Bishop the android's quick thinking and quicker reflexes that keep Newt from being sucked into outer space. The message of the second film is clear: however fierce you are, you can't make it without a team.

Second, in Cameron's sequel, Ripley is made into a mother. She takes charge of young Newt, and most of the second half of the film focuses on Ripley's desire to protect her. In doing this, the second film recurs to a far more traditional take on women's roles and on what gives women power. Indeed, in the final confrontation between the alien progenitrix and Ripley, Ripley screams at the alien, "Get away from her, you *bitch*!" taking on the role of angry, protective mama bear. It's compelling, but it's not the same Ripley that we met in the first film, isolated, fierce, indomitable, powerful, and unseduceable by either the claims of male attention or maternal desire. In the second film, it's her desire to protect Newt that gives Ripley her final burst of bravery, the burst that's required to dispatch the "bitch" alien once and for all. In the first film, Ripley was allowed to remain a free agent, a warrior, and a survivor. Ripley survived, ultimately, by *killing* Mother, not by *becoming* a mother. Ripley, in the end of the second film, is subjected to yet another feminist ambivalence: She's allowed to be fierce, but her ferocity is both curbed and structured by her subjection to maternal feeling. The Ripley of *Aliens* is a safer, more recognizable type of woman than the Ripley of *Alien*. She's fierce and powerful, but she knows she needs her friends to help her and now her child survive.

Of course, from the standpoint of domestic violence survival, that's almost always true. It's notoriously difficult for women—particularly women with children—to extricate themselves from situations of battery and domestic torture without third-party help, be that third party a lawyer, doctor, police officer, counselor, friend, family member, or colleague. For this realism about domestic violence, I can only commend Cameron. But on the other hand, this is part of why the original film—*Alien*—is so powerful and also so terrifying: Ripley is, like so many victims and survivors of domestic abuse, totally alone in the end. She has no backup. She has no one at all. And yet, somehow, she makes it through.

For that reason, I think it's safe to say that, of all the domestic horrors in this book, Ridley Scott's original *Alien* is in a strange way the most optimistic—naively optimistic, even. It has the most confidence in a woman's power to overcome truly unthinkable peril and violence. It has confidence in the possibility for an individual woman—even a woman like Ripley, with no formal combat training—to find within herself a warrior. Moreover, she finds within herself the capacity not just to escape but actually to destroy the abuser that wanted to assault, rape, impregnate, and kill her. (Or I should say, abusers plural. We must never forget that Ash was at least as much of a problem for Ripley's safety as was the stowaway alien.) Whereas Rosemary was psychologically and spiritually destroyed by her rape and abuse, whereas Chris wound up a shattered and solemn woman, whereas Joanna ended up dead and replaced by a robot, and whereas Kathy ended up battered by her son and murdered by his hench-nanny, Ripley escapes, and she kills her tormentors.

Which, of course, is not an option for real women, living on planet Earth. Quite the contrary, as legal scholars, advocates, and activists like Leigh Goodmark have argued, women who are proven survivors of catastrophic violence in the home, and who ultimately become violent against their tormentors, routinely find themselves serving long prison sentences. As strange as it is to say, it appears that things are better for battered women in outer space than they are on Earth—at least in the sense that Ripley can actually rid herself of her tormentors forever, blowing up her ship and blasting her enemies into the void.

In real life, as many women survivors of violence know, and as the families of many victims of femicide know, there is no decisive, permanent way out. Instead, most of the time, you move through the rest of your life knowing that the person who hurt you in the past could return, at any time, to hurt you again. Of course, the massive sequelization of *Alien* reminds us precisely of how tenacious the abuser can be, but at the end of the original film, as Ripley sails off into space asleep and all alone, there is a palpable relief and sense of safety, one we do not feel at the end of any other film we've discussed so far. This is part of why Ellen Ripley becomes such a powerful archetype for feminist horror ever after. For one shimmering, silent, sleepy moment, alone in deep space, it seems that this violent alien has been put to rest for good. The end is glorious, but it is also—very clearly—science fiction.

CHAPTER 6

The Shining: Only Just Fiction

The Shining probably has the largest cult following of any film in this book. It, like the others, was a box office success when it came out in 1980, but its rate of return was lower. The film is said to have cost $19 million to make, and it brought in $48 million at box offices worldwide. But *since* its release in 1980, *The Shining* has gone on to be obsessively studied by film and horror geeks the world over, including in the wonderful 2012 documentary film *Room 237*. Beyond that, the iconography of this film crops up everywhere in horror since 1980: Axes signal Nicholsonian craziness; the unforgettable interior design of the film pops up constantly; the haunting image of Jack Nicholson frozen to death at the end of the film has become a pervasive internet meme. Recently, the carpeting in the infamous hallway scenes of *The Shining* showed up in another horror hallway, in

Coralie Fargeat's award-winning 2024 body horror extravaganza *The Substance*. In the same year, the film's surreal scene when Jack sees Wendy and Danny walking through a model of a labyrinth on a table was echoed in *Heretic*. Everything about *The Shining* has become iconic.

In addition to its cult status and popularity as an inspiration for later horror films, *The Shining* is the film for which claims about domestic abuse and violence are the easiest to see, even from a distance. Classic movie posters for the film often show a terrified Shelley Duvall, her mouth gaping in a panicked scream, behind a bathroom door that a crazed Jack Nicholson is trying to carve through with an axe. The domestic violence is not subtle. From a sociohistorical standpoint, that makes sense. By 1980, when the film was released, Americans had grown broadly aware of domestic violence as a problem and aware that women and children in situations of domestic violence were trapped and isolated. What makes this film extraordinarily powerful is *how* it renders the dynamics of domestic violence, and in how it explores—in more fine-grained detail than in any other film so far—the psychology of the male abuser.

The opening scene of *The Shining* is long and ominous. From above and from a distance, the camera watches a small, vulnerable-looking car traversing mountainous roads into increasingly remote areas. We hear a heavy, low-pitched, chilling anthem pulsating in the background. The road gets snowier and snowier, more and more removed from the city, from society, from anything. Isolation is a clear, palpable dynamic the film. The ponderous soundtrack makes clear that the isolation—

far from being some kind of idyllic retreat from the mania of civilization—is going to be dangerous somehow, maybe even evil.

Eventually, the car pulls up to a resort in the mountains. The Overlook Hotel is large, wooden, very much a lodge-style resort, perched at the absolute upper perimeter of the tree line—indeed, about two hundred yards behind the hotel, we see the pine trees dwindle to nothing and only bare, rocky ground beyond—no roads, no structures, no people. A man, Jack Torrance, memorably played by Jack Nicholson, strikes out across the lobby to do a job interview. Watching him walk is unsettling; he looks like a man ill at ease in his body, ill at ease in reality. He can't decide whether to put his hands in his pockets or leave them out; he sucks his lip; when he introduces himself to the front desk clerk, he says "Jack Torrance" with a nervous, up-speak quaver. But the camera doesn't leave us there with Jack for long; as he settles in for his job interview with the hotel manager, we cut to his wife Wendy (Shelley Duvall) and their son Danny (Danny Lloyd) back at home in Boulder. They are talking about whether they're all going to go live in a hotel—this is the job Jack is interviewing for, the winter caretaker for the Overlook Hotel. Danny is unenthusiastic about the prospect and talks to the imaginary friend that lives in his finger—Tony—in a way that seems to smack at once of the boy's creativity and some kind of trauma. Something is amiss with this family, but we don't know just what it is.

The camera cuts back to the hotel and to Jack's interview. We learn that he's a former schoolteacher, but not much more than that about his backstory. Jack asks, sensibly, why the resort closes in the winter, given it seems so well positioned as a ski resort, and the manager tells him that it's not feasible to keep twenty-five miles of road clear all winter simply to enable access to the Overlook. This fact plays an important dramatic role: If he takes the job, Jack and his family will be alone, without even roads to drive on, isolated by a span of twenty-five miles all winter long. But Jack, a writer, is excited by the prospect of this arrangement, saying, "That just happens to be exactly what I'm looking for." Nicholson's smile as he says this looks false, more than a little unhinged. In that, the film adheres strictly to the novel on which it is based; Stephen King's novel describes Torrance's smile at the Overlook manager as follows: "Jack flashed the PR smile again, large and insultingly toothy." Nicholson's performance took that characterization to heart. Seeing that smile, we already know that something about Jack Torrance isn't quite right.

Quickly, things get more concerning. The manager, somewhat skeptical that Jack really understands the degree of isolation he and his family will endure, discloses that there was a tragedy in the hotel's past, when the previous caretaker had a mental breakdown during the winter and murdered his wife and children. The manager's disclosure gets very little reaction from Jack, who takes it entirely in stride, saying, in a painful *mise en abyme*, that his wife is "a confirmed ghost story and horror film addict." Of course, Jack's total failure even to flinch at this disclosure of extraordinary—indeed, mortal—domestic violence puts the audience on high alert for what's to come. For modern viewers, it reminds us of how the COVID lockdowns of 2020 revealed that domestic violence ramps up rapidly under conditions of isolation, not only because domestic tensions run high with cabin fever, but also because no one can see what's going on in the domestic space when people aren't regularly coming and going.

Amplifying our anxiety at the prospect of Wendy and Danny wintering over at the Overlook, back in Boulder, Tony tells Danny that Jack got the job. At this revelation, suddenly, Danny has some kind of seizure in which he sees a vision of two little girls and a river of blood in a hotel hallway, until things fade to black. When Danny comes to, Wendy has called for a doctor. The doctor tries to get Danny to reveal something about the nature of his friend Tony; like us, she's trying to work out whether Danny is suffering from something psychiatric, something somatic, or some kind of abuse. Wendy watches anxiously, her arms crossed over her chest. In the end, the doctor is not particularly concerned until Wendy reveals that there is a history of violent domestic abuse in the family. She tells about how Jack, when drunk, once hurt Danny badly, dislocating his shoulder: "On this particular occasion, my husband used too much strength and injured his arm." The doctor looks troubled, as well she should. Wendy, during her talk with the doctor, has looked terrified—smoking nervously, her hand shaking as she tries to light her cigarette, struggling to sustain eye contact, her face tensed. She looks like what she is, namely: an abuse victim trying to cover up for her—and her child's—abuser.

Child abuse had become a known and recognized sociomedical problem by the 1970s. A groundbreaking article published in 1962 in *The Journal of the American Medical Association*, "The

Battered-Child Syndrome," described family dynamics in which children were brutally beaten. That article led to a groundswell of change, resulting relatively rapidly—in about five years—in the national criminalization of child abuse. Doctors by the late 1970s knew about the psychology of abusers, they knew the prevalence of alcohol consumption as an amplifier of abusive behaviors, and they knew about how wives tended to cover up for or minimize the abuse inflicted by fathers. Watching the doctor's face, and watching Wendy's very apparent anxiety in telling this story—"It's just one of those things that happens with kids"—we feel more than a little anxious, already, that Jack may not be the best pick for winter caretaker of the Overlook, even though Wendy swears to the doctor that he's no longer drinking: "He hasn't had any alcohol in five months!" she proudly informs the doctor. The doctor—who clearly knows what child abuse is and clearly thinks something isn't right with Wendy's story—looks at her steadily and with skepticism but decides not to intervene. As a result, when Jack takes the job at the Overlook, Wendy and Danny accompany him, if somewhat less than enthusiastically.

At the Overlook, the family gets an orientation from the staff, during which the manager tells Jack that there's no alcohol on the premises, and Jack confirms what Wendy told the doctor: "We don't drink." Meanwhile, Danny meets the Overlook's chef, Mr. Hallorann. Mr. Hallorann sees something special in young Danny and takes him aside for some ice cream. It turns out that Hallorann and Danny have a rare psychic ability in common. This ability, which Mr. Hallorann refers to as "shining," enables him to communicate telepathically with Danny. Mr. Hallorann takes a few minutes to teach him about shining. Danny doesn't quite know what to do with this information. He shrugs his shoulders nervously, unsmilingly, at Mr. Hallorann's questions. Eventually, Danny reveals that Tony, the entity that lives in his finger, doesn't like for Danny to talk about his psychic abilities. Seeing that Danny is anxious, Mr. Hallorann tries to reassure Danny about the hotel but tells him, fiercely, to stay out of room 237. So we know, from the get-go, that Mr. Hallorann, despite his reassurances, is actually not all that comfortable with young, psychic Danny spending the winter at the Overlook. Piggybacking on Hallorann's perspective and combining it with what we know about Jack and the prior caretaker, we as viewers are not feeling very good about things for this winter, either.

After Hallorann and the rest of the staff take off for the winter, Wendy and Danny are alone, with Jack. The hotel quickly starts to seem too large, too empty. Its corridors begin to seem labyrinthine and disorienting. The camera is often placed at a significant distance from the actors, highlighting the sheer amount of empty, quiet, eerie space they have to traverse to get from one location to the next. Deepening the rising sense of danger and disorientation in the film, Jack's mind seems to be coming off the rails. He types maniacally, day after day, alone in a vast room. Sometimes, he hurls a ball ferociously and obsessively against a wall. One evening, Wendy goes to ask Jack a question while he's typing away at his manuscript. He blows up at her for interrupting him. He's cruel, he shouts, he mocks her; Wendy's eyes are wide, her face almost perfectly still, as though she knows anything else she says will merely provoke the bear. After

Jack tells her to "get the fuck out of here," she looks crestfallen, meekly mumbling, "Okay." She walks out, dejected, her hands jammed into the pockets of her dress. Something really *isn't* right with Jack, that much is clear, and Wendy and Danny are the only people there, in the twisting, creepy corridors and rooms of the hotel, to be on the receiving end of whatever it is that's wrong.

Making matters worse, they are without recourse to outside aid. A predicted snowstorm becomes a real snowstorm, and the phone lines go down. All Wendy has to communicate with the outside world is a radio; when she radios anxiously down to the rangers' station lower on the mountain, the rangers advise her to keep the radio on 24-7, because they don't think the phone lines will be repaired until spring. She is now officially locked into an archetypal situation for wife-battery: isolated from friends, family, and even the police, locked into a domestic space with a man known to have violent tendencies and an alcohol problem.

Danny asks Wendy one morning if he can go fetch his fire engine from the family's bedroom suite. But Jack is in the room, sleeping. Wendy pleads with Danny to leave Jack alone, saying that his father only went to sleep a few hours ago. This scene is crucial to establishing the degree of Wendy's entrapment, because it indicates that she is tracking his every move, his hours of sleep—in the way partners of alcoholics count their drinks or the way abused women track their abusers' patterns of behavior. Throughout this scene, which is shot from behind, almost as though we are spying on Wendy and Danny, we can see heavy, relentless snowfall coursing down outside, emphasizing the profundity of their isolation. Danny promises to be quiet and not to wake his father up, but he *really* wants his fire engine. This toy choice, of course, is marked: Danny wants a toy that portends the possibility of rescue from a potentially lethal situation, a truck that can extend its reach to the upper levels of a building, to pull people out of windows—something that Danny and Wendy will both specifically need but lack before the end of the film. Wendy relents, so Danny goes to get his fire truck.

In one of the most haunting scenes of the film, Danny finds Jack sitting upright in bed, in his bathrobe, looking utterly deranged. Jack calls Danny over and waits, unsmiling, as Danny nervously approaches. Jack holds him and kisses him while Danny stares ahead, wide-eyed, looking terrified. Danny seeks to reassure himself, so he asks Jack, "You would never hurt Mommy and me, would you?" And Jack responds, "What do you mean? Did your mother ever say that to you? That I would hurt you?" We can hear Jack's gorge rising at the thought of Wendy trying to turn his son against him, though we know that's the opposite of what's really happening. She is, against Danny's best interests, actually *protecting Jack*, while Danny is having psychic visions of murdered children.

But that changes very soon thereafter. We see Danny enter the forbidden room 237, and then the camera cuts away to Wendy in the boiler room, where she is doing Jack's job by maintaining the massive hotel furnace. Suddenly, she hears Jack upstairs screaming a wild, insane scream. She runs up to check on him and finds him asleep and having some kind of nightmare at his desk. When he wakes up, he reveals that he'd been dreaming of having killed her and Danny and cut them up into little pieces. Wendy freezes, as anyone would.

Suddenly Danny appears at the edge of the room. We don't know if he's heard what Jack confessed, but Wendy tries to cover for Jack, urging Danny out of the room to hide from him his father's state. When Danny doesn't leave, Wendy approaches him and realizes that something happened to his neck—it's very badly bruised and swollen—and that he's sucking his thumb, a classic childhood sign of trauma. Convinced Jack has attempted to strangle Danny, Wendy at last turns on him: "You did this to him, didn't you, you son of a bitch? *You* did this to him, didn't you! How could you? How could you?" Wendy runs off with Danny in her arms. But where can she go? She knows, just as we do, that there is nowhere to go: The roads are impassable, the phone lines are down. She has no car. All she has is a snowcat. And given the storm, making an exit from the hotel is all the more forbidding. We realize, in lockstep with Wendy, how very perilous her and Danny's situation has become. They are trapped and isolated in a labyrinthine building with a madman who is dreaming of murdering them both.

Things rapidly get worse as it becomes clear both that Jack is losing his mind *and* that the hotel is somehow possessed by malevolent forces. Jack goes into the "gold ballroom," muttering that he'd give his "goddamn soul" for a glass of beer. Suddenly, he sees a man named Lloyd, who has materialized as the bartender at the gold ballroom's lavish bar. The bar, previously emptied of booze, is now amply stocked. Viewing the film, we can't tell whether Jack is having a hallucination or the past history of the Overlook is supernaturally intruding on his present moment of life. As Jack starts complaining to Lloyd about his woes, he says, "Just a little problem with the old sperm bank upstairs"—referring to Wendy in this dehumanizing metonymy. He goes on to call her a "bitch" and to rail against her for refusing to forget about the arm-breaking scene from years before.

While Jack talks with Lloyd, we suddenly hear Wendy screaming Jack's name. She's running down the hallway in a blind panic, holding a baseball bat. Gasping and looking repeatedly over her shoulder as if she believes someone is pursuing her, Wendy bursts into the barroom. Her face stained with tears and pink from exertion, she screams amidst sniffling and heaving, "Oh, Jack, thank God you're here. There's someone else in the hotel with us. There's a crazy woman in one of the rooms. She tried to strangle Danny." Jack's response? He glares at her and asks, angrily, "Are you out of your fucking mind?" Here, the conflation of real-life, hard-core domestic abuse with the supernatural and haunted hotel becomes more acute. *We* the viewers know now that Jack is feeling full of rage against Wendy, that he's out of control of his addiction again, though we don't know whether he's *actually* drinking some kind of spectral booze or imagining drinking it at this point, and that his violent impulses are returning to him. We know that it's Jack who's out of his mind, not Wendy. What *Wendy* knows is only what Danny has told her, which is that there's a crazy woman in room 237.

Despite his rage and disbelief, Jack checks out room 237, where he finds a gorgeous naked woman in the bathtub. She rises to embrace him, and they kiss. Quickly, however, she transforms, and Jack realizes he's holding a dead and rotting corpse. He is, understandably, terrified and disgusted. Yet, when he returns from room 237, he lies to Wendy, telling her he saw nothing. He ventures that maybe Danny hurt his own neck—a common defense for child abusers, to blame the injury on the child. But this time, Wendy knows it's impossible and wants to get Danny out of the hotel. At the thought of leaving the hotel, Jack visibly starts to panic. He turns on Wendy, verbally abusing her and gaslighting her, blaming her for all his problems. "It is so fucking typical of you to create a problem like this when I finally have a chance to accomplish something! . . . Wendy, I have let you fuck up my life so far, but I am *not* going to let you fuck this up." Wendy sits alone and cries quietly. She is imprisoned with someone with only the loosest control over himself, someone who blames her for the failures in his own life, someone who struggles with addiction, and someone who has a history of violence. She is trapped with the absolute, perfect distillation of "compulsively masculine" domestic abuser, a figure well understood in the late 1970s. But there is nothing she can do to escape: the lines are down, the snows are in, the nearest neighbors are twenty-five miles away. There's no one to hear her scream.

The showcasing of domestic violence in the film soon directly activates the historical logic that underpinned and justified the battery of wives and children: the logic of correction. Remember, correction is the idea that the head of household, the *paterfamilias*, has both the right and obligation to regulate and control the behavior of his wife and children, by physical force when and as necessary. So now, Jack finds himself back in time in the hotel. He meets a waiter, who turns out to be Delbert Grady, the man who murdered his wife and children at the Overlook when he was caretaker years before. Grady starts grooming Jack to turn violent against Danny. Grady induces Jack to note that Danny "is a very willful boy." And Grady responds, "Indeed he is. A very willful boy. A rather *naughty* boy, if I may be so bold." Seeing that Jack is receptive to this line of influencing, Grady—whether truly a ghost or a psychic projection of Jack's own abusive consciousness, we do not ever fully know—goes on, "Perhaps they need a good talking to," says Grady, "perhaps a bit more . . . " Grady then talks about how he "corrected" his own wife and children; he uses the word twice, referring, of course, to how he brutally murdered them. Jack is, in Grady's view, the man of the house; it is incumbent upon him to correct misbehavior.

After this conversation with Grady, Jack's abusive tendencies overtake him. Wendy goes to find Jack. When she looks at his manuscript, she finds that it's simply an ongoing repetition, for hundreds of pages, of the phrase "All work and no play makes Jack a dull boy." With this incontestable revelation of Jack's diseased mind, Wendy begins to panic because she finally sees her and Danny's reality for what it is: domestic imprisonment. They are being held hostage by an insane domestic abuser. In that very moment of realization, we witness Jack looking at a terrified, wide-eyed Wendy. She starts to explain that Danny should be taken to a doctor; Jack begins to excoriate her for insensitivity to his work obligations to the owners of the Overlook—again, the compulsive masculinity argument comes in, where he feels his status as breadwinner is being challenged or threatened. She tries to get away, and Jack says, "Wendy, darling, light of my life! I'm not going to hurt you. You didn't let me finish my sentence. I'm not going to hurt you. I'm just going to bash your brains in. I'm going to bash them right the fuck in." Now she's screaming and starts swinging the bat.

Listening to this stretch of dialogue is agonizing as a viewer. Like Wendy, we allow ourselves to hope—in the face of a mountain of evidence to the contrary—that Jack may *not* be intending to harm her when he starts out with "Wendy, darling, light of my life" and promises he's not going to hurt her. Like her, we want to believe that. But at the same time, we know he's just trying to get closer to her so he can control her, maybe hurt her, maybe kill her. He smiles like a lunatic, moving slowly and menacingly, like a predator stalking his prey, up the stairs, and we feel unsafe, terrorized in lockstep with Wendy. Even so, at the last minute, when he arrives at his assertion that he's going to bash her brains in, we are somehow still startled by the brazenness of it, by the obvious pleasure he takes in terrorizing her.

The soundtrack is a shrill, scratchy non-melody as Wendy backs up the stairs; we watch her from below, seeing her hunched posture, her weeping face, her fragility, her fatigue, her terror. Somehow, miraculously, as she flails around with the bat, she hits him on the hand; as he moves to shield the injured hand, she knocks him in the head and sends him backward down a flight of stairs. Seeing him unconscious at the bottom, Wendy screams, and the camera fades to a close-up of Jack's face, now semiconscious on the kitchen floor, being dragged by Wendy into a food locker, where she locks him in. Although he says he's hurt and needs a doctor when he fully comes to, she holds her ground and refuses to release him.

For a fleeting moment, it seems she's going to be okay, until she finds out that Jack sabotaged their snowcat, the only vehicle that might be capable of getting her and Danny down the mountain during the blizzard. Now, in the twenty-first century, this is a known and recognized form of domestic violence—vehicular control, or restriction of movement or transportation—and has been criminalized or is in the process of being criminalized in some states. But in 1977 and 1980, when the novel and film were released, it was a cutting-edge recognition that the physical imprisonment of women and children by hiding or sabotaging a vehicle was often key to how the abuser could maintain control. Jack understood that physical flight was Wendy's only escape from death, and he took it from her.

The score of the film in this scene is screaming, sharp, discordant, and metallic. When we see Wendy outside in the garage, confirming the sabotage, her thin hair is plastered to her head, her breath comes out in jagged puffs on the frigid air, and she lamely palms a piece of machinery that Jack has physically sliced out of the snowcat. There's no way she can fix this, she realizes at the same moment as we do.

The next scene dispels any doubt we might have had about the realness of the supernatural forces at work in the hotel because Grady comes to the door to talk to Jack, urging him to punish Wendy and Danny, and expressing scorn at Jack's inability so far to do so: "I and others have come to believe that your heart isn't in this. You haven't the belly for it . . . Your wife appears to be stronger than we imagined, Mr. Torrance. Somewhat more *resourceful*. She seems to have gotten the better of you." Grady is goading Jack's wounded masculinity, his sense of his life as a failure. Then, having strummed the strings of Jack's already vibrating self-hatred, Grady ups the ante, urging Jack, "I fear you will have to deal with this matter in the harshest possible way, Mr. Torrance." Jack responds, with the sadistic brutality of someone bent on violence, "There's nothing I look forward to with greater pleasure, Mr. Grady." As Jack delivers this line, his jaw is set, jutted slightly forward, as if he's some kind of wild boar with tusks, hungry for blood. Indeed, he licks his lips, nodding in something like erotic pleasure as he agrees to slaughter his family. Nothing, after all, would give him greater *pleasure*. Somehow, Grady unlocks the door—whatever the spectral and supernatural presences are in the hotel, they are capable of moving matter, of acting both on people and on things.

Once released from the food locker by Grady, Jack grabs the infamous axe that anyone who has seen this film remembers. He finds Wendy and Danny, holed up in their suite, and begins to chop through the door with the axe, while Wendy screams and Danny appears entirely possessed by Tony. Wendy pushes Danny up and out a window in the bathroom, into the snow outside; this is the moment at which that fire truck would have come in handy. Tragically, Wendy, although thin, cannot fit herself through the window, so she is trapped alone in the bathroom while Jack—his eyes wild, his hair disheveled—begins quoting the story of the Big Bad Wolf, saying he'll huff and puff and blow the house in. With the conclusion of his deranged nursery rhyme, he begins to chop his way through the door. Wendy screams, her eyes round as coins, as she retreats into a corner. Accentuating her vulnerability, she's clad in a bathrobe throughout these final, horrifying scenes of the film. She is a perfect, abject, absolute picture of a domestic violence victim. Duvall isn't really acting in this scene but channeling. She's channeling the unheard suffering of untold thousands of American women every year who are subjected to terrifying, and sometimes lethal, domestic violence, both in 1980 and today.

In a reprieve for Wendy, Jack suddenly leaves her alone to go look for the source of a sound he hears—it turns out to be Mr. Hallorann, who's been summoned psychically by Danny from his winter home in Florida. Mr. Hallorann's arrival feels like a miracle, because suddenly Wendy and Danny are no longer completely alone with their abuser. Better still, Hallorann has arrived on a borrowed snowcat, which can easily hold Wendy and Danny as well as Hallorann himself, so there's now a very real possibility of escape from the domestic prison of the Overlook. Hallorann, alas, doesn't know quite what he's walking into, however. We see him walking down one of the main corridors of the hotel when—unexpectedly—Jack emerges from around a corner and chops into Mr. Hallorann's chest with his axe. Hallorann dies immediately; with his death, our hopes for Wendy and Danny's extrication sink once again.

Enraged that someone from the outside has attempted to help Danny and Wendy, Jack pursues Danny outside, eager to kill him. Throughout the scene, Jack's psychopathy is in stark focus: He's huffing and puffing, his eyes wild like a rabid animal.

Meanwhile, tiny Danny, dressed in very insufficient clothing for a Colorado blizzard, trudges desperately through deep snow, making for the hedge maze. Jack chases Danny in the blinding snow into the maze, and now we realize that Danny—who has done this hedge maze many times with Wendy—has the advantage. We see him from behind, backlit, running through the snow at top speed. He seems incredibly, impossibly vulnerable in the harsh blue light of the shot, a tiny little boy in a sweater, hiding from his murderous father in a snowstorm. While we watch him run, we hear Jack screaming "*Danny!*" in a blind rage, and strange, Satanic-sounding discordant music plays in the background. But Danny turns the forbidding and fast-falling snow to his benefit by retracing his footprints, walking backward, so that his path appears to end abruptly, for no reason. He does this slowly—agonizingly slowly for the viewer, who knows that Jack can't possibly be that far behind him. But clever little Danny keeps at it until he gets to a fork in the labyrinth that he can hop over to, using his hands to blot out the path to his hiding place. Jack, meanwhile, giggles sadistically and clutches his thin jacket to himself, his face lowered and his eyes gazing straight on in a bull-like expression. Finally, Jack catches up to Danny's last footprint, but there's no Danny. When Jack realizes Danny has subjected him to some kind of ruse, he puffs air into his cheeks and decides to look for Danny down another path—fortunately for Danny, the wrong one. Danny escapes the maze by racing back along his own footsteps. But Jack, in his mental disorientation, cannot escape and freezes to death overnight, as Wendy and Jack escape in Mr. Hallorann's snowcat. One of the final shots of the film shows Jack, frozen stiff and solid, sitting in the snow, his eyes still open and menacing, though no longer alive.

The domestic abuse dynamic in this film is far from subtle. We know that Jack is a child abuser—he broke Danny's arm in prior years. We know he's an alcoholic—and we know that, whether spectrally or actually, he's been drinking heavily again. We know he fits the "compulsively male" profile of wife beaters that 1970s-era sociological literature characterized. None of these dynamics are marginal or borderline; all are present in both the film and the novel it was based upon. *The Shining*, both on the page and on the screen, is a horror about domestic violence.

Kubrick's domestic horror changes King's ending, however, in a way that raises an important question about domestic violence in 1980 and beyond. In the novel, Hallorann's life is spared, and he helps Wendy and Danny escape; in the film, Hallorann is murdered by Jack's hand. So, when Wendy escapes with Danny, she does so with no assistance, all on her own, the "final girl" of the film. Empowered. Self-saving. Kubrick revised King's ending to make Wendy the uncontested heroine, kind of like Ripley in *Alien.*

To me, the change to the novel's ending is disappointing, even if more dramatic, because it understates the extraordinary difficulty that abuse survivors face in attempting to escape their abusers. If the 1970s studies of domestic violence had shown anything, it was that King's novel was closer to reality: Women *did* need help—usually a lot of help—to escape situations of domestic violence. Colorado in 1980 isn't the interstellar space of some futuristic sci-fi film; it's reality, part of the United States of America. The obstacles—social, financial, physical, psychological, circumstantial, legal, vehicular—faced by American women in situations of domestic violence were not just often but *almost always* too great to overcome on their own. Women needed shelters. They needed new laws. They needed more social support. They needed allies. They needed family members and friends. They needed someone like Hallorann to help them drive the escape vehicle. They *still* do. It's not weakness but vulnerability to need help, and I hope we all know by now that there's a huge difference between the two.

Abuse victims need advocates who *can hear them and who will listen*. And that's exactly what Hallorann does. Hallorann saves Wendy and Danny because, through Danny, he could *see and hear* what was going on. Because he chose to listen, he could act. What King insists upon in his novel is that more people need to be listening for the cries of abuse victims and to act, because those victims often cannot help themselves. The revision to the end of the film may indeed be feminist, from a certain viewpoint: Wendy gets powerful! Go, Wendy, go! However, it is also a simplification of the ways in which women might actually achieve safety in these situations. Women need *help*, not because they are weak but because their entrappers are demonic. Ripley's escape option appears to be the only one that works decisively: Blow up the domestic space altogether. Although, as we know from the sequels, even *that* doesn't really work.

In fact, the idea of destroying the domestic space of violence as a way of ending things decisively was in King's mind, too. In his novel, the hotel burns to the ground at the end—the boiler having exploded through Jack's lack of attention and care. Whatever violent malignancy haunted that place is put to rest. In the film, by sharp contrast, the hotel survives intact—and that particular aspect of Kubrick's revision works beautifully. Wendy and Danny escape in the snowcat, and Jack freezes to death, but the hotel remains, no doubt to ensnare and torment another family down the line. Indeed, the very last shot of the film slowly zooms in on a photograph, hanging on a wall in the Overlook, dated to 1921 that features our Jack in a party scene, front and center, gazing directly and brazenly at the camera. *I'm still here*, he seems to say. This place of domestic terror, it appears, will not be burned down or blown up by this film, and Jack Torrance will merely be absorbed into its host of violent, misogynistic, abusive ghosts. So even though Kubrick minimizes the importance of outside aid in Wendy and Danny's escape, he revises King's ending to accentuate the fragility and impermanence of that escape. Horror hangover extraordinaire.

So, *The Shining* is obviously a film committed both to its supernaturalness but also, crucially, to its realism. It's a film about a haunted hotel and a haunted person (Jack), but it's also a film—like *The Exorcist*—about the demonic, cruel, and altogether too real forces of violence that lie in the heart of patriarchy. Jack isn't just a scary monster; he's a stand-in for a very real and all-too-pervasive kind of person, an abuser, a domestic terrorist, a predator in the home. Wendy and Danny, meanwhile, represent the hundreds of thousands of domestic abuse victims in the United States every year. That's why I love the final zoom on the photograph so much: "Jack" is always there, staring, waiting to pounce again.

This hyperrealism is accentuated by the very casting choices of the film. It's surely no accident that the actor who plays Danny's real name is *Danny*, nor that the actor who plays Jack's real name is *Jack*. When Shelley Duvall screams "Jack!" in horror, she's screaming that at a person who is both a fictional man named Jack Torrance and a real-life man named Jack Nicholson. The depth of horror that Duvall's face registers throughout the latter half of the film is surely partially about the vertigo she must have felt, screaming for her life against this oddly twinned "Jack" who stood before her, looking way, way too malicious and predatory to be mere fiction. I should note that the infamous drugging and rape of the thirteen-year-old Samantha Geimer by Roman Polanski transpired in 1977—three years *before* the release of *The Shining—at the home of Jack Nicholson*. When Nicholson flaps his tongue lasciviously at Duvall on the staircase as he threatens to kill her, it's somewhere uncomfortably short of pure make-believe.

Indeed, Duvall has gone on record many times saying that Stanley Kubrick himself terrorized and tormented her, to elicit the most shattered and horrified performance from her that he could. The documentary film *The Making of "The Shining"* shows scenes where Shelley Duvall, drained and exhausted, is lying on the floor, being propped up with pillows and blankets, while female crew members stroke her hands and attempt to console her. In interviews for *The Making of*, Duvall says the filming was so stressful that it impacted her health. Also in *The*

Making of, we see a moment when Shelley Duvall's hair has been ripped out during shooting of the bathroom scene. She complains, and Kubrick says to the crew, "Don't sympathize with Shelley." When you watch Wendy come apart at the seams, you're seeing real psychological anguish on-screen. Shelley Duvall really was abused in the making of this film.

Precisely *because* of that dynamic, Shelley Duvall took a lot of heat for her performance in *The Shining*. Reviewers said she seemed weak and defeated. The harshest review of her performance that I've read characterizes her as follows: She "transforms from the warm, sympathetic wife of the book into a simpering, semi-retarded hysteric whom nobody could be locked up with for the winter without harboring murderous thoughts." A "hysteric" who's asking for it—sounds an awful lot like the pre-1970s justification for wife battery. One slightly more astute reviewer noted that she was "a cipher, a seeming amateur, a waif dragged into a house full of expert actors." She grated on reviewers' nerves, appearing more a "ludicrously helpless wife." But that is the genius of her performance, not its shortcoming: She *is* ludicrously helpless, because that is what it *means* to live in an abusive household. You are helpless beyond belief because you are being held hostage by a person who likes—maybe even *lives*—to terrorize and torment you. She channels a woman who has been slowly beaten down by an alcoholic husband who abuses her verbally and her son physically. In the scene in the bathroom, as we watch Jack's axe hack through the door, the horror that Duvall displays on her face and that Kubrick captures, telegraphs a radical and complete abjection. She truly *is* a cipher—a conduit for the agony and horror endured by hundreds of thousands of American women each year who live in a home that, far from being a safe retreat from a dangerous world, is itself a world of danger and peril.

But, as I suggested in the introduction, the power of art is that it *anticipates and accelerates* social change. Reviewers and many audience members at that time weren't ready to acknowledge the torture and psychological collapse of Shelley Duvall for what it was: the picture of domestic violence. Many Americans who viewed the film simply couldn't process what they were seeing, so they blamed their discomfort on Duvall's hair, or her mouth, or her scrawniness, or her "hysteria." As scholar Elizabeth Hornbeck also notes, people dismissed Duvall in a manner strikingly similar to how they often dismissed claims of domestic abuse—the women were asking for it, weak, or crazy somehow.

But despite those critiques of Duvall's performance, something about the film wormed its way into American public culture and stayed there. The film quickly became a classic of the horror genre and an absolute staple of Kubrick's oeuvre. Within a decade, it became enough of a classic—as did Duvall's performance in it—that reviewers sought her out to interview her about her method for channeling Wendy's abjection. Indeed, renowned film critic Roger Ebert interviewed Duvall ten years after the film's release to ask her what it was like to work on that set. "Jack Nicholson's character had to be crazy and angry all the time," she said, "and my character had to cry twelve hours a day, all day long, the last nine months straight, five or six days a week. I was there a year and a month. After all that work . . . the reviews were all about Kubrick, like I wasn't even there." Duvall's frustration at the reception of her acting in the film is telling: She wasn't entirely acting, she was experiencing pain, suffering, fear, and stress. When I watch Duvall's performance, I find myself thinking about the horrific Edvard Munch painting *The Scream*—like that painting, Duvall's performance is an embodiment of absolute fear. It's somewhat depersonalized, somewhat anonymous, somewhat ethereal. And it's all the more powerful for being that way because we can imagine ourselves—or anyone else we know—stepping into her life, into her horror, into her entrapment.

Within the same decade in which Duvall went from gangly hysteric to preeminent scream queen, the situation changed markedly for victims of domestic abuse in the United States. In 1979, only fourteen states provided any funding at all for battered women's shelters in the United States; by 1989, the US had 1,200 battered women's shelters, which provided aid to 300,000 victims per year. Much of this social change originated in activism, legal advocacy, successful prosecutions of abusers, media coverage, and pressure from grassroots organizations of women, but for American people to watch Shelley Duvall's complete and total entrapment would have driven home the point that so many shelter-focused activists were making: Women cannot leave if they have nowhere to go.

Duvall's performance drove home what had been right there in prior works of domestic horror art, but maybe *just* below the level of conscious gettability for audiences. Sure, Rosemary can't easily get away from the coven, but she can go see her doctors and, on occasion, her friends. Chris is in thrall to the demon every bit as much as Regan is, but she still manages to go out to see doctors and priests. Joanna has quite a bit of freedom of movement, until the end of *Stepford Wives*; same with Kathy from *The Omen*. Ellen Ripley is every bit as imprisoned as Wendy Torrance, but her imprisonment feels incidental because she's trapped on a floating domestic space, and everyone else is trapped right along with her. Wendy's entrapment feels obvious, manifest, total, unbreachable. She's trapped by the hotel; by Jack; by the weather; by the distance to any other person or place, to any kind of shelter. The horror of *The Shining* isn't ultimately the ghosts in the hotel. It's Jack and his total imprisonment of Wendy. And, as viewers, we are trapped with her.

I often think that what people dislike about Wendy's face, body, voice, and affect in the film is really that they see themselves too much in her. We don't want to see ourselves as weak, trapped, panicky, shrill, or hysterical. Wouldn't we all just find a way to get out of there? Of course we would, right? Well, historically and demographically, the answer to that question is no. And early viewers and reviewers of the film balked at that painful realization that they, too, might be made weak, terrorized, and powerless by an unstrung abuser in the house with them. *The Shining* is not just a supernatural horror story about a ghost-ridden hotel; it is first and foremost an allegory for sustained domestic violence, inflicted and justified by a man who honestly believes his wife and children owe him their lives.

And, of course, this belief is precisely what drives femicide in the United States today. As author and counselor Lundy Bancroft has amply shown in his revelatory work *Why Does He Do That?*, the core motivation for domestic violence against women isn't centrally psychopathology or alcoholism—though, to be sure, as in Jack Torrance's case, these things can be in play as well—but is instead the pervasive belief in the lesser humanity of women and children, the pervasive belief in the fundamental, categorical superiority of the male head of household and his basic right to expect and compel obedience, compliance, respect, and—if necessary—sacrifice and humiliation from those with whom he cohabits. Jack Torrance is moved to slaughter Wendy and Danny immediately by the ghosts that have invaded his mind; the reason the ghosts are able to invade, however, is that he already possesses the belief structures that enable them to get a toehold.

Many early reviews of the prior five films in this book didn't explicitly recognize the domestic violence and domestic horror dynamics at work in the films. With *The Shining*, however, contemporaneous reviews were very clear on the abuse dynamics that underpin the film, though all put their emphasis on Jack's portrayal of an abuser, rather than on Wendy's abject channeling of the abused. Roger Ebert asserted, in his luminous review of the film, that it was "not about ghosts but about madness and the energies it sets loose in an isolated situation primed to magnify them. Jack is an alcoholic and child abuser." Janet Maslin, writing for *The New York Times*, noted that it's relatively easy to scare people, but that the genius of *The Shining* was "to accentuate the horrifying aspects of things that are familiar." She goes on to note that Kubrick manages to make his movie thoroughly unnerving by keeping the horror so close to home." She even refers to *The Shining* as "domestic terror." Between 1968 and 1980, mainstream, prominent reviewers had become aware of domestic abuse. They'd become aware that familiar things, things and people in the home, are often where the danger lies. By 1980, domestic horror was a recognized type of horror, and *The Shining* was seen as its apotheosis. But *The Shining* stood on the shoulders of Rosemary, Chris, Joanna, Kathy, and Ripley, and it took another thirty years before filmmakers really started working through the overall inheritance of these films together.

CHAPTER 7

Bad Men Making Good Films: An Interlude

Between 1980 and 2009, the domestic horror genre went into hibernation. In fact, even though these classic six films were sequeled—multiple times in some cases—the domestic horror element of the remakes was either severely diluted or, more commonly, entirely absent (see appendix A for a survey of the sequels). During this same time period, however, the horror genre writ large absolutely exploded. Zombie horror, sociopathy horror, slasher horror, sci-fi horror, and serial killer horror all had their day in the sun, but there was next to no filmic action involving domestic horror. So what happened?

I have two necessarily speculative answers. First, things got better for American women between about 1980 and 2000. Not *fixed*, by any means, but perceptibly better. The ERA never became law, but women were able to advance in the military and in the workplace more generally. Opposition to *Roe* seemed, for a couple of decades, to level out, and, more important, the Supreme Court seemed disinclined to reverse it—until 2022. Domestic violence became a better-known phenomenon, both in the public eye and in the procedures of the American criminal justice system. Police, judges, lawyers, advocates, women's groups, shelters, and activists worked together to intensify consequences for abusers and to lower the threshold not only for criminal prosecution, but also for divorce, obtaining restraining orders, and entering into shelters. Marital rape was criminalized in a landmark decision in New York State in 1984, and nationally by 1993. Sex offenses across the board became more readily prosecutable. Sexual harassment was tackled as a social ill. Things got better for women—or, at least, they *seemed* to. With that seeming improvement, the demons, monsters, and abusers of the glory days of domestic horror seemed more like bad dreams, and less like reality. So, fewer domestic horror films.

The other reason—an extremely dark one—for the somnolence of the domestic horror genre has to do with the bench of directors who were making them. Half the directors of the original films—namely, Roman Polanski, William Friedkin, and Stanley Kubrick—were abusers of women themselves, students of how much strain and agony the female body and mind could take before crumbling. Everyone (I hope) knows about Polanski: In 1977, he was charged with five counts of sex abuse against a minor girl and an additional count of drugging a minor. When Polanski filmed the scene of Rosemary being drugged and raped, it felt so real and so powerful in part because Polanski was filming out of his own hoard of abusive desires. Polanski was a student of the vulnerability of women, and he made an excellent film about it. It's a revolting paradox, but that doesn't make it false. Sometimes very bad people make very good art.

The circumstances of the filming of *The Exorcist* typify this paradox in particularly excruciating ways. Indeed, there is a complication in calling *The Exorcist* a feminist masterpiece. That complication has to do with the physical risk and abuse that its actors—mostly Ellen Burstyn and Linda Blair—were subjected to during its filming. No matter how feminist the upshot and impact of the film, no matter how iconic the portrayal of Ellen Burstyn as a domestic abuse victim and survivor, director William Friedkin was not himself *straightforwardly* an ally of women. If he had been, surely, he wouldn't have subjected Blair and Burstyn to such striking and damaging physical trauma. Ellen Burstyn, who plays Chris in the film, was not warned about many of the special effects that would happen in the film. In one scene, Burstyn was attached to a rig, which would yank her to the ground. In between takes, she told Friedkin that the crew needed to go easier on her, or she would be injured by the rig. Friedkin agreed but secretly signaled to the crew to yank Burstyn *harder*. In the next take—which was ultimately included in the actual film—she is jerked violently to the floor, grabbing her back in what she herself later called "horrendous pain." Her screams in that scene are *real* screams of pain and fear and shock. Friedkin also put Linda Blair, who plays Regan, in a body harness to make her body appear to swing around wildly in the bed; the harness did significant harm to Blair's body, causing enduring spinal damage. So, William Friedkin's movie *about* domestic violence also *enacted* that violence. Friedkin took Alfred Hitchcock's oft-quoted dictum to heart: When making thrillers or horror films, "'Torture the women!' The trouble today is that we don't torture women enough." Friedkin tortured the women plenty. In doing so, he made a ton of money, got wildly famous, and, paradoxically, helped teach Americans to question the ideology that a woman should be "possessed" by the man she lived with.

So, when we watch—and feel horror at—Chris's battery, we are simultaneously watching the actual physical battery of the body of Ellen Burstyn. In the story of *The Exorcist*, the demon hurts Regan's and Chris's bodies. On the set of *The Exorcist*, William Friedkin hurts Linda Blair and Ellen Burstyn. William Friedkin is in parallel with the demon, just as Roman Polanski in *Rosemary's Baby* was in parallel with Roman Castevet—and likely also with the devil—even while he used all the devices of cinema to garner sympathy for Rosemary herself. One can make the claim that, perhaps, Friedkin just wanted the violence to seem as real as possible; and, indeed, it seems all the more real because it actually *was real*. The excruciating paradox is that, to witness the film's staging of the horror of domestic violence, audiences had to witness real-life and real-time violence against Ellen Burstyn and Linda Blair. Ebert notes this in an early review, saying, "Linda Blair, as the little girl, has obviously been put through an ordeal in this role, and puts us through one." That's exactly right: viewers are made to empathize with and even feel the suffering of the women on the screen, but it does come at a cost.

Although differently from how Friedkin had tormented Burstyn and Blair, Kubrick tormented Shelley Duvall in the making of *The Shining*. He kept her in a state of constant anxiety during filming. He verbally abused her, and he criticized her performances brutally, so that she was in an actual state of fear and insecurity throughout the film. The psychological torture to which he subjected her is palpable in her performance. It is not only true that Wendy is terrified of Jack (Torrance), but also that Shelley Duvall is terrified of Jack (Nicholson) and, likely even more, of Stanley Kubrick.

When we watch Duvall/Wendy in a state of palpable horror, we feel along with her the unthinkable chaos and agony of domestic violence, but we also, by praising the film, sanction the kind of psychological violence that male directors enacted on their female stars. Watching this film, like watching *The Exorcist*, isn't just watching a film about abuse—it's watching actual abuse, however attenuated and ultimately escapable it was, both for Burstyn and Duvall. When Roger Ebert interviewed Duvall ten years after the release of *The Shining* to ask her what it was like to work with Kubrick, she said, "Almost unbearable."

But long before that, back in October 1980, the short documentary film *Making of "The Shining,"* as discussed in the last chapter, clearly showcased Kubrick's cruelty toward Duvall. Ironically directed by Stanley Kubrick's own teenaged daughter—seventeen-year-old Vivian Kubrick—this film records the manic brilliance of Kubrick and his actors, but also immortalizes scenes of Shelley Duvall lying disconsolate on a floor, being verbally abused and mocked by Kubrick himself. Since this documentary aired on television rather than on the silver screen, it enjoyed a far narrower audience than the film. Even so, the documentary was significant, in that it gave the public a vision of a director as cruel, abusive, and tyrannical. This happened very soon after the scales had fallen from the public's eyes about Polanski, as well, in the wake of his 1977 arrest for the rape of Samantha Geimer and his 1978 flight from the United States to avoid prison time. These directors, people had to acknowledge by the end of 1980, weren't slam dunk feminists by any stretch of the imagination. Their *films* might have been, but they weren't.

Now, I'm not in a big hurry to say that, since 1980, Hollywood directors have treated women *well*, or even consistently *as human beings*. We have plenty of data to the contrary. But I do think that the extremity of the torture to which directors subject their female leads has waned—much more slowly than anyone would want but waned nonetheless—in the past fifty years. Part of the reason is that the feminist activism *works*: we have names for all these things now and awareness about them. We know about sexual violence, reproductive violence, domestic violence, gender-based abuse, and that has made many, many women much safer than they used to be—both in their homes and in movie studios. Or, at least, has made some women *somewhat* safer. Things got a little bit better for women—again, not *fixed*, just better—which made it harder to pull off the kinds of on-screen cruelty that typified half of the domestic horrors in this book.

It took about thirty years for filmmakers to start to register, thematize, and scrutinize the kinds of cruelty and dehumanization that went into the making of many domestic horror films in the 1970s, but the day did come. When it came, a group of new and very important domestic horror films were made: The first was *Paranormal Activity* (2009), the second was *Creep* (2014), and the third was *Creep 2* (2017). These films come charging headlong at the slumbering domestic horror genre and wake it up. *Paranormal Activity* and *Creep 1* and *2* all reanimate and reimagine the tropes of horror and domestic violence that had specifically animated many of the original domestic horrors of the 1970s. Put otherwise, they bring the 1970s into the 2010s. But interestingly, they do so in large part as an indictment of predatory directorial practices and of their tendencies to dehumanize and endanger the people they cast in their domestic horrors.

Paranormal Activity (2009)

Paranormal Activity was an independent film made on a tiny budget—reportedly only $15,000 for the initial shooting—that did astonishingly well upon its release. After it was acquired and distributed by Paramount, it brought in $108 million in the US and an additional $85 million worldwide. The math here is worth remarking on: This film grossed about 13,000 times its initial budget. People *loved* this movie, leading to its repeated sequelization between 2010 and 2021. The original film featured two unknown actors, Micah Sloat and Katie Featherston, who play eponymous characters—Micah and Katie. This choice, of course, echoes *The Shining*, which cast Jack Nicholson as Jack

Torrance and Danny Lloyd as Danny Torrance. As in *The Shining*, the effect of the eponymy is to blur the line between fiction and reality—though in *Paranormal Activity*, the effect of that blurring will serve a novel purpose, and it will be accentuated by the fact that the entire film is found footage, shot by the protagonists themselves, whose POV we are aligned with throughout.

In the film, young lovers Katie and Micah live in San Diego together. We learn early on that there are paranormal phenomena going on in their home, not because we see them, but because Micah has decided he wants to make a film about them, and about how they torment his girlfriend. Micah wants to capture it all on film, using a home video camera. Almost immediately, we can see that Micah's aspirations are partly to film and thereby diagnose the paranormal phenomena that bedevil Katie—a potentially laudable goal—and partly to shoot a porno with his girlfriend—substantially less laudable.

As Micah and Katie discuss Micah's plan to film the paranormal activity in their home, Katie registers that Micah is a little too focused on the film and a little too unfocused on her. She says, "You're supposed to be in love with *me*, not the machine." He responds, insouciantly, "Well, we are going to be sleeping with this camera, you know. We're going to put it in the bedroom." Not a question, not an offer, just a statement: *We will be sleeping with this camera, you know*. Through his assertion, the camera becomes, in effect, a third party to their relationship, and Katie is forced to comply with the plan. Micah may seem like a devoted partner, but he is actually a predatory filmmaker who's about to land his girlfriend in a situation of serious domestic horror precisely through his inability to respect her wishes and boundaries about the making of this film.

The next day, a psychic comes to see them for a consultation on the paranormal disturbances that follow Katie around; Katie hopes this psychic will be able to diagnose and perhaps dispel her paranormal phenomenon. While Katie talks to the psychic, Micah jokes that he'll play a spooky soundtrack to accompany their conversation. The film doesn't spell out Micah's motivations for being so flip, but it's strongly implied that he doesn't like the idea of the psychic taking charge of what Micah sees as *his* film project, wresting away Micah's authorial control. Katie explains the long history of her "haunting" to the psychic, though Micah intermittently interrupts to minimize what she's saying or to cast doubt on the psychic. This is going to be *his* film, damn it, and no one else can play a significant role in how things progress.

Micah becomes more interested in the psychic, however, when he reveals that Katie is not being haunted by a ghost but by a demon. Micah's filmmaking instincts kick into high gear. He suggests that they get a Ouija board in order to interact with the demon directly. Micah wants to remake *The Exorcist*, but make it as an action movie that he stars in as the hero. The psychic warns them against trying to communicate with the demon, but Micah doesn't care; he is bound and determined to direct his own sequel to Friedkin's 1973 film, casting himself as William Friedkin and Katie as Ellen Burstyn.

Katie wants to call a professional demonologist, but Micah tries repeatedly to talk her out of it. He minimizes her worry and questions her perceptions, much as Guy minimizes Rosemary's concerns about the coven in their apartment building and attempts to deny her access to outside information. And like Guy, Micah tries to paint his female partner as overly anxious, overly inflexible; he gaslights her, he manipulates her. He also violates her privacy. At one point, she calls out from the adjacent bathroom to turn the camera off because she's peeing—another reference to an iconic scene from *The Exorcist*—and he doesn't do it immediately. Before they go to sleep that night, he lies to her, saying the camera is turned off, while he tries to get Katie to have sex with him. *Paranormal Activity* sets up Micah as a predatory domestic abuser, whose mechanism of abuse is the camera itself. Micah uses the same coercive control tactics that we saw in Polanski's film, only here he is in the role of Polanski *and* Guy Woodhouse simultaneously.

In a scene relatively late in the film, we see Katie doing beadwork with a female friend when Micah aggressively intrudes upon what Katie calls their "intense girl time" with his camera. Katie says she needs a break from the camera, which angers Micah. "What the fuck?" he says. "I'm trying to show you something." Micah doesn't like when his control over Katie in the home is interrupted by this interloping woman, not any more than Guy liked it when Rosemary's friends hauled her into the kitchen at the party and shut him out. Building on the *Rosemary's Baby* echoes, the scene then veers sharply toward *The Exorcist* as a horror touchstone when Micah says he'll get a Ouija board.

Katie begins to experience disturbances more obviously akin

to demon possession than any she has encountered before. Up until now, she'd heard noises at night, had things moved mysteriously around in the house. Disturbing, but not terrifying. Not an indication of her being possessed. Now, she wakes up, stands perfectly still in front of the camera for two hours in the middle of the night, wanders down to the lower floor and out into the backyard, all without meaning to, and without remembering it the next day. When Micah learns this by reviewing the film, he is freaked out, but he simply channels his fear into more aggressive filmmaking. He whips out his Ouija board and challenges the demon on camera, "All right, you little fucker, you got something to say?" Like Guy in *Rosemary's Baby*, Micah facilitates the demon's access to his female partner and is utterly unyielding in his refusal to listen to her protests after the demon has shown up and begun to interact with her.

Micah asks Katie, mockingly, if she wants to call an exorcist; she shouts, "Yes, yes!" But Micah steps firmly into the *paterfamilias* role: "I'm taking care of this. This is *my* house, you're *my* girlfriend. I'm going to fucking solve the problem." No exorcist intervention, no demonologist. And definitely no Father Damien Karras. The dynamic here, with Micah programmatically rejecting professional help for his girlfriend, very strongly recalls Robert Thorn's reaction to Father Brennan's warnings about Damien. Robert sees Kathy as *his* wife, Damien as *his* son, and he will allow no outside interference in how he runs *his* household. Micah, of course, is wired the same way. Katie, like Kathy (both Katherines, perhaps not *totally* accidentally), is put in grave danger by her partner's mentality.

But unlike Kathy Thorn, Katie knows there's something supernatural going on, and, with that knowledge, she is able to make a decision on her own behalf. She finally insists on calling Dr. Averies, the demonologist, over Micah's protests. Micah complains, saying he's "in control" of Katie and their home. Finally fed up with his fatuous assertions, Katie says, "You're not in control. *It* is in control. If you think you're in control, then you're being an idiot . . . You are absolutely powerless." At long last, Katie takes a real stand, not only against Micah but against the fiction that patriarchy keeps women safe in the home. In so doing, Katie goes somewhere Kathy Thorn never dreamed possible.

And there's a reason she's able to do so. Katie has seen this movie before—*The Exorcist*, *Rosemary's Baby*, *The Stepford Wives*, *The Omen*. She knows the demon is in control, and she now clearly knows Micah is facilitating the demon's control through his cinematic ambitions. As she puts it, "Micah, you and your stupid camera are the problem." Katie's realization, however, comes too late. The demon takes possession of Katie so that she gets out of bed at night, stands creepily for a while over a sleeping Micah, then heads out into the hallway where we cannot see her anymore. Once there, she—presumably still possessed by the demon—screams for Micah, who jumps from the bed and races to help her. We don't see their interaction, but we hear it off camera. She screams, Micah screams, and then there are loud thunks followed by total silence. A few seconds later, we hear heavy footsteps coming back up the stairs, and Katie appears at the doorway, hurls Micah's corpse across the room, and reveals herself, covered in his blood. She starts sniffing Micah in an animalistic way that seems to indicate that she herself has killed him, perhaps as her prey. The sniffing continues until she registers that the camera is on and trained on her. Slowly, she lifts her gaze toward it and ultimately lunges toward it. Camera off. So Katie is possessed, Micah is slain, and the film survives to speak for both of them.

Now, the most obvious overall reading of this film is that it's a straight-up demon possession horror, very self-consciously in a lineage with *The Exorcist*. We can add to that reading that the film is a domestic horror about coercive control, very much in line with *Rosemary's Baby*. It also resonates very strongly with *The Omen*. But what I think is fascinating about this film's participation in the domestic horror genre is that it ends with the demon punishing the bad boyfriend, not the ostensible female victim. This demon may want to possess Katie, but it wants to *kill* the wannabe patriarch, the self-styled "director" of all the violence. In fact, Katie will go on to be in *five* of the sequels to the original film. She winds up being a survivor, albeit a survivor possessed by a murderous demon.

Paranormal Activity reboots and revises *The Exorcist*, *Rosemary's Baby*, and *The Omen*, then, but with a critical feminist twist. This time, the woman is not the ultimate object of attack. Instead, it's the male abuser, punished by the demon for his predatory filmmaking aspirations. Micah wanted to film Katie pornographically; he wanted to film her against her will; evidently, the demon didn't much care for that. Remember that in the final, final moment of the film, the demon (housed in Katie's body) lunges *at the camera*. This represents a huge swerve from the 1970s domestic horrors I've featured in this book. It's *almost* as if, in this revisionist engagement with the demonic domestic horror that *The Exorcist* inaugurated, the demon is fighting *for* Katie, not against her.

Fascinatingly, this critique of the male gaze on female suffering threads through many of the films in the franchise. There are numerous sequels, as I said, to the original *Paranormal Activity*, several released in very quick succession. Parts 2 and 3, like the original, center on a male figure who takes film footage of the demon-possessed women in his family. So, for three consecutive films, we see that the demon stalking and possessing Katie (and eventually also her sister Kristi) achieves his heightened power over the women's bodies in the domestic sphere because of a male relative (*Paranormal Activity*: boyfriend; *Paranormal Activity 2*: husband; *Paranormal Activity 3*: boyfriend) who decides to record their lives on video.

The series grapples with the idea that "demonic possession" of women originates in men who overextend their sense of ownership over their female partners to include those partners' stories, images, and voices. Indeed, there's something quite *Stepford*-y about it—remember how the Men's Association took Joanna's pictures and her voice? That's what Micah and the male leads of the first two sequels all do, too. This series, then, advances a thesis that resonates loud and clear with the classic domestic horrors of the '70s, a thesis that male domestic partners can cause horror to befall a woman through their desire to overexert their power over her through recording technology.

By doing that, on a meta level, *Paranormal Activity* also offers a stinging riposte to the likes of Polanski, Kubrick, and

Friedkin, as if to say to a new generation of domestic horror filmmakers that, if we *are* going to make horror films about the subjection of women's bodies, minds, sexualities, and souls to patriarchal abuse in the home, let's not rely so heavily on our male, directorial privilege as a proxy *paterfamilias* in so doing. No more "torture the women" in order to make a horror film. Let's figure out a way to do things differently while maintaining all the heat of the domestic horror genre. Let's let the Micahs get picked off for once, not the Katies.

Creep (2014)

Paranormal Activity's indictment of directorial abuse as a powerful if hard-to-perceive dynamic in American domestic horror gets revisited, with a crucial twist, in *Creep*, four years later. *Creep* is a masterpiece, both as a work of art and as a work of hair-on-fire horror feminism in the same lineage as the 1970s domestic horrors we've come to know and love, engaging with *Rosemary's Baby*, *The Shining*, and *The Stepford Wives*. But fascinatingly, despite its multiplicity of domestic horror sources and inspirations, the entire cast consists of two men and no women. Patrick Brice plays Aaron, and Mark Duplass plays Josef.

So, lacking female characters, how is this film feminist? Simple. It accomplishes its feminism not by overtly talking about feminist issues as feminist issues but by placing its own male protagonist into a role that is nearly always reserved for females in domestic horror films. Just as Micah became the object of prey for Katie's demon, a young, naive videographer named Aaron will become the object of prey of a sociopathic stalker and murderer named Josef. Our empathy will be aligned with him throughout the film, as was true with Rosemary, Chris, Regan, Joanna, Kathy, Ripley, and Wendy. But because of the added dynamic in which Aaron is our director and cameraman, filming everything that's happening to him, we will see almost the entire story of Aaron's domestic entrapment and torture directly through his eyes. The domestic horror in this film feels extremely direct, extremely immediate, because we are in total synchrony with the man who's making the film. Even though, as we will see at the end, he's not *ultimately* the one who's calling the shots.

Creep opens with Aaron (Patrick Brice), filming himself driving a car up to a remote mountain cabin. The opening strongly invokes the opening of *The Shining*, except that we are *in* the car with Aaron, rather than watching the car Jack Torrance is driving from above. He goes on to reveal that he's answering a personal ad for $1,000 to do a day of film shooting in a remote location, though he doesn't know whom he's meeting. He notes that the ad had said, "Discretion is appreciated," which immediately injects the idea of sex work into the film. Aaron recognizes that explicitly, saying, "So here's a thought. What if this is just some forty-something who's sitting alone in her apartment, waiting for some young, handsome boy to come up the hill and give rubdowns, money, and whisper sweet nothings." He, like a more benign and frankly naive version of Micah, is hoping he's walking into a porno situation. But of course, what's interesting about this moment is the gender dynamic. If Aaron were a female character, he wouldn't be thinking those things. He'd be packing a container of mace or stuffing a jackknife into his boot. Maybe he wouldn't be taking this particular gig in the first place. Instead, he imagines that this whole stupid enterprise he's signed up for might end in a cougar tryst and maybe a bespoke, low-budget porn film.

Aaron arrives at the cabin and trudges breathlessly up a set of stairs to the front door. We hear Aaron huffing and puffing while he lugs the camera up the stairs with him. This is important because it aligns our physiology with his; we're getting his POV, not just in what he sees, but down to his very breath. This filmic insistence on our physiological empathy with Aaron is going to be crucial to the horror dynamic of the rest of the film. We are very nearly in Aaron's body with him throughout the film.

No one answers the door when he knocks, so he pans his camera around to look down at the yard. There, he finds an axe embedded in a tree trunk. He zooms in on the axe. This clear reference to *The Shining* isn't lost on Aaron, who's now a little unnerved and starts muttering to himself. Like Katie reacting to Micah's proposal that they use a Ouija board, Aaron has seen this movie before. Wisely, he heads back to his car to take cover from the creepiness outside. All of this we see from his POV, as though we are one with him. When he gets back into his car with the window tightly shut, we, along with Aaron, feel a physiological relief.

Suddenly, Josef—the other main character, played brilliantly by Mark Duplass—materializes outside Aaron's car window and slaps his door. Aaron jumps; we jump. There are introductions, and Josef flatters Aaron by saying, "You have a nice, kind face." This soothes Aaron, of course, because in saying that, Josef acts as if *he* had been afraid of meeting Aaron—not the other way around. Surely someone who's relieved to encounter a "nice, kind face" wouldn't also be a sociopathic serial killer. Augmenting Aaron's burgeoning feeling of safety, when Josef opens the car door, Aaron's camera lands on Josef's wedding ring—as viewers, we are meant to feel reassured by that, and so is Aaron. Josef is just a regular, married man. This should be a relief, except, of course, if we're keeping track, Guy Woodhouse was a regular, married man. As was Walter Eberhart. And Jack Torrance. Maybe there's not quite so much comfort in that tiny golden circle around Josef's finger as Aaron might hope.

Up at the house, Josef reveals that he's a terminal cancer patient, and that he wants Aaron to document a day in his life for his unborn son, whom he refers to as "Buddy." With Josef's vulnerable self-disclosure, Aaron is endeared to him, and he lets down his guard yet further. Josef isn't just a married man but a cancer patient who is eagerly expecting a baby. What could be less threatening than that? Josef seizes that moment and grabs Aaron for a big bear hug. We feel Aaron flinch a bit, as does Josef, so Josef notes that, by the end of the day, it won't at all be weird anymore that they hugged like that. He keeps on hugging Aaron.

Now, think about this dynamic if Aaron were female. We'd be freaking out; she'd be freaking out. Why? Because Josef is using one of the oldest sex abuser tricks in the book, which is to violate someone else's physical boundaries in a relatively innocuous way—a hug—and to insist, counter to that person's resistance, that it's *normal*. Aaron is being told to disregard his fight-or-flight reflexes, and to allow this *total stranger* to get into his personal space. Aaron is being groomed for further incursions into his space, incursions that will go way past his boundaries.

Josef's boundary violations ramp up quickly when he informs Aaron "I'm going to go get in the tub" and confirms that he expects Aaron to come with him into the bathroom. He expects Aaron to film a naked, full-grown man—and a stranger to boot—in a bathtub. "We're going to go a lot deeper places than this," says Josef, smilingly and warmly. He's warning him about further boundary violations to come, but he does so in a normalizing way, with a smile on his face. The viewer experiences whiplash in sync with Aaron: Josef seems nice, but he's a little too familiar. When we get nervous about how overfamiliar he is, he doubles down by asserting—gleefully—that more intimacy is yet to come. What is with this guy? Is he a slightly weird, lonely man? Or something more insidious? We don't know and neither does Aaron, partially because Josef grooms him and us in unison, crossing little boundaries and then larger and larger ones.

In the bath, Josef starts talking about suicide and dunks himself under the water. Aaron calls to him to emerge from the water. Josef appears to be attempting to drown himself. When Josef finally does come up for air and registers shock on Aaron's face, he says, "Oh man, that was supposed to be a joke. I got a weird sense of humor, man. I'm sorry about that." Classic gaslighting move: *Oh, did my behavior make you uncomfortable? It was just a joke*. Moreover, if you read through literature on domestic and intimate partner violence, you'll find that suicide threats are a well-known and very powerful mode of controlling another person, because it's hard to leave someone who seems bent on self-slaughter. No one is thinking that Josef is a normal guy anymore. Not even Aaron. And yet, Aaron overwrites his instincts. He's hooked in. That's the horrific thing about grooming: It works.

Josef wants to take Aaron on a special hike, so he tells Aaron to go get a jacket from the hall closet. In the closet (camera still and always in hand), Aaron is startled by a huge, terrifying wolf mask. When Josef hears Aaron scream in shock, he explains that the mask is just "Peach Fuzz," a mask his father gave him. Josef sings a completely insane, nonsensical song about how Peach Fuzz is a good friend. To say that Peach Fuzz is a friendly wolf is absurd: The mask's grey hair is matted and wild; its teeth are long, fully bared, yellowed, and bloody; we can see bloody gums; its tongue lolls out hungrily; its eyes angle downward toward the nose in an expression of uncontrolled rage. Who's afraid of the Big Bad Wolf? Aaron is, and rightly so, because he's Little Red Riding Hood in this scenario. Or, perhaps, because he remembers the scene at the end of *The Shining* when Jack Nicholson, wielding his axe, recites a "Big Bad Wolf" nursery rhyme through the bathroom door to Shelley Duvall. Or maybe Aaron doesn't think of that scene, but *we* certainly might, especially prompted by the earlier shot of the axe in the yard.

Out on their special hike, Josef runs off for a second, only to sneak back and terrify Aaron by jumping out at him. He says, "That's what it feels like when you think you're going to die. It's incredible, isn't it?" This certainly feels—both to Aaron and to the viewer—like a threat, but Aaron (and we) can normalize it by thinking about how Josef is a terminal cancer patient who's simply trying to convey the feeling of knowing you are in mortal peril. The two men carry on hiking, our POV locked in tight with Aaron's through the camera. As they go deeper in, Josef says, "When you saw that axe outside of the house, was there a small part of you that thought I might kill you with it?" Josef is systematically messing with Aaron's sense of reality. And yet Aaron stays put. It's clear as day that Josef is crazy. We know it; Aaron knows it. But Aaron doesn't *act* on it. Why is that? Part of the answer is that Aaron is a *man*, and he can't quite accept the fact that he is being groomed by another man. Why would a straight, married cancer patient want to groom and attack a man?

But the film will soon reveal that sex and gender are no protection here. Night falls, and Aaron has a natural justification for leaving; he wants to drive down the mountain as carefully as possible before it gets any later. But Josef convinces him to come in for "one drink"—the classic line of the sexual predator. They have their drink, but then, right when Aaron finally tries to leave, Josef reveals that he lied about Peach Fuzz. At this point, the lens of the camera is covered; we only have sound, while looking at a black screen. Josef tells a story about how he discovered that his wife had a bestiality fetish. As a punishment for what he saw as her sexual crimes, he broke into the window of their own house with the wolf mask on his head, and he raped her. Josef says it was "Ravenous, animalistic sexual intercourse. I'd never seen her so happy. I have to admit, it didn't feel terrible on my end . . . Aaron, I raped my own wife." The camera lens pops back off, so we can see again, and Aaron has decided to leave.

Unfortunately for Aaron, he cannot leave because Josef has stolen his car keys and hidden them. This, again, is a well-known form of domestic violence—denying someone access to a vehicle in order to keep them imprisoned in the domestic sphere. At this point, Aaron can no longer normalize the situation in his own mind, nor can he rest comfortably with the idea that he's safe from harm because he's a man, because Josef has just deprived him of his chance to escape. So, aiming to preserve his own life, Aaron tries to make a run for it. Just then, Josef appears, now with the Peach Fuzz mask on, blocking the front door. He rocks his hips sexually, side to side, and starts growling. Aaron is the prey; Josef is the predator. But Aaron rushes the door, overpowers Josef, and escapes. We, as viewers, sigh in relief. He's made it, and we've made it with him.

But not for long. Back at home, Aaron receives a package from Josef containing a video, a baby wolf stuffed animal, and a knife. The DVD, which Aaron watches, instructs him to cut open the baby wolf with the knife; he does so. Inside, he finds a heart locket containing a picture of him opposite one of Josef. A couple of nights later, Aaron's got the camera trained on himself while he sleeps; we see Josef sneak into his room and, with a *very* long pair of scissors, slice off some of Aaron's hair. Josef sees Aaron as a fetish object, a plaything for him to terrorize, hunt, and eventually kill.

On another DVD that he slips into Aaron's house, Josef invites Aaron to meet up with him at a lake. Unfathomably, Aaron goes. But of course, it's not totally unfathomable: Once again, Aaron thinks he can outfox Josef with his masculine and, in this case, directorial know-how. We watch Aaron, from a camera he's left rolling in his car and aimed at a park bench by the lake. He approaches the lake at which he'd agreed to meet Josef, and he sits on the bench, waiting. Through Aaron's camera, we see Josef slowly, slowly sneak up behind him in a trench coat—a clear sartorial reference to the iconography of the sexual predator—then slip on the Peach Fuzz mask and reveal that he's carrying an axe—again, a clear reference to *The Shining*. Then, swiftly, he chops into Aaron's head. We hear a very quiet thunk. Aaron slumps over, dead.

The film of Aaron's murder suddenly pauses, and we realize we're watching live footage of someone recording a screening of the film of Aaron's murder. Obviously, it's Josef watching the film, back at home. Josef pops in front of the camera and says to us that he loves Aaron, and that Aaron will always be his "favorite." He takes the murder recording out of his DVD player, labels it "AARON," draws a heart on it, and then puts the DVD onto a shelf with dozens of other similarly labeled tapes and DVDs. All the while, Aaron thought he was in control because he had the camera. But in actuality, he was simply the cameraman, shooting a film that Josef was choreographing and directing all the while. A film about his own torture and death.

In Josef's DVD collection, we see that the labels in red are of women he's killed; those in black are of men. There's about a fifty-fifty balance in terms of gender. This balance is intimately linked to the film's incandescent and provocative politics. Indeed, *Creep* is a feminist domestic horror of the highest order, *not* because it's "about" women; it's actually not *about women* at all. It's *about* a more basic, human vulnerability to manipulation, coercion, grooming, and physical violence. By centering its exploration of these dynamics not on a wraithlike woman like Mia Farrow or Shelley Duvall but on a big, burly, bearded, bear-like, male, hetero videographer, the film makes a crucial intervention into the field of feminist horror. What if, it asks, stalking and domestic horror were social dangers directed with equal frequency at men? What would the world look like if men had to fear entrapment, sexual assault, and mortal endangerment at the same rates as women? I can tell you one thing: Our anti-stalking laws would be much, much stronger.

And what if men had to suffer the kinds of technological predation to which they so often subject women? What if, indeed, men were subjected at the same rates as women to the kinds of coercive control and gaslighting, the kinds of objectification and dehumanization, to which women are subjected all the time by men behind cameras? Because again, in the end, it's revealed that Josef, and not Aaron, is making the film we're watching. Aaron believed he was at the helm; he believed he held the power because he held the camera. But he was wrong all along: Josef was using Aaron as a cameraman to film a documentary that he, Josef, was scripting and directing all the while. Josef is the Polanski of this film, the Friedkin, the Kubrick. Josef is the filmic genius here, torturing Aaron for our viewing satisfaction and for his own. And in the end he steals the recordings Aaron had made to pad out his own personal Criterion Collection of murder documentaries with its crowning glory: the seduction, entrapment, and murder of Aaron, the aspiring director.

This is made all the more powerful by an even deeper irony. Patrick Brice, the actor who plays Aaron, is also the director of *Creep*. From a metatheatrical standpoint, this film then offers a powerful and pointed corrective to the likes of Roman Polanski, William Friedkin, or Stanley Kubrick: If you want to make domestic horror, make it about yourself. Put yourself in the hot seat. Brice is not tormenting a Mia Farrow, nor an Ellen Burstyn, nor a Katharine Ross, nor a Lee Remick, nor a Shelley Duvall, nor a Katie Featherston. In his exploration of domestic horror, he is his own target.

Creep 2: A Woman Calls the Shots

The sequel to *Creep* took yet one more step toward an unambiguously feminist kind of domestic horror—one in which, at last, we get a woman behind the camera and calling (most, though not all) the shots. After the opening credits roll, *Creep 2* (2017) shows a bunch of online personal ads superimposed on one another, and a female voice saying, "Hi, I'm Sara. Welcome to *Encounters*." Sara (Desiree Akhavan) will be the protagonist of *Creep 2*, a young vlogger who curates a show in which she answers personal ads and provides odd services to lonely and desperate men. Sometimes, the men want to be held like babies. Sometimes they want to show her their houses and garner her appreciation for their possessions and collections. None of these encounters appear to include anything we could fairly call sex work. There's no nudity, no kissing, no fondling, and certainly no sex. Her encounters are much more focused on the strangeness and vulnerability of isolated men than on sex per se.

On all her encounters, she brings her camera, turning the men who've hired her into the subjects of her own short films. It's not entirely clear that the men know about or consent to being filmed; what's clear is that she sees these men as her subjects, and herself as their director. We see her, in multiple scenes, sitting close to men on their couches, asking them questions. The interactions are generally extremely mundane. Like Josef from the first film, Sara often casts a knowing glance over at the camera as she does whatever activities her male clients require of her. She is the director, the shot caller, the woman behind the camera and the *auteur* of all she does. In a very real sense, what she's doing is predatory.

Alas, her show doesn't have many followers, possibly because all her encounters are, in fact, so mundane. She bemoans to her camera that her newest episode only has nine views. She announces that she's come to the painful conclusion that she may need to end the series. So when Sara comes across a personal add on Craigslist—offering $1,000 for a day of "emotionally brave" videography—she's ready to go, thinking this lonely, desperate man might help her make an episode of her docuseries that gets her some notice.

Soon, Sara is three hours from home, driving deep into the woods. We do not know she's heading to meet Josef because the location is different from the last time, but we suspect it, of course, because we know we are watching a sequel. The camera angle is similar to the camera angle capturing Aaron on his way up to meet Josef in the first film: She's got the camera riding shotgun while she drives, and it's angled up at her face while she talks about her feelings about heading up into the middle of nowhere. But of course, there's a profound difference. Aaron was going up to do videography for the day as a service to the other person; Sara is going up to do videography as a way of collecting material for her own rather predatory web series. So, from the outset, the film asks us: Who is the prey, and who the predator?

When Sara arrives, the man we know as Josef from the first film introduces himself as "Aaron" and offers her a green smoothie to drink. She drinks and says it's good; he replies, "It's also poisoned." She laughs awkwardly before he walks back his threat. And thus the gaslighting and grooming begin. But interestingly, Sara seems at least partially immune to her new mark's craziness—maybe her training in dealing with desperate, lonely men has inured her to bizarre interpersonal conduct. Regardless, he—Josef, whom I'll refer to as Aaron 2 from here on out—is clearly fascinated and somewhat disarmed by her sangfroid, and what he perceives to be her frankness and steely resolve. But *we* know that she's playing him: She tells him that she shoots wedding videos to make money.

When she asks him about himself, he says, matter-of-factly, "I am what is commonly known as a serial killer." There is no pretense of sanity—no cancer patient facade—this time. "I have killed thirty-nine people. This is something that I love to do; it's the greatest job in the world." But Aaron 2 then proceeds to tell Sara that he's having a midlife crisis. The camera, which she is holding, zooms in—not because she is afraid, but because she's starting to think that maybe, just maybe, this is going to be the episode that catapults her to internet fame. Aaron 2 appears to be entirely aligned with her, proposing that the two of them team up to make a documentary about the world's most prolific serial killer that no one knows about, together, right now. "I'm into it," says Sara. Again: Who is the predator? Who is the prey? Or, put only slightly differently: Who is directing this film, and who is the unwitting and unlucky main character?

Soon, Aaron 2 shows Sara the final scenes of his *Aaron* DVD, where he chops into Aaron 1's head. Then he grabs her camera and turns it on her. She is remarkably unperturbed. Realizing that he's having trouble frightening her, he suggests that they should do the filming naked. While Sara films him, he drops a towel he'd wrapped around himself and stands fully nude in front of her. There is a lot of penis in this scene, for a long time. We wonder if Aaron 2 will try to rape her. If she tried to run, would he grab the *Shining*-esque axe, familiar as the murder weapon from the first *Creep*, that's conspicuously mounted on the wall and cut her down? Instead of running or panicking, to Aaron 2's complete shock, she asks for her own "turn," passes him the camera, and takes off her clothes on camera. It turns out, evidently, that her past experience filming her "encounters" with strange men really has inoculated her against his particular form of craziness. It's starting to seem like Sara really *is* directing this picture.

What's yet more fascinating about this moment is the framing of the shot—which she calls attention to upon giving him the camera, saying, "Do you have your frame?" When she filmed him, she filmed his whole body, head to toe—genitals very much included. When he films her, he restricts his frame as she gets more naked; because of Aaron 2's oddly prudish camerawork, we don't see Sara's genitals, and we only see her breasts for a split second before Aaron 2 zooms in tightly on her face. Is he sparing her modesty from the public? Is he sparing himself? Is he *afraid* of her bravery? Flummoxed by her lack of fear? His camerawork doesn't read like that of a predator—*hers* does. She really *is* in control. She—not Aaron 2—is directing this film. This is *her* project.

We cut to a scene in the bathroom, when Sara films herself debating aloud as to what she should do. She's been with Aaron 2 now for maybe an hour, and she concludes that she's 99.9 percent certain he's not a killer, and she thinks he's the ideal subject for her. Just in case, she'll keep a jackknife in her boot. Immediately after that, he jumps out to terrify her, and she doesn't even flinch. Instead, she points out that his beard is patchy—calling into question the coherence of his masculinity. She acts toward him the way Kubrick supposedly acted toward Duvall—critiquing, nitpicking, mocking, deriding. This is her movie, and she'll point out the elements of it—including in Aaron 2's appearance—that don't work for her, even at the expense of her star actor's self-confidence.

As Aaron 2 drives her to their shooting location later in the day, he wears the Peach Fuzz mask. Somehow, in the broad daylight, with her pointing the camera at him, the mask looks absurd, not scary. Aaron 2 looks like a man playing at craziness rather than being an actual crazy man. This, of course, is what Sara thinks, too. Perhaps it's because he's driving a Hyundai sedan? Perhaps because he's got his hands firmly planted carefully at ten and two on the steering wheel? Sara's shot frame, by including these details, makes it hard for us to fear him in this scene despite what we know about the first film. When he asks her what she thinks about his mask, she points out—totally deadpan—that it probably reduces his effectiveness as a driver. When pressed, she reveals that she thinks he's "a cute little wolf." Because of the mask, of course, we can't see Aaron 2's facial expression. But we can imagine that he's getting pretty frustrated under there, since none of his tricks as an interpersonal terrorist and domestic abuser are working. Sara really seems to be immune.

Soon, as they walk along the same hike that Josef took Aaron 1 on in the first film, Sara begins peppering Aaron 2 with questions. Eventually, he snaps at her for asking too many. Her indifference to his terror tactics is really getting under his skin now. He doesn't like to be the *true* subject of the film; he prefers to be the secret director. Seeing his frustration, Sara urges him to think about what Francis Ford Coppola would do to make their movie great. She is acting, again, like a director, trying to be supportive of her high-strung, emotional lead actor—in this case, precisely by allowing him to continue to pretend that he is the director. Stunned by her wisdom, he points at her and barks out, "That's really fucking smart." Aaron 2, you have met your match! Whether she will prove your soulmate or your nemesis isn't clear yet, but there's something electric between the two of them. And that electricity is fueling a film that *she* is making, even though we know that Aaron 2 secretly thinks it will ultimately be his film.

Even with Sara's encouragement, Aaron 2 can't get the scene he wants, so he has a diva-style meltdown. We cut to Sara talking to the camera, referring to Aaron 2's behavior as a "tantrum." She says, "He's so vulnerable right now, and I know the decent thing to do is just give him some space. But at the same time, it would be so easy to go down there and provoke him." Realizing that another person is vulnerable and choosing to provoke them anyway, just to see how they'll respond and to test how much power you have over them? Sounds like abuse to me. It also sounds exactly like how Friedkin directed Burstyn, and how Kubrick directed Duvall. Sara is turning the tables on Aaron 2, more than she realizes, of course, because she still thinks he's a sad, lonely loser, rather than a sad, bored documentarian and murderer.

Soon, she finds him downstairs in his house, soaking in a hot tub, telling her to turn the camera off because he doesn't want her to make the documentary film anymore. But Sara, like Micah from *Paranormal Activity*, is far more interested in her film than in her interlocutor's personal boundaries. Despite his repeatedly telling her to leave, she gets into the hot tub with him, camera rolling all the while. She instructs him to close his eyes: "I don't want to," he says; "Do it," she commands, and he does. She places the camera down, trained on Aaron 2. She then goes over, sits wrapped around him from behind, and proceeds to massage him. She, as director of her own film, has stepped decisively into the role of the controller, rather than the controlled. The film reveals itself as a radical, feminist rebuttal to the domestic horror genre overall, in which the potential female victim takes the power into her own hands by wresting the camera from the abusive male director and making herself the maker of her own film. She who holds the camera holds the power.

After the hot tub scene, Aaron 2 briefly gets the camera, while Sara showers. He starts talking to Sara in the camera in the way he'd talked to Aaron 1 in the first film. Then he approaches the bathroom Sara is showering in. Everything is bathed in red light. He thinks he's finally going to get the drop on her and turn the tables on their power dynamic. When Aaron 2 goes to pull the shower curtain to the side, however, Sara jumps out at him and screams, with a mask of Scotch tape plastered on her face that twists her features into horrific monstrosity. He panics, screams, falls down, and gasps, "Oh my god, you got me." Once again, despite Aaron 2's best efforts to gain the upper hand, Sara remains in control.

But eventually, Aaron 2 starts talking about the thoughts he had while watching "a little show called *Encounters*." He knows she lied about being a wedding videographer. He knows she's using him and planning to make a film about him and about their "encounter." He knows she is trying to ingratiate herself to him through a combination of flirting and flattery. He tells her all this. Her cover is blown. Her tone of voice, which had been deep, low, and calm all along, shifts to jagged, halting, and anxious. Aaron 2 reveals that his big plan is for *her* to kill *him* on camera. Then, with the Peach Fuzz mask on his head, he coaches her in how to use an axe to kill a person. It's starting to look like maybe, just maybe, Aaron 2 has secretly been the director all along.

Aaron 2 takes her out into the woods at night for a "surprise," which is a locket inscribed with "J+A Forever," and with a picture of him and Aaron 1 on the inside. The shot is mostly black, with Aaron 2's head brightly lit by the camera spotlight, and with the silver locket in the foreground, also illuminated. Beyond, there is nothing. Sara is totally alone with this maniac. Soon, he reveals a freshly dug grave. He's not sure, he says, whether the grave is meant for her or for him, but he *thinks* he knows. *Now* the camera is trained on Sara. We hear a strange sound, and we watch the microexpressions on her face turn from confusion to concern to fear to shock. It turns out that the strange sounds were Aaron 2 stabbing himself in the abdomen with Sara's boot knife, which he stole. "This is cool right? We both stab each other, and then we crawl into the grave, and then we die like Romeo and Juliet." She turns and runs; he follows, the camera light swinging in the blackness. We hear his panting, his pained exertion, as he—at last—tries to wrest back control from her and call the shots.

Eventually, he catches her, attacks her, and drags her into the grave, and then crawls back to the camera to reveal that he's "not going to die tonight." We think Sara is dead, but wait for it: As he talks to the camera about how great her final episode was, we see her emerging from the grave behind him. Speaking to the camera and unaware that she's behind him, he refers to her as "his muse," much like Mia Farrow to Roman Polanski, much like Shelley Duvall to Stanley Kubrick, much like Katie to Micah. She was the beautiful woman who had to be destroyed so he could create his finest work. As he sighs in pleasure and pain at the vicious irony of it all, she creeps toward him, sneaks up on him, beans him hard on the back of the head, and runs. So, in the end, the prey strikes back at the predator. *That* feels like a riposte, both to the domestic horror genre and to the abusive men who contributed to it. It will be *her* movie after all, and she will survive the making of it.

But that's not the end. The final shots of the film show Sara, walking in the streets of Manhattan, near the Dakota/Bramford building, actually. Someone carrying a handheld camera is following her, at a slight distance. We feel afraid for her because we know it's Aaron 2 filming her. And yet she is wearing the "J+A Forever" locket that Aaron 2 gave her, presumably as a trophy of her survival. She looks strong, secure, comfortable in her own skin. Finally, Aaron 2 catches her eye, while they're both underground on the A train. Interestingly, her face remains impassive, almost as though she expected to see him there. Almost as though she *wanted* to see him there. Perhaps so that she can shoot her own sequel. The film cuts to black.

Bad Men Making Good Films: The End and Beginning of an Era

Taken together, these three films embody a sudden, emergent awareness among filmmakers in the 2010s that something was seriously wrong with having predatory men make movies about the entrapment, torture, and dehumanization of women. That awareness likely emerged from sociocultural changes taking place in the United States. First, of course, was the advent of the #MeToo movement. Social activist and sexual assault survivor Tarana Burke coined that phrase in 2006, and by 2009, when *Paranormal Activity* hit theaters, it was widely known that male filmmakers had been exploiting and mistreating their female leads for a long time, as well as the women they were partnered with, and the girls they sought out socially. In fact, as it happens, Roman Polanski was detained by Swiss police—under pressure from US lawyers—for the 1977 rape of Samantha Geimer on September 26, 2009, exactly *one day* after *Paranormal Activity* hit theaters. This, of course, is a coincidence, in the sense that nothing about *Paranormal Activity* caused the arrest of Polanski. But it's much *more* than a coincidence in the sense that both the arrest of Polanski and the release of the film body forth an emerging cultural awareness that male filmmakers—even very talented ones—were altogether too often also predators and dehumanizers, and that they should be held accountable for that. Ironically, Polanski was caught because he was en route to accept a lifetime achievement award at the Zurich Film Festival; the award was conferred on him, ultimately, in 2011. Were the filmmakers of *Paranormal Activity* consciously thinking about Roman Polanski? Possibly, but it doesn't matter. This film and the *Creep* films embody a cultural shift—a shift toward holding predators accountable for how they used their directorial privilege to abuse women.

Not only did these films embody that cultural shift, they also helped to accelerate it, highlighting the dangers of giving a camera to a selfish (Micah) or outright psychopathic (Josef/Aaron 2) man and letting him aim it at women to make horror films. This on its own was an important contribution to the horror genre because it coincided with and likely amplified the sudden inrush of women directors into the horror genre—a genre historically almost totally dominated by male directors. In the 2010s and 2020s, that changed dramatically, so that some of the most renowned horror directors working now are women: Issa Lopez, Ana Lily Amirpour, Coralie Fargeat, Julia Ducournau, Karyn Kusama, Nia DaCosta, Sarah Polley, Natalie Erika James, and Arkasha Stevenson have released brilliant, searing, and searchingly feminist works of horror in the past fifteen years.

In 2024, two of those directors—Natalie Erika James and Arkasha Stevenson—made new domestic horrors for the twenty-first century, and specifically for the post-*Dobbs* era. Both James and Stevenson deliberately styled their films as prequels to one of the original horrors in this book: James's film is the prequel to *Rosemary's Baby*; Stevenson's to *The Omen*. Their films are brilliant, excruciating feminist revitalizations of the domestic horror genre. Taking them alongside Michael Mohan's *Immaculate* (also 2024), we can see a new heartbeat in the domestic horror genre, one that has everything to do with the collapse of reproductive agency in the United States in 2022.

CHAPTER 8

Domestic Horror After *Dobbs*

In June 2022, the United States Supreme Court overturned *Roe v. Wade*. The highest juridical body in the land abandoned the idea that federal law would protect the reproductive autonomy of women; instead, decisions about women's reproductive rights would fall to individual states. As a result of that decision, many pregnant American women have died, and many more will die. Meanwhile, laws that criminalize domestic violence are under siege, and new laws, intended to protect women from emergent forms of violence (tech abuse, for instance, as well as other forms of coercive control) are slow to pass. Only a very small number of states have criminalized coercive control, despite lawmakers and clinicians having become increasingly aware that it exists and that it profoundly endangers the lives of women. New York State, for instance, has a measure before its legislature attempting to define coercive control as a class E felony; the legal experts I have consulted with about this law think it is wildly unlikely to pass, and that, even if it *does* pass, it's likely to be almost unenforceable. Topping things off, as of mid-2025, the ERA has still not passed. It's just not a compelling enough idea, I guess, that women should be guaranteed equal rights under the law.

Given all of this anti-feminist turmoil, I had been eagerly waiting for blazing reboots of classic domestic horrors to take these issues on. I've been hoping hard that these imaginary reboots would be directed by women and would run headlong at reproductive violence as a central concern. Much to my relief, I've been gratified with three clear, raging reboots in a single year, two of them directed by women: *Immaculate* (2024), directed by Michael Mohan; *The First Omen* (2024), directed by Arkasha Stevenson; and *Apartment 7A* (2024), directed by Natalie Erika James. All of these films charge at the *Dobbs* decision, highlighting how reproductive coercion lies at the heart of domestic horror—how it has lain there for a long time, and it lies there still.

Immaculate (2024)

The opening shot of *Immaculate* shows a painting of the Virgin Mary, clad in blue, while someone recites the Ave Maria in Italian nearby. A girl, who appears to be a nun, sneaks into an adjacent room. She finds a set of keys and runs off, trying to escape by the front gate. Floodlights come on, and a posse of dark-clad nuns pursue her. They brutally break her leg in an open fracture at the knee; she will not be escaping anywhere anytime soon. Fade to black as the young nun loses consciousness. When she comes to, we realize she's been buried alive. She screams for help, lights a match to see the interior of her coffin, and cries. And we fade to black again, assuming rightly that this young nun will die. Something evil is going on at this convent, and it's targeting young women. We get plenty of time to feel this young nun's panic, her isolation, her entrapment, and, of course, her mortality. As the opening credits roll in darkness, we hear her desperate screams echo impotently off the walls of her fatal prison.

When the camera again fills with light, we are looking at a young woman named Cecilia (Sydney Sweeney), in a nun's habit, watching Italian border control go through her bag. One of the agents keeps commenting on how beautiful and young she is, and how she is wasting her life as a nun. He strongly implies that she will regret her choice because she's opting out of having a sexual life, a married life, a reproductive life. That may seem like incidental information, but Cecilia's youth, sexual vulnerability, and fertility are *very* important to the logic of the film, so take note. Also important to the logic of the film is her name: deriving from the Latin word *caeca*, which describes a woman who is blind, dark, gloomy, hidden, or confused. Cecilia is the *perfect* name for this soon-to-be-sequestered, deer-in-the-headlights-looking, moody, and, as we'll soon see, naively blind young woman.

Cecilia gets picked up by a driver, who conveys her to the remote convent from the opening sequences of the film. As we move out into the countryside, our hackles rise—this feels too much like the opening sequence of *The Shining*, as we understand how isolated our heroine is about to be. The music in this scene is vaguely Christian chorale, with high women's voices, but there are low, heavy bass pulses in the background that again strongly invoke the opening sound design of *The Shining*. When the car pulls into the nunnery's parking area, Cecilia peers vacantly out into the rain, her face illegible, impassive. The building is clean but forbiddingly institutional. Inside, the Reverend Mother greets her warmly, but Cecilia can't understand a word she says because Cecilia doesn't speak Italian. She learns from another young nun named Isabelle that this place is where elderly nuns go to die and to be cared for by the other sisters of the convent. "Death is a part of everyday life here," Isabelle says, in a strangely hostile, menacing tone. The tour guide gives Cecilia precious little time to contemplate what's happening to her, instead ushering her deeper and deeper into the belly of the building. The scale and internal twistiness of the convent—aptly named Our Lady of Sorrows—seems to engulf and imperil her; by contrast with it, Cecilia seems woefully small, trusting, and simple.

Simple indeed: Cecilia's backstory is very spare. She's from Michigan and nearly drowned as a child under winter ice in the Saginaw River. She became a nun because she believes God saved her from that horrific death. Since her parish back in Michigan closed, she's come to Italy to find her true home among the sisters. She is, in effect, a refugee from her own childhood trauma. She presents as very humble, very quiet, very easily cowed. She has trouble making or maintaining eye contact and often appears dazed and disoriented. Her face wears a loose, open expression, as if she is chronically unable to make sense of what's around her. And no wonder: We soon understand that what's around her is really, really crazy. Soon, the Reverend Mother shows Cecilia a very large nail and reveals that it's a nail from the True Cross, on which Jesus suffered the Passion and died. Perhaps overwhelmed by religious devotion, or thunderstruck by the idea of being in the same room with a nail that contributed to God's human death, or perhaps because she had been drugged—indeed, she blinks hard and wobbles, looking very much like someone who has been roofied—Cecilia loses consciousness upon hearing this revelation.

In the following scenes, we follow Cecilia through a complex dream sequence—strongly reminiscent of Rosemary's when she is drugged by Guy and Minnie. In Cecilia's "dream," she attempts to make confession before a priest, only to realize that the priest is somehow moving away from her. She calls after him, but suddenly she is grabbed from behind and pulled through wallpaper into another room. Everything shifts: A loud, bass-heavy, hammering song with screeching metallic overtones slams in, and we're focused close on Cecilia's panicking face, lit by a flickering deep crimson light. She is lying down, and we are seeing things from her vantage point—recalling Rosemary's posture and point of view during her rape scene. At her feet, a group of masked nuns are doing something to her. Other nuns are pawing at her face and mouth. We see one nun lift up what appears to be the nail from the True Cross and drive it down toward Cecilia's abdomen, in an unmistakable and extremely sacrilegious figure for rape. Cecilia wakes up, shocked and terrified, in her bed. She, like Rosemary, thinks the whole thing was a dream. We, the audience of this film, know entirely too well that it was not a dream. Because we've seen this movie before, in 1968.

Cecilia attempts to move forward with her new life. There's a surprisingly cheerful training montage, in which Cecilia learns how to do the laundry, how to tend to the dying nuns' wounds, who the on-staff doctor is, and how to slaughter and butcher chickens for the nuns' dinner. During this time, Cecilia befriends a young Italian nun named Guendalina (Benedetta Porcaroli); we see them laughing and talking animatedly with each other and with the dying nuns whom they care for. Maybe, just maybe, Cecilia will be okay here, we think. This training montage is the emotional equivalent of the family snapshots of the Thorns that we get in *The Omen*, lulling us, along with our protagonist, into a false sense of comfort and security. They serve to establish the domestic sphere as a safe, comfortable, warm, loving place, when, in fact, the domestic sphere will soon turn ugly, violent, and abusive.

The film leans toward that reality in a bathing scene, when Guendalina brushes Cecilia's hair and reveals to her that she is a domestic abuse survivor. Evidently, Guendalina met some nuns at a domestic abuse support group and started to think that maybe the way out of patriarchal violence and abuse was to join the Catholic Church, take vows, become a nun, and forswear human heterosexuality forever. Guendalina thought to herself, "These women have a very good life. They have a place to live, a job where they can keep their clothes on, nothing to worry about, so I signed up." Marrying Christ and retreating into a convent, for Guendalina, appeared a far safer proposition than marrying a man and retreating into the domestic sphere, only to be battered again. Cecilia responds to these disclosures first with a blank, vapid smile, and then—out of nowhere—with severe retching and vomiting. Guendalina assumes that her story about domestic abuse and her pragmatic reasons for becoming a nun had turned Cecilia's stomach. There is no hint in this scene that she vomits due to pregnancy, but we—who have seen prior incarnations of this film—begin to suspect.

Unsurprisingly, it soon emerges through medical testing of Cecilia's urine at the convent that Cecilia is pregnant. At first, her superiors are critical of her, assuming she's had sexual relations with a man. But as they come to believe she has *not* had sinful relations—by checking and confirming that her hymen is still intact—everyone around her changes, becoming excited, enthusiastic, and fawning. It's as if they had somehow been planning for this, preparing for her pregnancy, which they understand as a miracle, a renewed prospect of a Virgin birth. Cecilia is far less sanguine about it. In fact, she retains her general air of confusion, disbelief, and disorientation throughout these scenes of interrogation and disclosure—even when she, surrounded by priests and doctors, is subjected to an ultrasound and sees a fetus growing inside her. The clergy rejoice; they tell Cecilia that it's a miracle, but she knows different. Miracles don't generally start with dreams of a nail being jammed into one's abdomen.

As soon as the clergy at the convent are convinced Cecilia has conceived without sin, they drape her in blue, flowing robes, following the traditional iconography of the Virgin Mary. Simultaneously, of course, the film thereby makes tangential contact with *Rosemary's Baby* and *The Omen*, in each of which a young, reproductively abused mother is routinely bedecked in blue. Everyone in the nunnery is made to worship Cecilia, standing at the altar in front of the chapel, while she appears lost and anxious. With good reason, because things start going south very quickly as she enters her second trimester.

Vomiting up her own teeth into a toilet, Cecilia comes to realize the physical danger she's in. Something is seriously wrong with her pregnancy, just as something was seriously wrong with Rosemary's. During an ultrasound performed in the convent by the convent doctor, she's informed that the baby "appears to be okay," and Cecilia haltingly asserts, "But, I'm, I'm, I'm not okay." She begs for access to another doctor and to a real hospital, where she can get better quality care. Father Tedeschi, who had initially invited her to join this convent and has emerged as her main contact person about her pregnancy, refuses, saying it's safer for the savior if she stays where she is. Safer, that is, for the presumed savior, who is a fetus. The film is running directly at the core conflict around abortion: Whose life matters more, a woman's or a fetus's? And the film is heavily loading the question, because the latent idea that animates much of pro-fetal logic—which is that every baby can be a miracle, if given the chance to grow and thrive—is literally, explicitly true here. Or, at least, that's how the clergy see it. Cecilia's safety, her bodily health, her needs, her wishes, all of these things are secondary to doing what's safest for the savior-baby. It is a terrifying situation for Cecilia, mostly because she doesn't entirely understand what's going on or what's happened to her.

We know, however, that she has somehow been raped and impregnated, and that she is now being forced to carry the resultant pregnancy to term. Made more than fifty years after *Rosemary's Baby*, this 2024 domestic horror is animated by the same understanding that animated the classic film: the awareness that—absent federal protections for women's reproductive agency—women can be forced to carry their pregnancies to term against their will. The reason for this resurgence of attention to this horrific possibility is simple: From the vantage point of reproductive rights, we are getting perilously close to 1968 again.

Pointedly, we are not alone in our understanding. The film makes clear that Guendalina, the domestic violence survivor, also has the requisite perspective to see what's really happening to Cecilia. Father Tedeschi tries to stop Guendalina from speaking out, but she, the domestic abuse survivor, says, simply, "*Non mi toccare*. Fuck this." "Don't touch me," of course, is a phrase domestic abuse survivors know entirely too well. But it is also what Jesus says to Mary Magdalene after his resurrection: *noli me tangere*. Guendalina here emerges, albeit subtly, as the true savior figure here, the one who, like Jesus, will speak truth to authoritarian power and advocate for those without it. She pushes past Tedeschi and makes an impassioned speech in Italian in front of everyone at the convent, at the top of a staircase. In her speech, Guendalina points out how impossible and mysterious the recent events have been—Cecilia's pregnancy, the sudden violent suicide of another nun. All the nuns stare at her in shock. Father Tedeschi tries again to stop her, and she turns on him, shouting out in Italian, "Let go of me! I know when a man is lying to me!" The film makes it clear that Guendalina is better equipped than anyone else to protest the obvious reproductive horror at work in the film because she has lived with the demon of domestic abuse, too. *Listen to survivors*, the film suggests. *They are the ones in the best position to identify domestic abuse when they see it, and they are often the most inclined to protest.*

After Guendalina has been roughly taken away, Cecilia starts to search for more information. She finds a file containing a newspaper clipping about her near-death experience as a child, as well as a chromosomal analysis of her genetics. Wandering around the convent late at night, she finds a torture chamber in which Guendalina's tongue is being cut out; evidently, marrying Christ was *not* a safer proposition for her than marrying a man. Understandably, Cecilia begins to assess her situation as one of the highest peril. She knows she has to try to escape Our Lady of the Sorrows in order to preserve herself from whatever lurid conspiracy is going on around her.

In the next scene, a group of nuns rushes into Cecilia's bedroom as she screams in pain. Blood appears to be flowing from her body onto the bed. It looks like she is experiencing a placental abruption or perhaps an ectopic pregnancy rupture. Whatever the exact nature of the problem, it is clearly an obstetric emergency, and even the conspiratorial nuns and priests immediately register that. So, in order to save the baby growing in her womb against her will, the nuns and priests at the convent rush Cecilia to a local hospital with her screaming in the backseat of the car. It's a painful scene to watch, and one we're likely to see more of in real life in the coming years.

Back at the convent, a nun cries and prays over the bloodied bedsheets Cecilia left behind, burying her face in them and kissing them. In so doing, she spies a mutilated chicken under the bed. Cecilia hadn't been hemorrhaging; she had doused herself in chicken blood to fake a gestational catastrophe. The nun contacts the priests in the car with Cecilia; they haul Cecilia back to the convent and bind and brand her. She's made into livestock, effectively—a brood sow. "This is not God's work," she says. The priest responds, "If it's not God's work, why isn't He stopping us?" A great question, and a chilling one.

What *Immaculate does* with that question is by far the most interesting choice the film makes. Provoked by the question of why God doesn't help Cecilia and stop the corrupt clergy, Cecilia decides *not* to reject God and instead gets weaponized by her faith. Put otherwise, she decides to have faith in the very relics and signs of faith that she, as a devout Catholic, has learned to venerate and love. When she's at last alone with the nun who's guarding her, Cecilia grabs a heavy, huge crucifix and slams the nun who is guarding her in the head twice. Then there's the gruesome kill shot, where Cecilia crucifixes her right into the eye and smashes up the rest of her face. It appears that in this case, God *is* stopping them after all; evidently, the Lord helps those who help themselves. Cecilia's escape doesn't happen because she turns *away* from God but because she leans *toward* Christianity as a kind of warrior religion for terrorized women.

As Cecilia escapes from her bedroom, with the nun she just killed splayed on the floor, she walks out into the hallway, moaning loudly, when her water breaks. Now in active labor, Cecilia tries to escape the convent through the catacombs, but Father Tedeschi finds her and attempts an unanesthetized C-section on her. We watch the blade slither across Cecilia's swollen abdomen; we hear her scream in agony as blood pours forth. To call this reproductive violence would be to wildly understate the case. Fortunately, Cecilia has swiped and pocketed the nail from the True Cross, and, wrestling with Tedeschi on the floor of the catacombs, she jams it into his jugular, killing him instantly. The Lord again helps those who help themselves—this time with relics of the Passion.

Covered in Father Tedeschi's blood and her own, Cecilia crawls out of the catacombs and gives birth outside. She looks at the baby, and we see her wide-eyed, horrified face; this is another obvious reference to *Rosemary's Baby*, when Rosemary gazes in transfixed horror at her and Satan's goat-eyed offspring. This scene, however, is when the most important difference between *Rosemary's Baby* and *Immaculate* comes into play; it is a difference that retroactively highlights the importance of this film's incessant references to the earlier one. Cecilia cuts the umbilical cord with her teeth and then grabs a huge rock; in the background, we can see the baby. Although it's very blurry, this baby does *not* look normal. Her face covered in her own blood, and her eyes frozen wide in horror both at what she sees and what she's about to do, Cecilia raises the rock above her head and smashes her offspring while screaming her head off. Cut to black.

So let's recap the relation of this film to *Rosemary's Baby*. In both, a virginal, virtuous, innocent woman is raped and impregnated against her will while in some kind of altered state. There is a group of religious worshippers (clergy in *Immaculate*; Satanists in *Rosemary*) who are coercively controlling the pregnant woman, denying her access to medical care, refusing to let her leave the premises, determining what she eats, drinks, and wears as well as whom she's allowed to associate with. In *Rosemary's Baby*, the baby is the Antichrist, and the Satanists are hoping for a new world order of Satan. In *Immaculate*, the baby is supposed to be the reincarnation of Christ himself—using DNA, as we learn, that's been culled from the nail from the True Cross. The Christ-baby, however, is supposed to usher in a new world order, too, one that, as Cecilia eventually realizes, may well be destructive. *Immaculate* reboots *Rosemary's Baby* for the twenty-first century, and loudly trumpets its affiliation with that lineage.

But "reboots" is actually slightly imprecise. Really, *Immaculate revises* the *Rosemary's Baby* story. In *Rosemary's Baby*, Rosemary ultimately bows to her own innate and irrepressible maternal instinct—despite herself, despite her own horror, despite her muted urge to scream, in the end she finds herself rocking baby Adrian to sleep in his black cradle, deciding ultimately she will indeed mother the Antichrist. She's a woman, after all; what choice does she have? In *Immaculate*, Cecilia veers sharply the other way. She refuses to accept the obligation put on her by malicious clerics, who have so badly perverted Christianity in her mind. She refuses to raise a baby whom she perceives not only as a monster, but as a potential threat to Christianity itself.

Immaculate demonstrates that the Church should be in no position to enforce pregnancies on women, and that Christ himself would not *want* to be invoked in the service of such things. After all, there's no comeuppance to Cecilia for murdering a nun with a crucifix or a priest with the nail from the True Cross. Quite the contrary: God allows Cecilia to get away—both from the convent and from her unwanted baby. It appears that all the sacred relics and objects in this film are *actively on her side*—advocating for her to have agency over her body, helping her to escape imprisonment and dehumanization at the hands of the cultlike or even coven-like convent.

I'm not sure whether the filmmakers were trying to make an anti-Catholic or even anti-Christian film, but if so, they didn't succeed. Instead, what they did was far more interesting. They made a film that actually asserts a fundamental *allegiance* between true Christianity—as embodied in the cross and the nail—and women's rights to freedom, bodily autonomy, and reproductive choice. When Cecilia emerges from the womb of the earth—the catacombs under the nunnery—doused in blood, it is *she* who is being reborn, not Jesus. She is being born into a new and newly empowered form of Christianity, one that prioritizes the life, bodily autonomy, and reproductive freedom of young women. What the filmmakers did in this film was to envision a world in which true Christianity could actually line up *in favor of* women's reproductive rights, even if that meant escaping from the institutions—like the convent—that would seem to represent true Christianity. In that sense, the film is decisively a post-*Dobbs* reproductive horror, fully aware of the way in which Christian doctrine gets deployed to curb women's reproductive choices, and fully aware that that deployment will put women's lives in grave danger unless they come out, like Cecilia, fighting for their lives.

The First Omen (2024)

This is a shockingly good prequel, particularly given that the film it prequels—*The Omen* (1976)—is one of the bumpier domestic horrors of the '70s in terms of overall film quality. Don't get me wrong: I *love* the original film for its delicate handling of the ostensibly benign patriarch as an insidious source of domestic horror. But there's no denying that *The Omen* is campy and awkward at times, with some really spongy scripting, inconsistent acting, and mortifying special effects. Moreover, *Omen II* and *Omen III* are perhaps my least favorite of all the remakes and sequels of the original six films prior to 2020—which is really saying something, because they're all pretty god-awful (see appendix A). So I had the bar in my mind set *quite* low for *The First Omen*.

My skepticism was misplaced, however, because *The First Omen* is truly excellent. But I won't spend a whole lot of time extolling the virtues of this film, nor swooning over how terrifying it is. What I want to do is address how the film jumps *right* into the very same controversies that animated its obvious forebear *The Omen*, as well as its only slightly less obvious forebear *Rosemary's Baby*. Namely, it's a film that's profoundly concerned with reproductive rights and with what it means when women lack them. As we've seen, *The Omen* and *Rosemary's Baby* make the argument—sometimes very subtly—that denying women their reproductive freedom not only endangers their physical safety, but also *literally brings the Antichrist into the world. The First Omen* receives that legacy from the original films and dials the volume way, way up.

The reproductive coercion in the original 1976 film is subtle enough that you can miss it, while the reproductive coercion in *The First Omen* is the explicit, overt storyline. A convent in Italy recruits girls—orphaned girls, no less—to be raped by Satan in hopes of producing the Antichrist. The viewer knows some of this going in, since the movie is the prequel to a story that almost every horror afficionado is familiar with—we know the goal of the film is to explain how Damien comes into the world. The circumstances of the convent are revealed to us brutally: There are numerous scenes in the film of women giving birth to demonic halflings; there are scenes of violent restraining of pregnant women; there are rape scenes—one of which, as in *Immaculate*, very specifically echoes the rape of Rosemary in *Rosemary's Baby*—that are facilitated by members of the clergy.

The film opens with a gorgeous shot of a stained-glass window being lifted into place on a cathedral. The stained-glass window positioning leads us to shots of an old priest making a confession about his participation in some kind of ritual involving young women and babies. The confession scene is intercut with shots of a young woman, lying on her back, with someone covering her head in a black fabric covering. We are meant to understand that these scenes are memories that the priest is confessing to his confessor—things he witnessed or participated in. The woman is strapped down to the table by her hands. She begins breathing in and out heavily; we can even see the black cloth being sucked tight to this woman's mouth as she draws in her jagged breath. It looks like—and is—a torture scene. Back in the present of the confessional, the priest says, "I can't do this anymore," and then the young, hooded, bound woman says the same thing, "I can't do this anymore." The crosscutting of lines serves a very important purpose: It shows us clearly that the secret workings of the clergy—whatever exactly they are—are somehow coterminous with the enforced suffering of this young woman.

As the repentant and newly confessed priest leaves the church, the other priest who had been confessing him runs after him—it's Father Brennan, who had tried to warn Robert Thorn in the 1976 film about young Damien. Here, in the prequel, Brennan (Ralph Ineson) addresses the priest who had been making confession; when that priest turns toward Brennan, we hear the pulley holding the window creaking, then a loud bang. Everything holds still for a moment as the glass crashes in beautiful extreme slow motion around them. The camera angles up to the sky, and we can see that the window depicts Jesus, and that a metal pole is piercing through the Christ Child, sending huge shards of glass down below. A discordant choral piece shrills in the background as we watch thousands of fragments rain down onto the repentant priest along with the metal pole, which rips through the back of his head. This scene is a direct homage to a scene from the original *Omen* when Father Brennan attempts to take shelter in a church but is impaled by a falling pole. Here, in the prequel, we see Father

Brennan witness a scene that anticipates his own impalement six years later. History, it would appear, repeats itself. This post-*Dobbs* film wants us to note that dynamic explicitly because, of course, women's history in the United States *is repeating itself*, as we slide back to a states' rights model of reproductive freedom, and one that is every bit as restrictive in many states as the laws that obtained prior to *Roe*.

From the impaled priest, we cut to a glorious shot of sunrise over Rome in 1971. A beautiful, happy, bright-faced young nun (Nell Tiger Free) makes her way up a staircase at an airport; she seems keen, focused, and palpably nervous. She reunites with a man named Cardinal Lawrence, and through their conversation, we learn that he's been a part of her life since she was a child. He is warm and friendly, embracing her and praising the grown young woman she's become, nun's habit and all. Riding around the city in a car, this young nun, Margaret, is enraptured by the sight of the Colosseum and everything else around Rome. She seems content, relaxed, and eager to begin her new life, until—bang—a student protester slams her hand onto the car window, startling Margaret badly. Cardinal Lawrence tells her that the students are rejecting authority and the Church. He invites her to "play her part" in the Church's effort to "win back" the youth. Eventually, they arrive at the convent school where Margaret will be living and teaching. It's in the city, and everyone seems friendly. The children seem happy, the nuns industrious. The children are playing, laughing, and socializing. The nuns often join them and seem attentive and concerned with the children's welfare. The interior courtyard is well manicured and bright, and the rooms of the school are old-fashioned but beautiful. It looks like the kind of place that very wealthy people would rent to host their destination wedding.

I *love* this as a cinematic choice. Rather than making the place scary from the get-go, as in *Immaculate*, this film chooses to allow Margaret—and the audience—to feel a sense of openness, possibility, and comfort upon her arrival at the convent. This sense of ease—which extends even to the beatific choral soundtrack—only makes the collapse into the horror to come all the more powerful and striking when it happens. It's the equivalent of the still shots of Kathy, Robert, and Damien in the part of *The Omen* before Damien has revealed his true, devilish character. We are lulled into a false sense of security, in lockstep with Margaret herself, before the rug is jerked out from under us, and we find ourselves in the freefall of domestic horror and reproductive violence.

Margaret tours the hospital wing; in this convent school, unwed mothers can give birth and be cared for by the nuns. It all seems fairly rosy, until Margaret finds her way to a room in which a very young girl named Carlita (Nicole Sorace) sits on the floor, drawing. Margaret attempts to bond with this girl, who is pale, thin, and terribly alone. Creepily, the girl crawls over to Margaret, only to grab her roughly by the face and lick her cheek. Margaret is repulsed and afraid. Something is perhaps not quite right with this place after all.

Fortunately, Margaret doesn't have to stay there right away. She'll share a room with another novitiate named Luz (Maria Caballero) until the time comes for them to take the veil, a short while hence. As the two girls share backstories, we learn that Margaret suffered from some kind of delusional state as a child, and that the cardinal—who had known her when she was just a young orphan—had helped her to understand that everything she feared was only in her mind. Perhaps for this reason, as Margaret starts working during the days with the girls at the school, she feels drawn to young Carlita—she sees something of herself in the tormented child. At one point, through a partially open door, she sees young Carlita being restrained by the nuns; watching this upsetting scene, Margaret recalls how nuns had subdued her during her own juvenile fits and visions years before.

A short time before Margaret is due to take the veil, Luz invites her out for a last night of partying. Luz goes through her own clothes and selects a silver lamé plunging neckline top for Margaret and makes her wear it. Margaret looks incredibly uncomfortable, frowning as she gazes at all the skin she's showing, but Luz praises how sexy she also looks. Out at a disco, Luz and Margaret do shots and pick up men, though Margaret is still clearly uncomfortable with it all. But eventually, the alcohol, music, and pheromones do their magic, and we find Margaret dancing with a young man named Paolo on the dance floor. With strobing blue lights around them, they dance, and eventually, Margaret licks Paolo's face—recalling what Carlita had done to her earlier. As viewers, we have a foreboding sense that something is about to go terribly wrong for Margaret.

The very next shot shows an extreme close-up on a hairy spider, which is revealed to be crawling along Margaret's face in an extreme close-up. As we zoom out, we see Margaret's head with her hair spread out like spiders' legs over a pillow, her makeup blurred and smeared. Our first thought, and seemingly also Margaret's, as she comes to consciousness and checks herself over to confirm that her clothes are still on, is that she might have been raped or seduced the night before. Luz is nearby and explains blithely as Margaret comes to consciousness that nothing too out of control happened the night before, but Margaret is badly shaken nonetheless. She smiles weakly, with chagrin playing around her eyes, while she sits wrapped in a blanket, her mascara streaked along her cheeks. The soundtrack has shifted from choral or happy disco to creepily ethereal chanting, in minor keys.

Soon, Father Brennan tracks her down and warns her that "evil things" will start to happen around young Carlita. Margaret doesn't know what to make of him, but he seems agitated, unhinged. She pulls away to leave, but not before he can share his address with her, promising that if she comes to see him, he will "tell her everything." Back at the convent, the little girls Margaret is teaching tell her that Carlita is "in the bad room." Margaret intervenes, advocating for Carlita with the higher-ranking nuns, questioning the very idea that there should be "a bad room." After Carlita is released, Margaret comforts her; the two bond.

Immediately thereafter, however, Margaret hears panicked screaming and goes to investigate. Through a small window, she sees a young woman in labor in the hospital wing. She's strapped down, her eyes frozen in terror, screaming, until the doctors and nuns administer laughing gas. As Margaret watches her, the woman's face contorts into one of sadistic mirth; she looks like a demon and turns her head toward Margaret, giggling and smiling evilly. Suddenly, she breaks into seizures as the doctors and nuns unceremoniously pick up cutting tools, presumably to do an episiotomy. The woman's face isn't just in pain; it's in abject terror, her eyes wild. Soon, Margaret can see why: In a truly graphic close-up on the woman's genitals, we see a large, claw-like, bluish hand reach out of her body and paw the air. This is *not* a normal human baby, not by a long shot. And these doctors are also *not* trying to do good for this woman. Margaret is horrified and overwhelmed by this scene, her eyes rolling back into her head as she faints in horror. When she comes to, however, she doesn't quite yet know what to do with what she saw; we get a sense she doesn't trust her own reality. Had it been a dream?

Margaret's suspicions that something insidious may be going on at the convent are gradually confirmed. After she sees a drawing Carlita has made of herself strapped to a bed with a fetus in her belly and two Munch-like nuns standing on either side of the bed, her fears start to take more concrete shape. She asks both Carlita and a strange nun, named Sister Anjelica (Ishtar Currie Wilson), why a young girl would draw such an image, and is informed that Carlita drew the image of herself strapped to the bed, but Anjelica drew the "ragazzo," or little boy, who's growing in Carlita's belly. Margaret cautions Anjelica that such a drawing is not "very appropriate." Anjelica responds in anger, roughly snatching back the drawing from Margaret's outstretched hand.

Moments later, Carlita gets pulled into a party game the little girls are playing in the convent courtyard. During the game, Carlita looks up. Sister Anjelica is high up in a windowsill. She appears to be doused in something. The camera looks up at her from below as she stands there and says to Carlita, "It's all for you," in a direct quotation of the line that Damien's nanny shouts out in the original *Omen* just before jumping to her death at his fifth birthday party. Anjelica then sets herself on fire and jumps; the rope she had around her neck snaps hard, and her body flies back through a window on a lower level—exactly as Damien's nanny did in 1976, minus the fire. History repeats itself: The 1970s are born again in the 2020s, and this film is bound and determined to make us feel that truth through its citations of its parent film.

Anjelica's bizarre suicide convinces Margaret that maybe some of what Father Brennan had told her was true, so she visits him. Brennan tells her that "There are two Churches. The one that follows the teachings of Christ—the one that you and I are part of—and the other. The Church that will turn a blind eye to torture, to rape." He reveals that the impure Church's greatest fear is secularism. He explains to her that a culture that is outspoken and rebellious—like the emergently secular culture of the 1970s—is not a culture that the Church can readily control. So this dark, power-hungry Church will create something for the people to fear, to lead them all back to the ostensible safety of the Church. As Margaret listens, her eyes are wide open, unblinking, alert, and her brows are knit in concern and confusion. "These priests," says Brennan anxiously and conspiratorially, but with great conviction, "believe they can birth the Antichrist and then control him." This, according to Brennan, will drive people back to the Church. Margaret responds exactly as any sane person would: "That's insane!" He goes on to suggest that Carlita has been selected as the mother of the Antichrist. Margaret smiles gently, looks down at her lap, and says quietly, "You're crazy." Undeterred, Brennan begs Margaret to search for the birth records at the school to confirm that Carlita was born at 6 a.m. on June 6—666. As Margaret listens to all this, we watch dawning horror coupled with disbelief spreading across her face. Finally, she stands up abruptly and heads nervously for the door. Brennan grabs her and begs her to help him. Margaret continues to protest, saying, "Carlita is a little girl! And she is not pregnant." There may be something sinister going on at the convent school, but surely Brennan's theory is fantasy. Her parting words to him clearly indicate that she thinks he is more insane than whatever is going on at the convent: "You need a doctor. I'm sorry I can't help you."

But the seed of suspicion has been planted, and soon the sinister incidents at the convent pick up again. The nuns harshly discipline Carlita, locking her into solitary confinement in "the bad room." Eventually, Margaret is told to stay away from Carlita by Sister Silva, the highest-ranking nun at the school, and to postpone her taking of the veil. She watches her friend Luz take the veil, don the ring of Christ, and become His bride. Jealousy and self-doubt play across Margaret's face as a tear escapes down her cheek; her desire to be accepted by God and by His community is almost all-consuming. Almost, but for the increasing skepticism she feels about the nuns, and the gnawing belief that Father Brennan may not be so insane after all.

During Luz's initiation, Margaret slips out and sneaks into the convent record office as Brennan had asked her to do and looks for any information related to Carlita's birth. She finds the birth certificate, which reveals that Carlita was, in fact, born on the sixth day of the sixth month, at 6 a.m. But there's more. Carlita Scianna is evidently the fourteenth of fourteen reproductive experiments, all performed on orphaned girls given the last name Scianna. When Margaret looks at the folder for the thirteenth Scianna baby, she finds that it was stillborn and terribly deformed. Looking further back, she ascertains that all the prior Scianna babies were female, most were deformed, many stillborn. This convent is, indeed, is at the center of some kind of cruel and often lethal reproductive conspiracy.

At this point, the audience realizes that Arkasha Stevenson's *First Omen* is not simply a prequel to *The Omen* and the backstory of Damien's mother. It's about reproductive abuse, *tout court*. But where the original *Omen* laid the responsibility for that abuse jointly at the husband's feet and the feet of a Satanic conspiracy, this film lays it squarely and exclusively at the feet of the Catholic Church. More specifically, it lays responsibility at the feet of a Church that is in a blind panic about the rise of "secularism" and about the lack of faith among the young. *The First Omen* portrays Christian moral panic as the point of origin for the horror of reproductive violence. There is a reason that this film, set in 1971, was conceived, directed, and released post-2022. And there is a reason that it was a woman who directed it:

Arkasha Stevenson is suggesting that a Christian moral panic about the rise of secularism today is to blame for the sudden danger in which thousands and thousands of young women now find themselves plunged, through state restrictions on their access to reproductive care, reproductive medicine, and reproductive agency.

After Margaret and a sympathetic priest named Gabriel smuggle the birth files out of the convent to bring them to Brennan, the three of them sit on the floor, puzzling through the files to figure out who the one baby is that the nuns seem to be planning to impregnate with the devil's son. They have realized it's not Carlita—there's someone else in queue ahead of her. Gabriel, Margaret, and Brennan see photographs of deformed, often stillborn, children. Gabriel, a devout member of the Church, gasps in horror at what he sees, and his reaction is important. Gabriel is shocked by the fates of children, the cruelty to the mothers, the cruelty of a Church that enforces this accursed pregnancy on people; his shock models for the audience how anyone—even someone utterly devout in his Catholicism—should feel at these horrors.

Set in 1971, this film takes place before *Roe v. Wade* and, indeed, is set in Italy, which had similarly restrictive reproductive laws in the 1970s. This scene of photographic revelation allegorizes actual reality in the early 1970s, when the Catholic Church, both in the United States and in Rome, was so adamantly opposed to abortion that it wouldn't allow even therapeutic abortions in cases where a growing fetus was too badly deformed or sick to survive outside the womb. In *The First Omen*, we're talking on the surface about a twisted scheme to prop up a failing Church by forcing women to carry ill-begotten pregnancies. But on a deeper level, we're seeing a cautionary narrative about the possibility of going back to a world in which the Church prevented abortion even in cases where the mother's life was in danger, or a fetus was known to be deformed beyond viability.

Eventually, Brennan and Margaret work out that it's Margaret herself who's destined to give birth to the Antichrist. She suddenly recalls the final events on the night of her disco rebellion in an extended, gruesome, color-saturated, strobing flashback. She remembers herself drugged, strapped down, and surrounded by shrouded clergy. Like the woman at the beginning of the film, she is hooded, while manic female voices chant in Latin. She remembers a demonic face with a monstrous eye perched over her—clearly referencing *Rosemary's Baby* with both the demonic face and the hooding of the rape victim—and remembers a small spider crawling across her abdomen toward her genitals. She remembers the leathery claw of Satan rake across her belly—exactly as it had done fifty-six years earlier across Rosemary's body. In full possession now of her recovered memory, Margaret collapses into screaming sobs while Brennan and Gabriel attempt to hold her and help her. As she recovers her wits, she says, simply, "If I am pregnant, I need it out of me. I need it out of me now."

This, of course, is where *The First Omen* parts ways decisively with *Rosemary's Baby* and situates itself decisively in lineage with the original *Omen*: Rosemary didn't want an abortion, even when it appeared her pregnancy was going to kill her. Margaret and Kathy Thorn, on the other hand, believed they should have some right to determine whether they would carry a pregnancy to term. That was an impossible belief to act on, however, when the entire shadow Church was lined up to keep the baby in utero until it was fully formed and ready to emerge on its own.

Indeed, as Margaret's pregnancy supernaturally accelerates, so that she goes from invisibly to very obviously pregnant in a matter of minutes, she is picked up by members of the shadow Church. Tearing at her own clothes to allow her belly to expand with the suddenly burgeoning Antichrist, Margaret loses consciousness. When she comes to, she is strapped to a table, with Cardinal Lawrence hovering above her, assuring her that he loves her and will be with her. Heavily drugged, she is wheeled into a subterranean operating room where she gazes upon row after row of blunt, old-looking gynecological instruments. Her tormentors—the nuns and priests of the shadow church—perform an awake C-section on her, with her gasping, "I'm in pain!" Soon, Cardinal Lawrence lifts a baby from her belly, still in its amniotic sac. He pierces the sac, revealing not one, but two babies, fully formed. The first child, to everyone's disappointment, is a girl. When Margaret hears Cardinal Lawrence joyfully announce that the second child is a boy, she bursts into tears: against her will, without her knowledge or consent, and in spite of her desire to prevent it, she has been forced—literally forced, being bound, drugged, and ripped open by a priest—to give birth to the Antichrist. Just at this moment, in a truly brilliant moment of synergy with the 1976 *Omen*, the same song that plays when Kathy is murdered by Mrs. Baylock starts thrumming: "Sanguis, bibimus! Ave Satani!"

The boy is taken from her by the evil nuns and priests who

have been coercively controlling and reproductively abusing her all along. Margaret asks to hold her son, and the clergy joyfully agree, thinking that she, Rosemary-like, is going to succumb to maternal feeling. Instead, she uses this opportunity to jam a scalpel into Lawrence's jugular. She then turns the scalpel on the Antichrist himself, but is stopped before she can murder him by Luz, who stabs Margaret with another scalpel. The shadow clergy grab the Antichrist and decide to incinerate Margaret and her unwanted baby daughter together. But Carlita arrives and helps rescue the very seriously injured Margaret and the baby girl.

The final shots of the film are of Margaret, Carlita, and Margaret's daughter trying to make a life for themselves in a secluded cabin in a wintry wilderness. The room they're in is lit by dozens of candles and decorated with dozens of bouquets of hanging dried herbs and flowers. They are all laughing and smiling together. *The First Omen*, then, leaves room for another chapter in the story, in which a superhuman girl-baby, raised in an all-women environment in the middle of nowhere, could grow up to challenge and perhaps defeat the Antichrist and the wrongheaded clergy who brought him to life. If that sequel gets made, I can only hope it is directed by Arkasha Stevenson, with her finely attuned sensitivity to how women experience their own bodily suffering as well as the suffering of other women around them.

Apartment 7A (2024)

Natalie Erika James's *Apartment 7A* tells the story of Terry Gionoffrio, a young woman who was groomed to bear the Antichrist *before* Rosemary and Guy Woodhouse's story began. In this film, Terry (Julia Garner) is an aspiring dancer who breaks her ankle and becomes addicted to painkillers in the aftermath of her injury. Walking in a drug-induced haze around the Bramford apartment building in New York, Terry is found by none other than Roman and Minnie Castevet. Played by Kevin McNally and Dianne Wiest, the two crotchety Bramford residents bring her up to their apartment and put her to bed. She wakes up, disoriented, but eventually Roman and Minnie prevail upon her—with the same characteristic bluster and odd joviality that spiced the original film—to move into their spare apartment so that they can care for her and help her get back on her feet. Terry is confused by this but also pleased: She sees it as an opportunity to straighten out her life, though she is warned by her roommate when she gets home that all of this is very, very strange, and that the Castevets could be maniacs for all she knows. Overriding all practical protest, Terry decides to take them up on their offer.

James's film is a faithful homage to the original film in many ways. First, once she is installed in the Castevets' second apartment, Terry finds herself subjected to the same—and I mean sometimes line-by-line and shot-by-shot repetitions—of what Rosemary and Guy were subjected to in the 1968 film. Terry, a performer like Guy, hears from Minnie that she has "a most interesting inner quality," and that she has the potential to be a star. This conversation happens in Minnie's kitchen while she and Terry wash and dry the dishes together—just as Minnie and Rosemary had done back in 1968. The color palette is the same, as are the camera angles, as the original film.

Dianne Wiest tries to convey that same brassy, no-boundaries nosiness Ruth Gordon did more than fifty years prior. Kevin McNally, meanwhile, emulates Sidney Blackmer's oily friendliness and saccharine manners.

Of course, the largest and most obvious debt of this film to its 1968 predecessor is the reproductive conspiracy at its heart. The central drama of the film is that Terry is unwittingly drugged by her neighbors and raped by Satan so that she will become pregnant with the Antichrist. Like Rosemary, Terry initially believes this rape and impregnation to have been a terrible dream, and she only slowly recovers her awareness of what really happened to her—partially through talking with people, partially by reading books that she finds in the Bramford. She wears the tannis root necklace that we remember from *Rosemary's Baby*; her obstetrician is Abe Sapirstein; her neighbors are nosy and overinvolved in her life. The very end of the film includes the opening lullaby from *Rosemary's Baby*, though sung in a lower key.

But the newer film also makes explicit some crucial ideas that the first film left unstated. Toward the end of the film, Terry goes to a church—having begun to understand the truth about the baby she's carrying—and she meets a nun. The nun turns out to have known a previous young woman whom the Castevets groomed; evidently, Terry is not unique or special but is merely one in a long line of potential vehicles for the Antichrist. The nun quickly realizes that Terry is not just a potential vehicle but actually already impregnated with the Antichrist. The nun drops to her knees and begins praying to God: "If this baby is born, God have mercy on us all!" James's film makes the powerful but implicit theology of *Rosemary's Baby* explicit: No one, especially a member of the Church, should be rooting for the survival of this pregnancy. It is actively un-Christian to want this baby to come into the world. *Apartment 7A* sees in *Rosemary's Baby* a template for how to terrify Americans about the straitened circumstances of women's reproductive rights but makes that template starker, less ambiguous.

Nowhere is this clearer than when Terry visits an abortionist. *Rosemary's Baby*, remember, centers on a young woman who desperately wants to have a child and rejects the idea of an abortion outright, even when pressed by her friends to consider one in order to save her own life. Like *The First Omen* and, before it, *The Omen*, *Apartment 7A* centers instead on a young woman who has *no desire whatsoever* to have a baby, here because she knows it will derail her dancing career. As a result of this knowledge, and spurred by the nun's panicky warning, Terry goes to speak with her former roommate, who knows of an abortionist. Of course, since the film is set in the mid-1960s, abortion was still illegal in New York State—even in cases of rape—and so Terry is forced to seek an abortion from an illegal abortion provider. Together, Terry and the former roommate journey to a back-alley, secret abortion provider. They both look afraid but determined.

In the abortionist's office, we see Terry lying flat on her back on a very thin set of towels on a table with an older woman poised at her feet with a tray of formidable looking tools and instruments. Terry is awake and unanesthetized, like many of the American women who underwent illegal abortions before 1973 in the United States. We see her face, gripped in fear and pain, as the abortionist begins the procedure. But Terry panics, kicking the woman away from her, and then the woman seizes up in a horrific state of rictus—evidently, Satan's spawn is able to exert real and direct power in utero, even over people who are outside the womb. Terry and the friend who had accompanied her to the abortionist flee. The scene—both for them and for the viewer—is suffused with both panic and uncertainty. We don't understand what just happened to Terry any better than they do; the scenes afterward are breathless, disorienting.

Apartment 7A ends in a significantly different fashion from the other two 2024 films about reproductive horror. Cecilia in *Immaculate* and Margaret in *The First Omen* both manage to get away in the end. Sure, they are forced to carry their demonic pregnancies to term, and they give birth under extraordinary duress and very much against their will. But they survive. Terry, in the final scene of *Apartment 7A*, manages to halt the Satanic conspiracy, but it costs her her life. With a somewhat numb look on her face, she shouts to the crowd of conspirators she is surrounded by in Minnie and Roman's apartment, "Hail Satan!" Then she begins the final and best dramatic and dance performance of her life. The song "Be My Baby" comes on the hi-fi, and Terry—her makeup smudged and her face still oddly numb looking—performs a bizarre interpretive dance, at once provocatively erotic and extremely aggressive. At some moments, she swings her hips seductively, and at others, she lunges forward, seeming ready to bite the men and women who are watching the mother of the Antichrist perform for them. At the end of the song, she jauntily poses, seating herself on the frame of an open window. Before anyone can stop her, she just tips herself out, and the song goes quiet. She deliberately plunges both herself and her baby to their deaths.

Now, James had to end the film with Terry's defenestration because this is how Terry's death happens in Ira Levin's novel and Roman Polanski's film *Rosemary's Baby*. But in both the novel and the original film, we never learn exactly how Terry got launched out the window. I always assumed Minnie and Roman pushed her out the window deliberately, once they realized that they had a more suitable Satan-spawn-vehicle in their cute new neighbor Rosemary Woodhouse. In James's interpretation, Terry's death is a suicide, undertaken because she realizes she cannot and will not bring the Antichrist into the world.

This interpretation of Terry's death may have originated in James's imagination, but I suspect it originated in James's reading and interpretive extension of Ira Levin's novel. In the book *Rosemary's Baby*—but not in Polanski's 1968 film—Rosemary goes through an agonizing process of debating what to do with herself and her baby once she sees that he is, in fact, Satan's son. The first and most compelling option, to Rosemary, is to grab the baby and hurl herself and him out the window, to their deaths. I have given a lot of thought to why the original *Rosemary's Baby* film cut this moment. It may have been because interior monologue is hard to convey in film. But the film does that brilliantly at other points, simply by having Mia Farrow talk to herself. So I've come to the conclusion that Polanski's film wants to leave Rosemary's agency in the end in a far more reduced, qualified state. Perhaps this should not be surprising, coming from Polanski. His film doesn't even allow Rosemary the option of imagining any other way out, apart from becoming the unwilling, semi-catatonic mother of Satan's son. James's film wants to restore that way out and give it to Terry. There is a way to defeat and defraud the malign forces that have gathered against Terry: She can choose to die.

Now, that's an extremely distressing place for the blistering feminism of this film to turn. Is James *really* offering up suicide as a serious alternative to forced pregnancy? I think yes and no. On the one hand, the film points out a bitter reality: Women who are denied access to abortion but need one will find a way to get one, even if it ultimately costs them their lives. This is no horrific fantasy but well-established historical reality. This was indeed the reality all over the news in the 1950s and 1960s before the legalization of abortion. On the other hand, what we already know as we come to this film—assuming we've all seen or at least heard of *Rosemary's Baby*—is that Terry is *not* the last woman to fall to the diabolical rape schemes of the Bramford coven. Rosemary's next, and is already in queue. In fact, *Apartment 7A* shows us a final scene shot from behind of Rosemary and Guy seeing Terry's mangled dead body in front of the Bramford. Terry's ultimate sacrifice, which, remember, she undertakes to save humanity from Satan, is simply not enough. It's not enough to sacrifice herself. Because there's always another woman waiting afterward, clueless as to her imminent conversion into a vessel for Satanic reproduction.

This awareness in the film of the ultimate inescapability of the coven's malicious and Satanic plans lies at the heart of James's feminism. She casts the horrific reproductive violence and dehumanization committed against the young women in the Bramford as generalizable, not specific to Rosemary or to Terry. The mechanisms by which women are trapped and oppressed in reproductive horror aren't about one specific woman but are applicable to any and all women of reproductive age. They are systemic, pervasive, and orchestrated. This is the second reason why the film's emphasis on dance is so important: Terry's entrapment in the coven's scheme is literally *choreographed*. It is made possible only by the orchestration of many different actors, agents, directors, and other dancers. The brutality to which she is subjected is not merely a one-on-one brutality. Instead, it involves dozens of people, acting in conjunction with a vast patriarchal plan to bring Satan's son into the world. The film's emphasis on choreography updates the domestic horror of *Rosemary's Baby* for the 2020s, making that horror *structural*. Natalie Erika James's ultimate contribution to the domestic horror genre is to remind us that it's not ever just about the oppression, dehumanization, and abuse of *one* particular woman. It's about the structures of power, patriarchy, and belief that make the categorical oppression of women a thinkable—and tragically desirable—thought.

Of course, this idea of the structural vulnerability of women to reproductive violence is something this film shares with Stevenson's *First Omen* and with Mohan's *Immaculate*. In all three of these reboots of the classic domestic horrors of the 1970s, there is a very strong sense that there is a long line of women, unwittingly waiting to be exploited and destroyed by a world that cannot bring itself to see women as human beings. It's not about Rosemary's special, perfect, Marian Catholicness anymore, nor about Kathy Thorn's sweet, devoted motherliness. The only required qualification for being tormented and abused into bearing the Antichrist is being a woman of reproductive age. The vulnerability to domestic horror and reproductive violence isn't personal anymore; it's structural and intentional. In focusing on domestic and reproductive horror as structural, there's something maybe even slightly darker in the 2024 prequels and remakes than in the original films of the 1970s. Or maybe it's not fair to say that the 2024 reproductive horrors are darker, but I do think it's fair to say they're more desperate than their 1968 and 1976 predecessors. Because in the '70s, the general trajectory of women's liberation was clearly upward; in 2024, in the wake of the *Dobbs* decision and popular slogans like "your body, my choice," the trajectory is clearly down.

Reviewers and audience members haven't failed to notice the political ambitions of these films nor the precipitous downturn in the fates of American women that they allude to. Keith Harris wrote a great review of *Immaculate* for *The Racket*, calling the film "a war over Sweeney's body," and notes that it's perfect to have Sweeney in such a role "just two years after the Supreme Court's *Dobbs* decision legalized forced birth in the U.S." Bilge Ebiri reviewed *The First Omen* for *Vulture* in similarly political terms: "So why should anyone be surprised that suddenly, in the wake of the Supreme Court's overturning of *Roe v. Wade*, as state after state attempts to enact religious laws depriving women of bodily agency, America is getting horror movies about people forced into monstrous births by religious institutions worried about their growing irrelevance? Whether it's from a direct desire to be topical or a subconscious need to make our anxieties tangible, horror throws our world back at us." James's film *Apartment 7A*, which has generally not been particularly well reviewed, has still gained notice for its politics: Casey Allen noted for Utah Public Radio that Terry's reproductive autonomy was manipulated in a way that "feels very mindful . . . especially since this year has seen a lot of people in the US fight each other over abortion and a woman's right to choose." Women's political reality in 2025 may be terrifyingly close to what it was in 1970, but our discourse around how feminist horror can do political work has finally started to crystallize. And it's crystallized with the help of feminist directors like Mohan, Stevenson, and James.

EPILOGUE

Women Talking, Women Screaming, Women Writing, Women Directing

Domestic horror in the 2020s is a call to speak out, a call to protest, and a reminder that we've been at this moment in history before and that the consequences of failing to resist are extremely high now. Violence against women continues to take the forms it has taken for countless years—reproductive violence and coercion, physical battery, psychological torture, entrapment, emotional abuse, and dehumanization. But domestic horror in the 2020s is also hell-bent on reminding us—all viewers, not just women—that the danger becomes infinitely graver if we allow ourselves to be silenced. This is why it's important for Cecilia to scream at the end of *Immaculate*, for Margaret to assert her pain in her C-section scene, and for Terry to whisper into Minnie's ear, right before she jumps out the window, "You were right, Minnie:

This is the role of a lifetime." All three films end with the main character using her voice.

The finest domestic horror of the 2020s, in my opinion, takes that theme of using your voice to a glorious precipice. Not usually classified as a work of horror at all, the film is Sarah Polley's magnificent *Women Talking* (2022). This film is an aria on the grief, pain, and fear of living as a woman in a history that seeks to erase you. Winning the Academy Award for Best Adapted Screenplay, the Independent Spirit Robert Altman Award, and numerous other awards besides, the film clearly hit a nerve, appearing on American screens at a historical moment when women's bodily autonomy and basic human rights to self-determination are precariously positioned at the verge of a new era of autocratic patriarchy. Indeed, this film was released only two months after the *Roe* decision was reversed. The timing there—like the timing of Polanski's arrest and the release of *Paranormal Activity*, or the timing of the ERA's failure and the wrapping of *Alien*—is coincidental in the sense that neither event caused the other. But it's also much more than coincidence. Polley's movie was reading the tea leaves about a political culture—our political culture—that was slowly, progressively, and determinedly turning its back on women.

Women Talking is based on a real-life domestic and reproductive horror—a bracing and horrific story, be warned. Between 2005 and 2009, more than one hundred Mennonite women in a colony in Bolivia were systematically raped by their Mennonite menfolk, who drugged them with animal tranquilizers. The men raped their sisters, nieces, wives, and neighbors. They raped little girls—girls under the age of six. Horror beyond horror; violence beyond words. Sarah Polley wanted to take this horror to the American public to make us bear witness to what these women and girls suffered. In fact, Polley's adaptation of the story—itself based on a novelistic adaptation of the actual historical events written by Miriam Toews in 2018—deliberately alters setting details to make it appear that this Mennonite colony is located somewhere in the United States. She is bringing the horror home to roost.

In her film, we do not see the sexual assaults in real time—only in scattered, fragmentary flashbacks. The attackers have already been taken to the police, and the rest of the colony's men have left to post their bail. Suddenly, and for the first time *ever*, the women are alone and unsupervised in the colony, and they have two days to decide what to do before the men return. They conclude together that they can choose to leave the colony, but then be unsure of divine salvation when they die. They can choose to do nothing and hope the men will not continue their violence after they've made bail. Or, third, they can choose to stay and fight.

Leave. Do nothing. Stay and fight.

These women are illiterate, but they decide to take a vote—their first ever. They vote by making their tiny *x* on a large paper, under a picture of their choice. They can place their *x* under a drawing of fields, to mean "do nothing," or under a drawing of a man and a woman fighting, to mean "stay and fight," or they can make their *x* under a picture that means "leave." The vote is tied between "stay and fight" and "leave."

For the next day, a small group of these women have been deputized to decide the matter. They debate between the two remaining options. During their conversation, the women try to imagine what being free would look like, feel like. They have never been part of the world beyond the colony. If they stay, what they may be fighting for is an equal role in decision-making in the colony; none of them know if this will work or what it would look like. If they leave, they must face a vast and mysterious world about which they know *nothing*: They have never seen so much as a map of the world nor any part of it.

They ultimately decide to leave because they realize that staying is incompatible with their own pacifism. Either they will knowingly subject themselves and each other to further sexual violence or they will murder the men to prevent it. Neither is a spiritually acceptable outcome, so they choose to go.

The film is grueling and mostly very quiet. The colors are muted, generally pale and washed out, apart from the dark dresses of the women. The sound design is minimalist. Almost the entire film takes place in a barn, and it mostly consists of dialogue. The film reads much more as a staged theatrical play than as a big-budget Hollywood film.

The entire movie is an invitation to enter into grief, through domestic horror. There's the surface grief of these women and their daughters, who have been violated in a profoundly brutal fashion, again and again. That grief is red, angry, molten, and vengeful. But there is also the hard, quiet, grey grief—the grief of women throughout history who have been kept illiterate and silent, unable to write, unable to have a voice for themselves.

Women who have been denied any decision-making power. Who have not been allowed to vote. The film takes place in the early 2000s, like the events on which the film is based, but the women depicted have a level of autonomy and independence comparable to the most repressed women in history. It's hard to stomach—this is a film about women *in contemporary times* who are totally debarred from power, from knowledge, and from reading and writing. Women who know that there's another world out there, somewhere beyond their "colony," but also know that they do not have access to it. Women who, when given for the first time the right to some kind of self-determination, barely know how to wield it.

The grief of *Women Talking* is conjoined with its horror, although again, I haven't read any reviews of the movie that classify it as horror. And maybe for good reason: It's not a slasher film, nor a psychopathy thriller, nor is it supernatural. Even so, by my lights it's a hard-core feminist horror film, a domestic horror in which the main action—the conversation among the women—takes place *after* the horror of sexual violence has been interrupted. Even in the flashbacks, we are watching the horror hangover of an entrenched, atavistic, predatory patriarchal scheme in which women were systematically dehumanized, made to satisfy—entirely unwillingly—the violent lusts of their menfolk in their domestic spaces. We are watching them try to come to terms with what has happened to them and to their daughters in their own homes, again and again. It is agonizing; it is watching not just one woman who is made a prisoner and victim of sexual violence in her own home but an entire community of women, over the course of a long period of time. It is a collective domestic horror and one of extraordinary magnitude. In some ways, the horror is made worse by the fact that the men were *not* trying to enact some kind of diabolical scheme. They were simply drugging and raping women because they wanted to. And, of course, because they were off the grid enough to be beyond detection and prosecution. At least, for a time.

It was surprising to me that, despite my well-established tear duct condition—which kept me in tissues for the entire researching of *Scream with Me*—there was only one scene in *Women Talking* that actually brought me to tears. But what tears they were. They came on like a torrent—I didn't feel them coming at all. Just a sudden lachrymal tsunami.

In this scene, the women are taking a break from their deliberations, and they hear a truck drive by the colony. It's the 2010 census truck, we learn. The census taker calls through a loudspeaker as he drives by to say that anyone who lives in the houses should come out to be counted. No one goes, except for two teenage girls. They run out, and they are counted. They are numbered in the annals of public life. They choose to become part of the historical record. Part of time. Part of a history shared with a larger world.

Count me, I want to be counted. How many women in history have had this thought, versus how many women have been able to make it happen? *I want to stand up and be counted. Include me in history.*

Watching those girls run clumsily toward the truck in their antiquated calico frocks and ask to be counted? That broke me.

They have grown up into a life in which they have had no possibility of playing a role in history. They were trained never to stand up and ask to be counted. But now, they will; they do; they did. However small that mark of legibility on that one census, they will have been counted. Not even their names but just the simple fact that they exist. They will have been numbered as part of something larger than the confines of the colony.

When I recovered from my tears, I started to think about the future anterior tense of verbs: *will have been*. That tense is so important to the history of feminism. *It will have been worth it. I will have survived. I will have learned something. I will have been heard. I will have been counted.* Because it envisions a future in which the present has become not just a past, but a *meaningful* past. It's a tense of auguring, a tense of divination. You are predicting the future in a way that shapes the present into a form you can use and think about. *All this pain will have been for something. I will have been counted.* That means that even if I die the next second, I will have been woven into history.

But there's a problem with the future anterior, even as there's a consolation in it.

One character in the film says, making an analogy between the women's situation and the way she felt when she was driving her two-horse carriage on a bumpy road: "It was only when I learned to focus my gaze far down ahead of me—and not on the road immediately in front of Ruth and Cheryl—that I started to feel safe." Put otherwise, she felt safe when she learned to drive her horse-drawn carriage in the future anterior. She looked up ahead, and she imagined the bumpy part of the road she was currently on as the past. Look far down the road, and you will feel safe. Look to the future for consolation.

The problem with the future anterior is that, as you cast your eyes forward on the future, you are still in the Bad Place *now*, and that the future is never guaranteed. You are quietly committing to the present as something ineluctable and unchangeable in your mental reach toward the future. You are staying stuck even while telling yourself you will get out.

The horror of *Women Talking* is the knowledge that these women—who have a choice, at last—are standing on the shoulders of generations of other, prior women. Those women *will not have been counted*. They will *never* have been counted. They were raped, hurt, silenced, muted, not taught to read, not shown a map, not allowed to scream. They were excluded from the book of the living, and they are excluded from the book of the dead. They will be forever silent. We will know nothing of them. Ever.

The meeting among the women in *Women Talking* is recorded by the one adult male they allow in their presence—a young man who left their colony long ago but returned with a college education to teach the boys. He takes the minutes of the women's meeting by hand. It's kind of a background dynamic in the film; you don't focus centrally on it. But the women say, early on, that he needs to write large enough for others to read it in the future. The women *all know* that what they are doing—their central and ultimate act of resistance and reclamation—is writing themselves into history. They are putting their names onto paper, their stories, their deliberations, their thoughts. He will take their words, their subjectivities, their views, their thoughts and make them stay still, make them be part of the world of the written word, part of history. They are transforming their horror into *an archive*.

Thinking about contemporary American political culture, doing nothing appears to me to be a non-option at this point. And I am not going to leave our "colony," for three reasons. One, I love the colony. Two, I love too many people in the colony. Three, I am a pacifist, but I'm not opposed to fighting with words. So I am going to stay and fight, and I'm going to do it by writing. And, when I need to, by screaming. I hope you will, too.

So I am going to end this book on domestic horror with a plea. Please write. Write journals. Write nonfiction books. Write histories. Write op-eds. Write biographies. Write blogs. Write books. Write letters to your children. Write letters to your abusers. Write letters to your congresspeople. Write essays. Write memoirs. And above all else, write screenplays. And then go direct them. Help us all to find our voices and help us use them to scream.

APPENDIX A

Brief Synopses of the Terrible Remakes of the Original Six Horror Films

These six outstanding films created domestic horror to meditate on the impossible domestic situations facing women—particularly women in their reproductive years—in the late 1960s and 1970s. Even now, they urge viewers to think seriously and carefully about what's at stake in women's having or being denied reproductive agency, the freedom to move, the freedom to make their own choices. As they prompt us to think seriously and carefully about the specter of male control over domestic space, through violence and reproductive restriction, these six works of domestic horror urge us toward a vertiginous realization. That realization, time and again, is that domestic abuse and the regulation of women's bodies and rights *is horror*. Sure, these films are ostensibly "about" witchcraft, Satanism, possession, aliens, and the Antichrist, but the point of origin of the horror, in all of them, is the abuse and dehumanization of women. Without the domestically facilitated control and domination of women's minds and bodies in these films, there would be no Satanic rape, no possession, no systematic murder of wives, no physical battery, no endangerment of children, no ghosts, no Antichrist.

Disappointingly, however, with the exception of *Aliens*, the remakes of all six of these films between 1980 and 2010 lose focus on the domestic horror elements of the originals. The extraordinarily terrible film *Look What's Happened to Rosemary's Baby* (1976) doesn't have one scintilla of the domestic horror of the original film, nor does it contend in a real, sustained way with the dynamics of sexual abuse that animate its infinitely superior forebear. Instead, we meet an adult Adrian—the son of Rosemary—who's become a kind of feckless rock star and playboy, prior to realizing that he's the Antichrist. Once his fate becomes clear to him, he's rather unwilling to follow through with it, so he fights back. But a conspiracy surrounds him, through which he impregnates a woman named Ellen with his son, the presumed new Antichrist. Nothing about the film is subtle, redeeming, or even particularly frightening.

The Exorcist franchise doesn't fare much better, veering hard from an examination of domestic violence to a bizarre exploration of colonialism in the Near East and Africa. *Exorcist II* has nothing to do with domestic violence, instead focusing on Sumerian demonology and the power of Catholic Christianity to set the world aright. *The Exorcist III* fuses a Sumerian demon with a serial killer to produce the weirdest horror move I've ever seen. *Exorcist: The Beginning* is the franchise's fourth film, released in

2004. The film is set in Africa, in a white-run colonial outfit that is oppressing a local African tribe. What there isn't in the film, at all, is domestic horror. No one is imprisoned in their own home by a male malefactor. There's no serious engagement with reproductive horror, domestic violence, or the categorical dehumanization of women.

Similarly, the 2004 remake of *The Stepford Wives*, starring Nicole Kidman and Matthew Broderick as the Eberhart couple, drains the domestic horror out of the original ending of both the novel and film. In fact, I wouldn't call the *Stepford* reboot horror at all. It isn't scary, nor does it elicit compassion, and it certainly doesn't leave us with a horror hangover. In fact, in this ultra-anodyne remake, Broderick's character, Walter, ultimately can't do it—he can't consign his wife to becoming a robot—so he and Joanna team up to fight against the bad guys who are dehumanizing women in the film. So, rather than being a tragedy-adjacent work of domestic horror, this film is really a dark comedy—in that it ends with an upbeat, even goofy, happy ending, in which the husband is redeemed and the wife unharmed.

In keeping with the feminist stagnation of the other sequels, the sequels to *The Omen* entirely omit the original film's blistering focus on the dangers of benign patriarchalism. *Damien: Omen II* (1978) centers on Damien, now an orphan raised by his uncle, who attends a military academy for boys with aspirations of serious careers in the military or the government. Initially, Damien doesn't realize he's the Antichrist, but he comes to accept it pretty quickly and grows almost instantaneously to relish the role carved out for him by the malign forces of darkness. He comes to understand that his sole goal in life is to bring about the reign of the Antichrist on earth and to oppose Christianity at all turns. Through the Satanic power that surrounds and suffuses him, Damien is able to bring about the deaths of anyone who might oppose him, as we see in a scene in which his opponent falls through ice on a lake and drowns. Over the course of the film, it becomes clearer and clearer that there are supporters of Damien all around him, including his uncle's wife, and that he will come to his ascendancy and power without much opposition. He appears to be poised to take over the US government, in part by taking over the massive corporation that his family is the head of. So, what had been an allegory about the dangers to women of ostensibly benign patriarchy has become a not even thinly veiled allegory about the decay of American politics in the 1970s. *Damien: Omen II* presents a vision of an actively anti-Christian and anti-moral American political and corporate landscape and a vision of the possibility that the reins of America's political chariot will fall into the hands of someone so undesirable that the very soul of the nation will be imperiled. It's still a highly political horror film, but it's not about domestic horror anymore so much as national horror. The film was released in 1978, when Carter was president, but you can feel the specter of Watergate looming in the background. You can also feel the general stagnation of the US economy that persisted throughout the 1970s; the '70s era panic about the possibility of nuclear holocaust; the general unsafety that Americans experienced in the 1970s. But you don't feel it as a problem especially targeted at women. In the sequel, that's been drained away.

In *Omen III: The Final Conflict* (1981), Sam Neill plays an adult Damien, the leader of one of the most powerful corporations in the world, Thorn Enterprises. He's close with the US president; he visits him regularly in the Oval Office to give counsel. He's made ambassador to the United Kingdom—just like Papa Thorn had been years before. Everything is looking bright and sparkly for the advent of the era of Satan, except that Damien is aware that the second coming of Christ—whom he refers to throughout as "the Nazarene"—will soon be born somewhere in England. But no fear, Satanists: Damien's new gig as ambassador to the UK puts him in a good position to execute the Nazarene before he can reassert his beneficent divine power over the world. But in the end, it's hard to call this film horror at all. If we accept one of my own main criteria for horror as a requisite for the genre—the horror hangover—this film fails to qualify. Because in the end, Damien gets defeated by the Nazarene. The film ends with uplifting Christian music and bold Christian rhetoric about the restoration of the realm of God to earth.

However pronounced they were in *Alien* and *Aliens*, the dynamics of domestic horror—and in particular of reproductive violence—got significantly dampened in *Alien 3* (1992). In this installment of the franchise, Ripley is the sole survivor of a crash on a prison planet—when the escape pod hit the surface, her adoptive daughter, Newt, and her love interest, Hicks, from the second film were killed. She is the only woman the inmates have seen in years; the threat of rape hovers around her, but there's no sense that her reproductive agency is ultimately what's at stake. All that made the first two films in the franchise compelling from a feminist standpoint is lost. The aliens even change physical form, becoming quadrupedal rather than bipedal; Ripley notes that "They move differently" than they did before. These aliens are not monstrous allegories for a world in which there is no reproductive self-determination. In fact, they don't even appear to impregnate their prey in this film; they simply kill on sight. They're not interstellar rapists; they're just regular sci-fi alien monsters. And the film, correlatively, is not a domestic horror.

In *Alien: Resurrection* (1997), reproductive horror comes surging back, but in a decisively campy way. A clone of Ellen Ripley is brought to life two hundred years after her death using harvested DNA. She is incubated and grown very rapidly to adulthood. She is called "number 8." Ripley 8 is "born" pregnant with a queen alien, which scientists harvest from her womb and grow to full size in a lab. In one scene, Ripley 8 stumbles across a large number of prior Ripleys, many suspended in embryo jars. Ripley destroys all her sister-clones in a blazing inferno. Eventually, Ripley's alien-hybrid baby is born and appears to have imprinted onto her. Alas, Ripley must destroy her offspring to save humanity. So, definitely some attention to reproduction in this film, but it owes a *lot* more to the very bizarre 1976 film *Embryo* for its thinking through of these dynamics than it does to the original *Alien* and its emphasis on rape, violence, and resistance.

In the newest and perhaps worst installment of the *Alien* franchise, *Alien: Romulus* (2024), we follow a group of ambitious teenagers who want to hijack a derelict spaceship in order to escape their horrible home world. When they discover a whole bunch of alien larvae—the "face huggers" from prior films—we realize what's going to happen. Navarro (Aileen Wu) is the first to get attacked. But when the alien hatches out of her, it comes out through her upper chest, not her abdomen. This change to the iconography of the original film matters, because it erases the iconographic meaning of Kane's death as death by *pregnancy and parturition*. When Navarro dies, we see broken ribs and cardiac tissue. It's no longer a pregnancy but a parasitic infection in her chest. Later, Kay (Isabela Merced), one of the other teens—this one pregnant already with a fully human baby—believes she is dying, so she injects herself with a non-Newtonian alien blood DNA extract serum. Her experiment accelerates fetal development violently, causing the fetus to be born as a half-human, half-alien hybrid. Kay quickly discovers that her breasts are leaking a mucus-like black fluid; the alien then suckles her *to death*. So this film, however clunkily, is returning to the idea of reproduction as something potentially lethal. But it abdicates the focus on rape that had been so central to *Alien* and *Aliens*.

Stephen King sequeled *The Shining* in the novel *Doctor Sleep* (2013). That book got made into a film six years later, directed by Mike Flanagan. *Doctor Sleep* is about how Danny Torrance, as an adult, has a psychic link with a young girl, Abra Stone, and how the two of them take down a ring of monstrous, witchy, soul-eaters. It's a fun movie, but it's about as far from domestic horror as it could possibly be. Danny plays an avuncular role for Abra, and they team up to fight bad guys. It *is* true that Danny

Torrance has grown up to be an alcoholic, just like dear old Jack. But he beats back his addiction, attending AA religiously for eight years and working the system. He is somewhat inwardly haunted by his father, and by all the spirits of the Overlook, but he learns a way to contain them all. All the things that make *The Shining* the extraordinary work of advocacy and awareness for women in domestic violence situations that it is are elided from the remake.

What made the original six domestic horrors great works of art and great works of social commentary simply melted away from their own sequels—with the exception of James Cameron's *Aliens*. The horrified empathy we feel for Rosemary, Chris, Joanna, Kathy, Ripley, and Wendy just isn't present in the later remakes. There isn't even the barest attempt to make us feel fear and empathy for twentysomething rock-and-roller Adrian; if anything, the film tries to make us jealous of him. Chris isn't even *in* most of the remakes of *The Exorcist*; when she is, she's not the focus. The early sequels of *The Omen* barely qualify as horror at all since they are told from the perspective of the villain, rather than the victim, and are scary primarily in a philosophical, rather than physiological, way. Danny Torrance gets his happy ending at last in *Doctor Sleep*, so no horror hangover there. And yes, we still are meant to identify with Ripley in the later *Alien* films, but they lean so far over toward the ridiculous that it's hard to feel much of anything in watching them, except maybe revulsion at the increasingly gruesome special effects. These sequels aren't trying to drag viewers kicking and screaming into the barely veiled lives of real American women who are raped, forced to carry dangerous pregnancies to term, physically battered, silenced, terrorized, broken, dehumanized, and killed. They aren't trying to make us feel unsafe in our own bodies, in our own homes. Maybe, as I suggested earlier, they didn't feel they needed to, since, in the 1980s and 1990s, American feminism was on the upswing. The domestic sphere didn't seem like it was in a state of emergency, as it had been in the 1970s. Nor as it appears to be again in the 2020s.

APPENDIX B

Further Reading for Victims and Survivors of Domestic and Reproductive Violence, and for Their Friends and Families

Lundy Bancroft, *Why Does He Do That? Inside the Minds of Angry and Controlling Men* (Berkley Books, 2003).

Jill Laurie Goodman and Dorchen A. Leidholdt, eds., *Lawyer's Manual on Domestic Violence: Representing the Victim* (Appellate Division, Supreme Court of the State of New York, 2006).

Cynthia Harrison, *On Account of Sex: The Politics of Women's Issues, 1945–1968* (University of California Press, 1988).

Jess Hill, *See What You Made Me Do: Power, Control, and Domestic Abuse* (Black Inc., 2019).

N. E. H. Hull and Peter Charles Hoffer, *Roe v. Wade: The*

Abortion Rights Controversy in American History (University Press of Kansas, 2001).

Jane J. Mansbridge, *Why We Lost the ERA* (University of Chicago Press, 1986).

Del Martin, *Battered Wives* (Volcano Press, 1976).

Sarah Polley, *Run Towards the Danger: Confrontations with a Body of Memory* (Penguin, 2022).

Leslie J. Reagan, *When Abortion Was a Crime: Women, Medicine, and Law in the United States, 1867–1973* (University of California Press, 1997).

Diana E. H. Russell, *Rape in Marriage* (Macmillan, 1982).

Susan Schechter, *Women and Male Violence: The Visions and Struggles of the Battered Women's Movement* (South End Press, 1982).

Rachel Louise Snyder, *No Visible Bruises: What We Don't Know About Domestic Violence Can Kill Us* (Bloomsbury, 2019).

Evan Stark, *Coercive Control: How Men Entrap Women in Personal Life* (Oxford University Press, 2007).

Suzanne K. Steinmetz and Murray A. Straus, eds., *Violence in the Family* (Harper & Row, 1974).

ACKNOWLEDGMENTS

This book would not exist without the support, counsel, perspective, and bravery of many friends, allies, activists, attorneys, clinicians, survivors, students, and colleagues. My gratitude goes first to my colleagues: Jeremy Dauber, whose idea to co-teach a history of horror class several years ago was the point of origin for this book; Brooke Holmes, Joy Connolly, and Julie Peters, my bold and brilliant writing compatriots, who read every word of the first draft of this book, and who held my hand and my thoughts as I leaned further and further out of my comfort zone; Sharon Marcus and Nicholas Dames, for encouraging me to publish earlier and shorter versions of a few pieces of this book in the Film section at publicbooks.org. Next, I'd like to thank my patient and stalwart de facto legal staff: Judy White for her razor-sharp insights about women in the eyes of the law, as well as for her advice about how to frame this project to have the greatest impact; Robert Michaels and Nicole Trivlis for helping me see things clearly, always; Dorchen Leidholdt, for her brilliance, perspicacity, and absolutely fearless devotion to the cause of women's safety and women's rights—you set the standard high, Dorchen, and I'm so grateful for it. Moving on to my agent and editors: huge thanks, of course, to Celeste Fine, John Maas, and Charlotte Sunderland at Park, Fine & Brower for always having my back and believing in me; I'm still counting my lucky stars that I get to work with you and your team. Profound thanks to Kate Napolitano at Atria, for seeing what this project was trying to do, and helping me get it to the finish line; it's an amazing privilege to work with an editor like you. Adoring and humble thanks as always to my incandescent students; I am perpetually in awe of you—your minds, your hearts, your vision of a better future for all of us. I bow in gratitude to my pack of beloved friends: Marie, Catherine, Sarah, Beth, Emily, Miriam, Erin, Mark, Ellen, Julia, Olivia, Meredith, Anna, Fauzia, and Sally, you have been my strength when I could barely stand, and I love you all. Thank you to my beautiful aunt Denise, for your love and support, for believing in me, and for our wonderful conversations over the years—I value your perspective more than I can say. Thanks to my parents, to whom I owe so much of myself. The other women who were most instrumental in my decision to make this book wish to remain anonymous, so I will acknowledge them this way: I hear you screaming, and I will never shut my ears on you. Finally, as always and most of all, I thank my children, who are the soul of my soul, the heart of my heart, and the fire of my mind. What I have learned from you two luminosities cannot be put into words, so I will just say this to you: It is all worth it when I hear the sound of your voices, fierce and bright, so keep speaking your truth to me and to everyone else around you.

NOTES

Introduction

2 *art takes on its fullest life once it interfaces with an audience*: For some of my other work on this idea, pertaining to ecological consciousness in the Middle Ages, see *Waste and the Wasters* (University of Chicago Press, 2023). For foundational work on the idea of how literary art in particular makes meaning, see Hans Robert Jauss, "Literary History as a Challenge to Literary Theory," trans. Timothy Bahti (University of Minnesota Press, 1982), 3–45.

3 *readers or viewers can witness—and to some extent experience—those dynamics*: On the experiential or participatory quality of art, see Eleanor Johnson, *Staging Contemplation* (University of Chicago Press, 2018), and Charles Altieri, *Reckoning with the Imagination* (Cornell University Press, 2015).

3 *we* feel *like we're right there with the horror protagonists*: Carol Clover notes this phenomenon, whereby viewers are induced by horror actively to empathize with protagonists, in her book *Men, Women, and Chainsaws* (Princeton University Press, 1992), specifying that, particularly in slasher films, the empathy of the audience is trained closely on the female protagonist—not on the usually male assailant.

4 *female monstrosity as something powerful and countercultural*: See Clover, *Men, Women, and Chainsaws*, and Barbara Creed, *The Monstrous-Feminine* (Routledge, 1993).

5 *a work of art should not be reduced to the intention of the person who made it*: See W. K. Wimsatt and M. C. Beardsley, "The Intentional Fallacy," *Sewanee Review* 54 (1946): 468–88. For a very different approach but the same general take on this issue, and one that directly speaks to some of the directors in *Scream with Me*, see Claire Dederer, *Monsters: A Fan's Dilemma* (Knopf, 2023).

7 *some say it's about the experience of the uncanny*: Julia Kristeva, *Powers of Horror: An Essay on Abjection* (1980), trans. Leon S. Roudiez, rereleased 2024 by Columbia University Press. For the idea of the uncanny, the most cited source text is Sigmund Freud, *The Uncanny* (Penguin, 2003).

7 *both are designed to trigger a physiological response in viewers*: Linda Williams, "Film Bodies: Gender, Genre, and Excess," *Film Quarterly* 44 (1991): 2–13.

7 *they can experience a catharsis at the end*: The locus classicus for this definition of tragedy is Aristotle's *Poetics*, book 6. For an easily accessible English translation, see https://www.amherst.edu/system/files/media/1812/The%252520Poetics%252520of%252520Aristotle%25252C%252520by%252520Aristotle.pdf.

8 *Tragedy is prosocial*: Kathy Eden, *Poetic and Legal Fiction in the Aristotelian Tradition* (Princeton University Press, 1986); see also Kathy Eden, "Aristotle's Poetics: A Defense of Tragic Fiction," in *A Companion to Tragedy*, ed. Rebecca Bushnell (Blackwell, 2009).

8 *share in the commonwealth we recognize as our humanity*: Katerina Bantinaki, "The Paradox of Horror: Fear as Positive Emotion," *Journal of Aesthetics and Art Criticism* 70 (2012): 383–92.

8 *there's usually an accompanying sense that the violence is done now*: One exception to this rule is Euripides's *The Bacchae*, which, I have argued elsewhere, is actually better understood as a horror play—perhaps the first in the Western tradition—than as a trag-

edy. See Eleanor Johnson, "Euripides' Bacchae and the Birth of Western Horror," eleanorshorrors.substack.com.

8 *we get what I call the* horror hangover: See Eleanor Johnson, "Beowulf: A Horror Show," publicbooks.org.

12 *climbing again, since 2022*: The *infant* mortality rate has gone up by approximately 7 percent—and the rate of severe congenital anomalies present at birth has gone up by 10 percent. See Parvati Singh and Maria Gallo, "National Trends in Infant Mortality in the US after *Dobbs*," *Journal of the American Medical Association, Pediatrics* 178, no. 12 (2024): 1,364–66.

For statistics about women, see Kavitha Surana, "Maternal Deaths Are Expected to Rise Under Abortion Bans, but the Increase May Be Hard to Measure," *ProPublica*, July 27, 2023, https://www.propublica.org/article/tracking-maternal-deaths-under-abortion-bans. For data on Texas, which has had abortion bans in place longer than other states, see Erika Edwards, Zinhle Essamuah, and Jason Kane, "A Dramatic Rise in Pregnant Women Dying in Texas After Abortion Ban," *NBC News*, September 21, 2024, https://www.nbcnews.com/health/womens-health/texas-abortion-ban-deaths-pregnant-women-sb8-analysis-rcna171631.

12 *have the force of law*: Annie Karni, "Can He Do That? Here's What Biden's Move on the Equal Rights Amendment Means," *New York Times*, January 17, 2025.

Chapter 1: This Is No Dream; This Is Really Happening: *Rosemary's Baby*

17 *eventually brought up on charges*: "7 Arrested in Raid on Abortion Mill," *New York Times*, April 4, 1951.

17 *he illegally performed on her at his office*: "Doctor Held in Homicide," *New York Times*, November 22, 1953.

17 *with abortion as the presumed cause of death*: "Woman's Death Studied—Victim Found in Bronx Home, Abortion Suspected," *New York Times*, April 5, 1954.

18 *they dismembered her and hid her body parts*: "Two Men Accused in Fatal Abortion," *New York Times*, January 13, 1956.

18 *obligations to provide abortion care to pregnant women*: Robert K. Plumb, "Law on Abortions Called Too Strict," *New York Times*, June 17, 1960.

19 *they would seek a legal abortion for her elsewhere*: "Mother, Rebuffed in Arizona, May Seek Abortion Elsewhere," *New York Times*, August 1, 1962.

19 *mental health justified an abortion*: "Sweden Accedes to Abortion Plea," *New York Times*, August 18, 1962.

19 *it was indeed severely deformed*: Megan Brenan, "Gallup Vault: Public Supported Therapeutic Abortion in 1962," news.gallup.com. See also "Mrs. Finkbine Undergoes Abortion in Sweden," *New York Times*, August 19, 1962.

19 *or any time a fetal deformity was suspected*: "Change Advised in Abortion," *New York Times*, December 14, 1964. It was noted in the coverage of this recommendation that therapeutic abortions were routinely performed in hospitals, but that they were illegal, and that, fearing legal consequences, women were turning in larger numbers to extra-hospital abortions, which were often dangerous or fatal.

19 *favored their passage*: "A New Abortion Law," *New York Times*, February 13, 1965.

19 *urgent need to decriminalize abortion*: Sandra Koch, "Re: Abortion," *New York Times*, May 9, 1965; and Diane Shaktman Tirado, "The Ladies Speak," *New York Times*, May 23, 1965.

20 *(also known to cause birth defects) was murder*: Koch, "Re: Abortion."

20 *medical attitudes toward the procedure*: Harold Schmeck, "Abortions Found Easier to Obtain," *New York Times*, June 22, 1965.

20 *due to illegally performed abortions*: "A Sensible Abortion Law," *New York Times*, December 8, 1965.

20 *to back abortion law reform*: "Psychiatrists Back Abortion Reform," *New York Times*, March 31, 1966.

20 *supported the liberalization of abortion laws*: Austin Wehrwein, "Abortion Reform Supported in Poll," *New York Times*, April 24, 1966.

20 *backed the liberalization of abortion law*: "Obstetricians Back New Abortion Law," *New York Times*, July 20, 1966.

20 *came out in support of therapeutic abortions*: "Lutherans Back Some Abortions," *New York Times*, October, 25, 1966.

20 *in favor of liberalizing abortion law*: "Women MDs Back Abortion," *New York Times*, November 6, 1966.

20 *in cases of rape or incest*: "New Abortion Law Urged by Doctors at Meeting Here," *New York Times*, December 6, 1966.

20 *in support of that position a week later*: Sidney E. Zion, "State Council of Churches to Seek Abortion Law Liberalization," *New York Times*, December 13, 1966.

21 *by a vote of 15–3*: Sydney H. Schanberg, "Abortion Change Killed in Albany by a Vote of 15–3," *New York Times*, March 8, 1967.

21 *with the horror* inside *the heroine!*: Ira Levin, "Stuck with Satan," Criterion Collection, https://www.criterion.com/current/posts/2541–stuck-with-satan-ira-levin-on-the-origins-of-rosemary-s-baby.

22 *eighty-five-year-old abortion statute*: Sydney H. Schanberg, "Rockefeller Asks Abortion Reform," *New York Times*, January 10, 1968.

22 *potential effects of liberalizing New York's laws*: Sydney H. Schanberg, "Governor Orders Study of Abortion," *New York Times*, January 21, 1968.

22 *rejected the year before*: Sydney H. Schanberg, "Abortion Panel Expected to Ask Sweeping Change," *New York Times*, March 20, 1968.

22 *again failed in the New York State Senate in April*: John Kifner, "Abortion Reform Dies in Assembly," *New York Times*, April 4, 1968.

25 *had reason to in 1967*: Levin, "Stuck with Satan."

28 *a hallucinatory dream*: I should note that many early reviewers of the film thought Rosemary was delusional and had not in fact been Satanically raped. This reading, although very common in the 1960s, flagrantly violates the logic of the film, and reflects the entrenched inability of male reviewers in the 1960s to bear witness to the torture of domestic women.

31 *having such trouble liberalizing abortion law*: Karyn Valerius

discusses *Rosemary's Baby* in relation to abortion law as well, and notes that "Her pregnancy hyperbolically involves the circumstances in which the American Law Institute's model penal code provided for legal abortion: Not only was she raped, but pregnancy compromises her physical health, while the third circumstance—potential birth defects—is established through anachronism" (Karyn Valerius, "Rosemary's Baby: Gothic Pregnancy and Fetal Subjects," *College English* 32 (2005): 116–35). Valerius goes on to note parallels between Rosemary's pregnancy and that of Sherri Finkbine, the Arizona woman who sought and was denied a legal abortion in the US (126).

37 *25 million tickets to the film were sold*: Grant Suneson, "From Pocket Change to Nearly $10: The Cost of a Movie Ticket the Year You Were Born," *USA Today*, August 29, 2019, https://www.usatoday.com/picture-gallery/money/2019/08/29/cost-of-a-movie-ticket-the-year-you-were-born/39998369/; and "Rosemary's Baby (1968)," The Numbers, https://the-numbers.com/movie/Rosemarys-Baby#tab=summary.

37 *"slouch toward East 72nd Street to be born"*: Renata Adler, "'Rosemary's Baby,' a Story of Fantasy and Horror," *New York Times*, June 13, 1968.

38 *"a wicked argument against planned parenthood"*: "New Movies: *Rosemary's Baby*," *Time*, June 21, 1968.

39 *were not loose enough*: "Abortion Experts, Saying Women Should Decide on Birth, Ask End to Curbs," *New York Times*, November 24, 1968.

40 *left entirely to a woman and her doctor*: "Need for Abortion Reform," *New York Times*, November 18, 1968; and Ruth Proskauer Smith, "Abortion Law Repeal," *New York Times*, November 30, 1968.

40 *were denied them*: Keith Monroe, "How California's Abortion Law Isn't Working," *New York Times*, December 29, 1968.

40 repealing *New York's abortion laws*: "Presbytery Encourages Abortion Repeal," *New York Times*, February 12, 1969.

40 *demanding abortion law repeal*: Edith Evans Asbury, "Women Break Up Abortion Hearing," *New York Times*, February 14, 1969.

40 *basis of individual conscience, not by law*: Untitled, *New York Times*, February 21, 1969. Although New York State was at or near the forefront of this sentiment, it wasn't alone: New Hampshire and New Mexico were pursuing abortion reform, and Maryland had liberalized its laws in 1968, with the result that the state had a flood of out-of-state women seeking help. See "Three Baltimore Hospitals Curb Abortions," *New York Times*, March 2, 1969.

41 *decided according to "individual conscience"*: "Gains for Abortion Reform," *New York Times*, March 8, 1969.

41 *a relatively new move in the fight against abortion law*: David Bird, "Women and Doctors Sue to Upset Abortion Laws," *New York Times*, October 8, 1969.

41 *heard by a Federal Supreme Court panel*: "Changing the Abortion Law," *New York Times*, November 10, 1969.

41 *eventually be recognized by the Supreme Court*: Fred P. Graham, "Abortions: Moves to Abolish All Legal Restraints," *New York Times*, November 16, 1969.

41 *abortion laws as unconstitutional*: Linda J. Greenhouse, "Constitutional Question: Is There a Right to an Abortion?" *New York Times*, January 25, 1970.

42 *moved to ease abortion restrictions*: "Washington Senate Votes for Abortion," *New York Times*, January 31, 1970.

42 *antiabortion laws were unconstitutional*: "California Ruling Stands," *New York Times*, February 25, 1970.

42 *abortions performed by licensed doctors*: "Liberalized Abortion Law Voted by Arizona House," *New York Times*, February 27, 1970.

42 *public attitudes toward abortion*: "Legalizing Abortion," *New York Times*, March 3, 1970.

42 *exclusively by a woman and her doctor*: Bill Kovach, "Abortion Reform Approved, 31–26 by State Senate," *New York Times*, March 19, 1970.

42 *without interference from the law or the police*: Bill Kovach, "Abortion Reform Is Voted by the Assembly," *New York Times*, April 10, 1970; and Bill Kovach, "Final Approval of Abortion

Bill Voted in Albany," *New York Times*, April 11, 1970. Inspired by the successes in Hawai'i and New York, state abortion laws started to fall like dominoes: Alaska and Washington state were next; abortion was relatively easy to obtain in California, Colorado, and Washington, DC; and many other states were trying at least to reform extant abortion laws.

44 *perpetual fear, dehumanization, and entrapment*: See Evan Stark, *Coercive Control: How Men Entrap Women in Personal Life* (Oxford University Press, 2009).

46 *with no way out*: Kathleen Carroll, *Daily News*, June 13, 1968. Later feminist critics of the film have seen that fears of maternity and Rosemary's lack of agency during her pregnancy are central to the film. See Rhona Berenstein, "Mommie Dearest," *Journal of Popular Culture* 24, no. 2 (1990): 59.

Chapter 2: There's a Demon in My House: Domestic Violence in *The Exorcist*

51 *it disadvantaged their children*: Jane Mansbridge, *Why We Lost the ERA* (University of Chicago Press, 1986), 20–28. This book offers by far the most thorough and important treatment of the ERA's fate; I strongly recommend it to anyone who wants to understand where women's rights stand now.

54 *wasn't given an X rating*: Pauline Kael, "The Exorcist," *New Yorker*, January 7, 1974. "If *The Exorcist* had cost under a million, or had been made abroad, it would almost certainly be an X film, but when a movie is as expensive as this one, the M.P.A.A. rating board doesn't dare to give it an X."

56 *a child says the word "fuck" onscreen*: The first American film that used the word "fuck"—*M*A*S*H*—was released a couple of years earlier. See Paul Byrnes, "Well, I Swear: A Brief F---ing History of Profanity in the Movies," *Sydney Morning Herald*, September 7, 2014, https://www.smh.com.au/entertainment/movies/well-i-swear-a-brief-fing-history-of-profanity-in-the-movies-20140901-10axdu.html.

58 *"That it received an R rating and not the X is stupefying"*: Roger

Ebert, "The Exorcist," *Chicago Sun-Times*, December 26, 1973, https://www.rogerebert.com/reviews/the-exorcist-1973.

60 *"she performs every thing"*: William Blackstone, *Commentaries on the Laws of England*, vol. 1 (Clarendon Press, 1970), 442.

61 *up to 1969*: *New Women's Times* 3 (1977): 1. A 1978 article in the *American Journal of Nursing* notes that "battered wife" and "wife battery" were new terms, and that the problem of domestic violence was only just starting to be taken seriously or responded to appropriately by medical professionals (*American Journal of Nursing* 78 [1978]: 650, 651). See Richard Gelles, "Violence in the Family," *Journal of Marriage and the Family* 42 (1980): 873–85. Gelles notes that "the prevailing attitude in the sixties was that family violence was rare, and when it did occur, was the product of mental illness or psychological disorder" (876).

61 *"nervous" and needed medication*: Del Martin, *Battered Wives* (Volcano Press, 1976), 2–3.

62 *among better-educated respondents*: Ibid., 19.

62 *approved of a husband slapping a wife*: Ibid., 19–20.

63 *so few of them were reported*: Nearly half of all major crimes except murder committed against women in Chicago in 1965–66 were committed in their own homes (Martin, *Battered Wives*, 11). In 1971, one-third of women murdered in the state of California were murdered by their husbands. Again, very few successful prosecutions emerged.

63 *whatever act of violence he did to his wife*: Reflecting the deep-set American beliefs about the fundamentally compromised legal personhood of a wife—her lack of rights to her own sexual and physical safety—the procedures a woman had to follow to get any kind of redress for domestic violence were forbidding. Although it was true in most states by 1975 that a woman could bring a criminal case against a husband who beat her, the mechanisms and procedures required to do so were so taxing that most abuse cases never saw criminal prosecution. See Martin, *Battered Wives*, 32–33.

63 *"sufficient" pattern of physical battery*: Martin, *Battered Wives*, 166–67.

64 *what intimate partner violence really was*: Larissa MacFarquhar, "The Radical Transformations of a Battered Women's Shelter," *New Yorker*, August 12, 2019, https://www.newyorker.com/magazine/2019/08/19/the-radical-transformations-of-a-battered-womens-shelter.

64 *outgrowth of normal male aggression*: Suzanne Steinmetz and Murray Straus, eds., *Violence in the Family* (Harper & Row, 1974), 7, 10.

65 *did not have a place to seek shelter*: Martin, *Battered Wives*, 2, 3, 83, 119.

68 *for an extended period of time*: Ibid.

73 *"same direction as Roman Polanski's* Rosemary's Baby*"*: Ebert, "The Exorcist."

74 *had a miscarriage, he said*: Judy Klemesrud, "They Wait Hours to Be Shocked," *New York Times*, January 27, 1974.

74 *fainting or vomiting*: Edward B. Fiske, "*Exorcist* Adds Problems for Catholic Clergymen," *New York Times*, January 28, 1974.

74 *in the wake of seeing the film*: Ibid.

75 *opened in California*: See Kathleen Tierney, "The Battered Women Movement and the Creation of the Wife Beating Problem," *Social Problems* 29 (1982): 207.

76 *situations of severe domestic battery*: A 1976 survey says that "at least 1.8 million American women are severely beaten in their own homes every year." Murray A. Straus et al., *Behind Closed Doors: Violence in the American Family* (Doubleday, 1980), 40.

76 *zero articles about the problem*: Tierney, "The Battered Women Movement," 212.

Chapter 3: Trad Wives Forever: *The Stepford Wives* and the Equal Rights Amendment

79 *men won't let them go*: Ira Levin, *The Stepford Wives* (Random House, 1972), unnumbered page. The full quotation from *The Second Sex* reads, "Today the combat takes a different shape: instead of wishing to put man in a prison, woman endeavors to escape from one; she no longer seeks to drag him into the realms of

immanence, but to emerge, herself, into the light of transcendence. Now the attitude of the males creates a new conflict: it is with a bad grace that the man lets her go."

80 *"And so is my husband"*: Levin, *The Stepford Wives*, 2.

80 *change the archaic organization "from inside"*: Ibid., 5–6.

81 *Bobbie Markowe*: Ibid., 9.

81 *"This is Zombieville!"*: Ibid., 57.

96 *likely have been minimal*: Jane Mansbridge, *Why We Lost the ERA* (University of Chicago Press, 1986), 2, 36.

96 *wait until 1972*: "Rights Amendment Faces Delay in Busy Senate Till '72 Session," *New York Times,* October 14, 1971.

97 *both to women's and men's gender roles*: Mansbridge, *Why We Lost the ERA*, 69.

97 *housework as an occupation they enjoyed*: Ibid., 105–7.

98 *implicitly to devalue domestic labor*: Ibid., 107.

98 *and passing the ERA*: Bella Abzug, "Power to the Majority—Women," *New York Times*, August 26, 1971.

98 *preferential treatment in family law*: "Yale Lawyers Urge an End to Sex Bias," *New York Times*, September 26, 1971.

99 *traditional roles in a family structure*: Jonathan H., "Letters to the Editor," *New York Times*, October 24, 1971.

99 *a lifestyle bill*: Throughout winter 1972, the *Times* ran articles about the Equal Employment Opportunity Commission, about presidential candidates for the coming 1972 election, and about women's attitudes toward those candidates with respect to their attitudes on the ERA. The message, during this period, was mixed: powerful Democratic candidates like Senator George McGovern were boosted by feminists like Gloria Steinem, while other feminist organizers worried that the women's liberation movement had not reached the women who needed its help most, and that the movement remained a "frightening" idea to many. See Christopher Lydon, "Gloria Steinem Aids McGovern's Cause," *New York Times*, February 12, 1972.

99 *voice his support for the ERA*: Eileen Shanahan, "Nixon Aid Sought on Equal Rights," *New York Times*, March 18, 1972.

99 *before the Senate vote was to take place*: Eileen Shanahan, "Sena-

tors Bar Weakening of Equal Rights Proposal," *New York Times*, March 22, 1972.

99 *84-to-8 vote was announced*: Eileen Shanahan, "Equal Rights Amendment Is Approved by Congress," *New York Times*, March 23, 1972.

99 *Hawai'i became the first to ratify*: Ibid.

99 *inclusion in the US Constitution*: "Amendment on Equal Rights Now Approved by Six States," *New York Times*, March 26, 1972.

99 *five more states had ratified the amendment*: Ibid.

100 *Kansas became the seventh on March 28*: "Kansas for Women's Rights," *New York Times*, March 29, 1972.

100 *require them to lift heavy objects*: "Oklahoma House Rejects Equal Rights Amendment," *New York Times*, March 30, 1972.

100 *"loved and protected by our men"*: "They're Housewives and Proud of It," *New York Times*, April 3, 1972.

100 *"every 90 days"*: *Ladies' Home Journal*, August 1975, 57.

100 *volatile roller-coaster ride*: *New York Times*, January 15, 1973; *New York Times*, January 25, 1973; *New York Times*, January 26, 1973; *New York Times*, February 2, 1973; *New York Times*, February 3, 1973; *New York Times*, March 3, 1973; and *New York Times*, April 10, 1975.

101 *Republican Women in 1967*: *Washington Post*, April 16, 1969.

101 *"before my six children were born"*: Judy Klemesrud, "Opponent of ERA Confident of Its Defeat," *New York Times*, December 15, 1975.

101 *jam to legislators*: Ibid.

102 *out of the screening room when she saw it*: Judy Klemesrud, "Feminists Recoil at Film Designed to Relate to Them," *New York Times*, February 26, 1975.

103 *a robot housekeeper*: Ibid.

103 *served them snacks and sex*: Judy Klemesrud, "A Controversial Film," *Press Democrat*, February 28, 1985.

103 *"and their living deaths"*: Roger Ebert, "The Stepford Wives," *Chicago Sun-Tribune*, January 1, 1975, https://www.rogerebert.com/reviews/the-stepford-wives-1975.

103 *"anti-men" and not "anti-women"*: Devan Coggan, "*The Stepford*

Wives: Inside the Making of the 1975 Feminist Horror Classic," *Entertainment Weekly*, October 23, 2017.

106 *as early as about 1980*: "In July 1980, only Oregon, Nebraska, and New Jersey had completely abolished the marital rape exception, and California, Delaware, Hawai'i, Minnesota, and Iowa had partially stricken it" (Diana Russell, *Rape in Marriage* (Indiana University Press, 1982), 21). New York State famously struck the marital exemption in the landmark case *People vs. Liberta* in 1984. In response to this case, the *New York Times* ran an article by David Margolick entitled "New York Joins 17 States that Deny Wives Are Property: Rape in Marriage Is No Longer Within the Law" (*New York Times*, December 23, 1984). When *Stepford* was released in theaters, there were still nine years between it and the criminalization of marital rape in the state of New York.

Chapter 4: Benign Patriarchy Turns Malignant: *The Omen*

110 *just two days after* Roe *was decided*: "Vatican's Radio Criticizes Abortion Ruling by Court," *New York Times*, January 24, 1973.

110 *would be excommunicated*: "Abortion to Mean Expulsion for Catholics in Cleveland," *New York Times*, February 26, 1973.

110 *involvement of* any *kind with abortion would be excommunicated*: "Cooke Warns Catholics on Abortions," *New York Times*, October 8, 1973.

110 *make abortion illegal*: "Abortion Foes to Seek Ban by Amending Constitution," *New York Times*, June 12, 1973.

110 *March for Life event on October 7, 1973*: "Abortion Ruling Protested," *New York Times*, October 9, 1973.

110 *to press their case*: Nancy Hicks, "Both Sides Press Abortion Views," *New York Times*, January 23, 1974.

110 *life of the mother was at grave risk*: Linda Charlton, "Forces Against Abortion Assemble, with Optimism," *New York Times*, June 2, 1974. The opposition to the pro-life movement sometimes appeared alongside them, either at the Capitol or at rallies, carrying counterimages: women dead from botched abortions or from self-induced ones.

111 *if a woman was under 18*: Missouri, for instance, in 1976. See N. E. H. Hull and Peter Charles Hoffer, *Roe v. Wade: The Abortion Rights Controversy in American History*, 3rd ed. (University Press of Kansas, 2021), 195.

111 *made at the state level*: James M. Naughton, "Ford Says Court 'Went Too Far' on Abortion in '73," *New York Times*, February 4, 1976.

112 *the kind of man who might beat a woman*: Karen Durbin, "Wife Beating," *Ladies' Home Journal*, June 1974.

122 *consent before terminating a pregnancy*: Many states had passed legislation soon after *Roe* that mandated a woman get her husband's consent before securing an abortion. The landmark case that contested this mandate came in 1976—the same year *The Omen* was released. See H. W. Smith et al., "The Politics of Abortion: Husband Notification, Self-Disclosure, Marital Bargaining," *Sociological Quarterly* 31 (1990): 585–98. The seminal case on husband notification came in *Planned Parenthood of Missouri vs. Danforth* 428 US 52, in 1976, which overturned a then-current Missouri law requiring women to gain spousal consent for abortions.

132 *far less bewitching one at that*: Roger Ebert, "The Omen," *Chicago Sun-Times*, June 28, 1976, https://www.rogerebert.com/reviews/the-omen-1976.

132 *like its predecessors*: Richard Eder, "The Screen: 'Omen' Is Nobody's Baby," *New York Times*, June 26, 1976, https://www.nytimes.com/1976/06/26/archives/the-screen-omen-is-nobodys-baby.html.

133 *"realization-of-dawning-horror" scenes*: Ebert, "The Omen."

Chapter 5: Reproductive Violence in Outer Space: *Alien*

136 *they have loved it ever since*: Indeed, this film has been sequeled at least four times—more if you count some of the *Alien*-adjacent films, like *Alien vs. Predator*. For a brief treatment of the main sequels, see appendix A.

136 *willpower, resourcefulness, and bravery*: James Kavanagh, "'Son of

a Bitch': Feminism, Humanism, and Science in *Alien*," *October* 13 (Summer 1980): 90–100; and Barbara Creed, *The Monstrous-Feminine: Film, Feminism, Psychoanalysis* (Routledge, 1993), 16–30. The sequel, *Aliens*, is also generally accepted as a feminism horror or sci-fi film; see, for example, Lynda Buntzen, "Medusa, Grendel, and Now *Alien*," *Film Quarterly* (1987): 11–17.

137 *thought it should be illegal*: "Gallup Poll Finds Little Change in Views on Abortion," *New York Times*, April 22, 1979.

138 *chanting "Life, life, life!"*: "Abortion Foes March on Capital on Anniversary of Legislation," *New York Times*, January 23, 1979.

138 *set the clinic on fire*: Robert D. McFadden, "Abortion Clinic Set Afire on L.I.," *New York Times*, February 16, 1979.

138 *known to be antiabortion*: "Carter Health Program Seeks to Hire Abortion Foe," *New York Times*, February 8, 1979.

138 *public funds to support abortion*: "Abortion Snag Expected in State-Budget Passage," *New York Times*, April 2, 1979.

138 *sought to terminate pregnancies*: "Abortion and the 99 Percent," *New York Times*, March 12, 1979; see also Karen De Witt, "Foes of Abortion Seek to Tighten Restrictions on Medicaid Funds," *New York Times*, March 1, 1979.

139 *"gigantic, cavernous, malevolent womb"*: Creed, *The Monstrous-Feminine*, 19.

142 *"a penis with teeth"*: Veronica Cartwright, *Memory: The Origins of Alien* (2019).

142 *"a kind of science-fiction* phallus dentatus*"*: Kavanagh, "'Son of a Bitch.'"

142 *the Freudian* vagina dentata: Creed, *The Monstrous-Feminine*, 23.

143 *no head and no eyes*: Think of Jordan Peele's alien in *Nope*. Nothing anthropomorphic about that alien.

144 *toward the end of the film*: Indeed, Carol Clover, the author of the feminist masterpiece of horror studies *Men, Women, and Chainsaws*, notes that men have no trouble identifying with Ripley. See also Carol Clover, "Her Body, Himself: Gender in the Slasher Film," *Representations* (1987): 187–228.

144 *and could be lethal*: Some of the finest extant criticism on this film focuses precisely on the gender dynamics at work. Barbara Creed

sees the alien mother (whom, again, we don't see in this film, but her presence is implied as the thing that laid all the eggs Kane sees) as a rendering of the archetypal psychoanalytic "ancient mother" who threatens to destroy us by eradicating the symbolic order. She has to be cast out by society in order to make it function: She is a powerful, brutal, nonhuman female force that violates Kane "in an act of phallic penetration" (Creed, *The Monstrous-Feminine*, 19). She goes on to note that there is a strange kind of sex reversal at work: "From this union, the monstrous creature is born. But man, not woman, is the 'mother' and Kane dies in agony as the alien gnaws its way through his stomach."

150 *"be open to women"*: Lesley Oelsner, "What Rights Amendment Could and Couldn't Do," *New York Times*, May 29, 1978.

150 *coming home in body bags*: Jane Mansbridge, *Why We Lost the ERA* (University of Chicago Press, 1986), 72.

150 *make women eligible for the draft*: "Rights Amendment Defeated in Nevada," *New York Times*, February 20, 1975.

151 *barred from most naval vessels*: Oelsner, "What Rights Amendment Could and Couldn't Do."

151 *warrior roles for women as "unthinkable"*: George Gilder, "The Case Against Women in Combat," *New York Times*, January 28, 1979.

153 Alien *wasn't "fun"*: Janet Maslin, "Critic's Notebook: What's Happened to Movies That You See for Fun?" *New York Times*, June 8, 1979.

154 *the "values" of* Alien *weren't very "enlightening"*: Derek Malcolm, "Alien," *The Guardian*, 1979, accessed at https://www.theguardian.com/film/2009/oct/13/derek-malcolm-alien-review.

156 *having women in the military*: Recent articles about the film have emphasized this element. See Dillon McCarty, "James Cameron's *Aliens*: A Classic Tale, Brimming with Female Empowerment and Social Resonance," *Medium*, September 6, 2019, retrievable at https://medium.com/incluvie/james-camerons-aliens-a-classic-tale-brimming-with-female-empowerment-and-social-resonance-5efd428094f5.

160 *serving long prison sentences*: See Leigh Goodmark, *Imperfect Victims: Criminalized Survivors and the Promise of Abolition Feminism* (University of California Press, 2023). She writes on page 9 about the ways in which women who fight back against abusers get punished while more passive, "victimized" women get the support of the law: "To benefit from legal system reforms, survivors of violence had to perform their victimization in very specific ways: they had to be perfect victims. The gendered rhetoric of criminalization created unrealistic stereotypes of people subjected to abuse. Blameless victims (usually meek, passive women) were pitted against monstrous perpetrators (usually men)." Put in the vocabulary of *Scream with Me*, the idea is that we pity the Rosemarys and Kathys when we see them in court, but we're inclined to condemn the Ellen Ripleys.

Chapter 6: *The Shining*: Only Just Fiction

166 *"large and insultingly toothy"*: Stephen King, *The Shining* (Doubleday, 1977), 7.

167 *regularly coming and going*: Alex Piquero et al., "Domestic Violence During the COVID-19 Pandemic," *Journal of Criminal Justice* 74 (2021): 1–10.

168 *the national criminalization of child abuse*: Stephen Pfohl, "The 'Discovery' of Child Abuse," *Social Problems* 24 (1977): 310–23.

175 *he brutally murdered them*: Hornbeck also notes this deployment of the logic of correction and, citing Pfohl's study on the "discovery" of child abuse, notes the commonness of that idea about the rights of parents to physically discipline their children. See Elizabeth Hornbeck, "Who's Afraid of the Big, Bad Wolf? Domestic Violence in *The Shining*," *Feminist Studies* 42 (2016): 689–719, at 702.

177 *being criminalized in some states*: See Cindy Lamothe, "How to Recognize Coercive Control," Healthline, October 10, 2019, https://www.healthline.com/health/coercive-control#restricting-autonomy. See also Vermont, Hawai'i, and Cali-

fornia state laws at https://vtlawhelp.org/node/2714/printable/print and https://www.californialawreview.org/print/coercive-control-legislation#_ftn26. For the current statutes in New York State, see https://www.nysenate.gov/legislation/bills/2023/A2707 and https://www.nysenate.gov/legislation/bills/2023/S6695.

178 *acting both on people and on things*: Hornbeck notes this as the second of two instances in which the hotel reveals its "supernatural intervention." The first is when the woman in 237 tried to strangle Danny; the second is this one. As Hornbeck notes, however, this is the more unambiguous instance, since we don't know with certainty that a ghost—and not Jack—tried to strangle Danny. See Hornbeck, "Who's Afraid of the Big, Bad Wolf?" 695.

181 *sociological literature characterized*: In scholar Elizabeth Hornbeck's view, credit for the film's representation of domestic violence lies with screenwriter Diane Johnson, who, as Hornbeck points out, already had a history of thematizing domestic violence in her other works. See Hornbeck, "Who's Afraid of the Big, Bad Wolf?" 690–91.

181 *the "final girl" of the film*: Hornbeck sees this dynamic as well; see Hornbeck, "Who's Afraid of the Big, Bad Wolf?" 710 and 713–14.

181 *to make Wendy the uncontested heroine*: See Hornbeck, "Who's Afraid of the Big, Bad Wolf?" n. 18, citing James Hala, "Kubrick's *The Shining*: The Specters and the Critics," in *The Shining Reader* (Starmont House, 1990), 215 n. 6.

184 *attempt to console her*: *The Making of "The Shining"* (1980), directed by Vivian Kubrick, Stanley Kubrick's teenage daughter. The relevant clip is viewable here: https://www.dailymotion.com/video/xkq12a.

185 *she seemed weak and defeated*: Even reviews that praised her in many ways found at least some fault with her appearance, as in *Cosmopolitan*, where Lawrence Eisenberg said, "Yes, yes, we know that she's skinny and gangly and that her teeth are on the longish side." Lawrence Eisenberg, "Shelley Duvall," *Cosmopolitan* 191 (1981), 64.

185 *"without harboring murderous thoughts"*: Jim Harwood, "Film Reviews: *The Shining*," *Variety*, May 28, 1980, 14.

185 *"a house full of expert actors"*: David Thomson, "Bits and Pieces," *Film Comment* 17 (1981), 13.

185 *"ludicrously helpless wife"*: Wendy Lesser, "Actors as Characters," *Threepenny Review* 5 (1981): 23.

185 *abuses her verbally and her son physically*: See Hornbeck, "Who's Afraid of the Big, Bad Wolf?" 706–9.

187 *"like I wasn't even there"*: Roger Ebert, "Isolated Madness," *Chicago Sun-Times*, June 18, 2006, https://www.rogerebert.com/reviews/great-movie-the-shining-1980.

187 *300,000 victims per year*: "Domestic Violence Timeline," Pennsylvania Child Welfare Resource Center, https://www.pacwrc.pitt.edu/Curriculum/310DomesticViolenceIssuesAnIntroductionforChildWelfareProfessionals/Handouts/HO3DomesticViolenceTimeline.pdf.

189 *those with whom he cohabits*: See Lundy Bancroft, *Why Does He Do That? Inside the Minds of Angry and Controlling Men* (Penguin, 2003), 49–76.

189 *"an alcoholic and child abuser"*: Ebert, "Isolated Madness."

190 *"domestic terror"*: Janet Maslin, "Flaws Don't Dim *The Shining*," *New York Times*, June 8, 1980, https://archive.nytimes.com/www.nytimes.com/library/film/060880kubrick-shining.html.

Chapter 7: Bad Men Making Good Films: An Interlude

192 *nationally by 1993*: The best overview on the path to criminalizing marital rape is Diana Russell, *Rape in Marriage* (Indiana University Press, 1982). For a compressed treatment, see Eleanor Johnson, "The Criminalization of Marital Rape: 40 Years after *The People vs. Liberta*," *Dame Magazine*, January 2025.

193 *very bad people make very good art*: For an extended and sensitive meditation on what it is to love a film made by a monstrous misogynist, see Claire Dederer, *Monsters: A Fan's Dilemma* (Knopf, 2023).

193 *"horrendous pain"*: See Burstyn's interview about this: https://www

.youtube.com/watch?v=0E1dV3YovZo. She said of Friedkin's choice, "I was so furious and said, 'Turn the effing camera off!' because I couldn't stand that he was willing to just get a quick shot of it before they called the ambulance." Later in the same interview, she went on, "It was way beyond what anyone needs to do to make a movie."

193 *causing enduring spinal damage*: Ed Power, "Why William Friedkin's 'The Exorcist' made Linda Blair's Head Spin," *Telegraph*, August 8, 2023, https://www.telegraph.co.uk/films/0/pushed-edge-exorcist-made-linda-blairs-head-spin/.

194 *"we don't torture women enough"*: Cited in Carol Clover, "Her Body, Himself: Gender in the Slasher Film," *Representations* (1987): 187–228.

194 *"puts us through one"*: Retrieved from rogerebert.com, originally published December 26, 1973.

195 *insecurity throughout the film*: See Elizabeth Hornbeck, "Who's Afraid of the Big, Bad Wolf? Domestic Violence in *The Shining*," *Feminist Studies* 42 (2016): 709, also citing Roger Luckhurst, *The Shining* (British Film Institute, 2013) and Geoffrey Cocks, *The Wolf at the Door: Stanley Kubrick, History, and the Holocaust* (Peter Lang, 2004).

195 *"Almost unbearable"*: Roger Ebert, "Isolated Madness," *Chicago Sun-Times*, June 18, 2006, https://www.rogerebert.com/reviews/great-movie-the-shining-1980.

207 *stuffing a jackknife into his boot*: Indeed, in the sequel, the main character, Sara, who is female, does exactly this.

210 *It works*: One reviewer of the film spent a great deal of time thinking through how easy it would be to overlook all the red flags about Joseph as Aaron is dragged toward his demise—but he doesn't think of it as Aaron being groomed but rather his wish to avoid being rude to Joseph. See "My Streaming Gem: Why You Should Watch *Creep*," *Guardian*, June 8, 2020.

215 *he is his own target:* Reviewers have given the film credit for its extremely metafilmic deployment of the found-footage genre (Andy Webster, "*Creep*: A Horror Film with the Look of Found Footage," *New York Times*, September 1, 2015). Interestingly, how-

ever, Patrick Brice in numerous interviews routinely points out that he felt that the film was also supposed to land as humorous—a reading I simply don't find anywhere in either film.

Chapter 8: Domestic Horror After *Dobbs*

229 *many more will die*: These deaths are already happening, and they are predicted to rise in frequency. A study from the University of Colorado predicts a 24 percent increase in maternal deaths with the abortion bans in various states, and a 39 percent increase for Black women. See Kavitha Surana, "Maternal Deaths Are Expected to Rise Under Abortion Bans, but the Increase May Be Hard to Measure," *ProPublica*, July 27, 2023, https://www.propublica.org/article/tracking-maternal-deaths-under-abortion-bans; and Nicole Mueksch, "Abortion Bans to Increase Maternal Mortality Even More, Study Shows," *CU Boulder Today*, June 30, 2022, https://www.colorado.edu/today/2022/06/30/abortion-bans-increase-maternal-mortality-even-more-study-shows.

229 *slow to pass*: To learn more about tech abuse, which is becoming more and more prevalent as a form of domestic violence in the United States, see Cornell University's wonderful resource page for the Clinic to End Tech Abuse: https://ceta.tech.cornell.edu/.

229 *endangers the lives of women*: As of June 2024, only seven states have passed legislation curbing and prohibiting coercive control, Massachusetts being the most recent. See Lisa Fontes, "Massachusetts Governor Maura Healey Signs Coercive Control Bill into Law," *Ms.*, June 20, 2024, https://msmagazine.com/2024/06/20/massachusetts-coercive-control/. For an overview of coercive control laws in the United States, see Brionna Crawford, *Coercive Control Codification Matrix*, Battered Women's Justice Project, https://bwjp.org/wp-content/uploads/2024/03/2024-CC-Statutory-Matrix-UPDATED-FINAL.pdf. New York State is in a slow process of attempting to classify coercive control as a class E felony: https://www.nysenate.gov/legislation/bills/2023/S6695.

230 *class E felony*: See https://www.nysenate.gov/legislation/bills/2023/A2707.

230 *ERA has still not passed*: Katherine Jackson, "US Equal Rights Amendment Blocked Again, a Century After Introduction," *Reuters*, April 27, 2023, https://www.reuters.com/legal/government/us-equal-rights-amendment-blocked-again-century-after-introduction-2023-04-27/. For an overview of ERA's fate in the twenty-first century, see "What Comes Next for the Equal Rights Amendment," *American Progress*, August 26, 2024, https://www.americanprogress.org/article/what-comes-next-for-the-equal-rights-amendment/.

243 *mortifying special effects*: When I show clips of it in my classroom, my students giggle, especially at the scene where Jennings gets decapitated.

253 *the horror of reproductive violence*: In locating reproductive violence squarely in the Catholic Church, the film is aligned with the historical realities of opposition to reproductive choice in the 1960s and 1970s: it was primarily the Catholic Church that opposed abortion reform in the US, even though, in the 2020s, most of the anti-choice fervor in the United States originates with Protestant evangelicals.

262 *extension of Ira Levin's novel*: As Natalie Erika James said to *The Hollywood Reporter*, she and her team tried to stay as close to Levin's novel as possible.

263 *I think yes and no*: James herself has said that the end is "quite dark" and "quite tragic," but that "she does take back control in the only parameters that she can." See Brian Davids, "'Apartment 7A' Director Natalie Erika James on the Challenges of Making a 'Rosemary's Baby' Prequel," *Hollywood Reporter*, September 28, 2024, https://www.hollywoodreporter.com/movies/movie-features/apartment-7a-director-rosemarys-baby-1236017080/.

265 *forced birth in the U.S.*: Keith Harris, "Woke Libs Rejoice! *Immaculate* Really *IS* about Abortion!" *Racket*, March 29, 2024, https://racketmn.com/woke-libs-rejoice-immaculate-really-is-about-abortion.

266 *"throws our world back at us"*: Bilge Ebiri, "Behold, an Actually

Good *Omen* Movie," *Vulture*, May 30, 2024, https://www.vulture.com/article/review-the-first-omen-is-actually-a-good-omen-movie.html.

266 *a woman's right to choose*: Casey Allen, "*Apartment 7A*: A Review," Utah Public Radio, October 17, 2024, https://www.upr.org/podcast/flix-at-48/2024-10-17/apartment-7a-movie-review-with-casey-t-allen.

INDEX

Index

G

H

O

P

ABOUT THE AUTHOR

Eleanor Johnson is a professor of English and comparative literature at Columbia University. She is the author of four nonfiction books: *Scream with Me*, *Practicing Literary Theory in the Middle Ages*, *Staging Contemplation*, and the award-winning *Waste and the Wasters*, as well as two collections of poetry, *The Dwell* and *Her Many Feathered Bones*.

Atria Books, an imprint of Simon & Schuster, fosters an open environment where ideas flourish, bestselling authors soar to new heights, and tomorrow's finest voices are discovered and nurtured. Since its launch in 2002, Atria has published hundreds of bestsellers and extraordinary books, which would not have been possible without the invaluable support and expertise of its team and publishing partners. Thank you to the Atria Books colleagues who collaborated on *Scream with Me*, as well as to the hundreds of professionals in the Simon & Schuster advertising, audio, communications, design, ebook, finance, human resources, legal, marketing, operations, production, sales, supply chain, subsidiary rights, and warehouse departments who help Atria bring great books to light.

Editorial
Kate Napolitano
Hannah Frankel

Jacket Design
Claire Sullivan

Marketing
Erin Kibby
Morgan Pager

Managing Editorial
Paige Lytle
Shelby Pumphrey
Lacee Burr
Sofia Echeverry

Production
Benjamin Holmes
Vanessa Silverio
Lisa Liu
Davina Mock-Maniscalco

Publicity
Falon Kirby

Publishing Office
Suzanne Donahue
Abby Velasco

Subsidiary Rights
Nicole Bond
Sara Bowne
Rebecca Justiniano